# Part 11 and Computer Validation Guidebook

By Daniel Farb, M.D., and Bruce Gordon

Please send any correspondence regarding permissions to:
UniversityOfHealthCare
419 N. Larchmont Blvd., #323
Los Angeles, CA 90004

Part 11 and Computer Validation Guidebook

ISBN: 1594912602

Library of Congress Catalog Number: 2005925205

UniversityOfHealthCare website: www.uohc.com

# Contents

# Introduction

This book is a text-only version of the acclaimed CD product with the same name. We have made it for those who prefer books. However, we have tried to retain the flavor of the CD approach with a conversational tone and the use of stories.

Using the CD as a supplement to enable testing and documentation is recommended.

# About the Authors

M. Daniel Farb, CEO of UniversityOfHealthCare and UniversityOfBusiness, is a leader in the field of interactive management and healthcare e-learning. He received a BA in English Literature from Yale (where he set an academic record and studied with writers like Robert Penn Warren), an M.D. from Boston University, a degree in Executive Management from the Anderson School of Business at UCLA, and is currently working on a degree at UCLA in International Trade. He is a practicing ophthalmologist. He also has received two patents in ophthalmology and is working on others, has worked with the World Health Organization in Geneva and the National Institutes of Health in Washington, D.C. He has written scientific and popular articles, and has worked as a newspaper reporter. He helped Dr. Robbins edit one of the editions of Robbins' "Pathology" textbook for readability. He wrote an article on humor for the Massachusetts Review. He has experience in theater and television, including acting, directing, and stage-managing. He has programmed his own patient records database. He has written and edited hundreds of e-learning courses. He has taken FDA-level training on Part 11.

Dr. Farb is a member of the American Academy of Ophthalmology, the Union of American Physicians and Dentists, the AOJS, the American Association of Physicians and Surgeons, the ASTD (American Society for Training and Development), the E-Learning Forum, the Southern California Biomedical Council, the PDA (Parenteral Drug Association), and the Medical Marketing Association.

BRUCE GORDON is the Creative Director for UniversityOfHealthCare, LLC, and plays an important role in writing the more creative projects, especially those with stories.

After receiving a BA in Economics from UCLA, he began a freelance writing career that included technical writing (such as a manual for Princess Cruise Lines), stand-up comedy routines for nationally known comedians, and screenplay writing.
He has done production support work with famous Hollywood personalities on such well-known productions as Aaron Spelling's "Dynasty" and "Love Boat" TV shows.

An audio-visual software specialist, he is a versatile artist, with published works in a variety of media, including music, motion graphics, and digital video short film. He has taken FDA-level training on Computer Validation.

# Agent GXP FDA Part 11

At the end of the points covered by the course, this title reprints the text of…
- Part 11, Final Rule
- 1999 FDA Guidance for Industry
- Compliance Policy Guide 160.850 on Part 11 Enforcement
- ORA FIELD MANAGEMENT DIRECTIVE No. 146
- FDA Part 11 Compliance Manual excerpts
- Guidance for Industry August 2003

The FDA (Food and Drug Administration) and other international regulatory organizations use the abbreviation GXP to refer to "Good X Practices." That can include *GMP* (Good Manufacturing Practices) or *GCP* (Good Clinical Practices), and so on. In this title, we refer to GXP for the Part 11 regulations because they are relevant to several different areas of pharmaceutical practice.

The body of the course will present the material in a way that will provide some entertainment in the learning process.

## INTRODUCTION

In the Federal Register of March 20, 1997, at 62 FR 13429, the Food and Drug Administration issued a notice of final rules for 21 CFR, Part 11, Electronic Records; Electronic Signatures.

Many people in industry who try to adopt these regulations (abbreviated as "Part 11"), have considerable difficulty with their interpretation. Companies are faced with the many issues involved in maintaining legacy systems and/or installing brand new systems.

This course will provide the knowledge necessary to break down the electronic submissions regulations into manageable elements--all in an entertaining manner. It gives insight into how management must understand and implement Part 11 requirements so as to be in compliance.

Part 11 went into effect on August 20, 1997. The FDA designed Part 11 to create criteria for electronic record-keeping technologies but to also maintain the agency's role in protecting and promoting the public health.

Regardless of the new technological tools, the FDA's priorities continue to be: facilitating timely review and approval of safe and effective new medical products, conducting efficient audits of required records, and pursuing regulatory actions when appropriate.

All FDA program areas are subject to Part 11, but the regulations do not mandate electronic record keeping.

The purpose of Part 11 is to describe the technical and procedural requirements that must be met if a person chooses to maintain records electronically and use electronic signatures.

Part 11 applies to those records required by an FDA compulsory rule and to signatures required by an FDA compulsory rule, as well as signatures that are not required, but appear in required records.

Certain older electronic systems may not have been in full compliance with Part 11 by August 20, 1997, and modification to these so called "legacy systems" may take more time.

The final rule's provisions are consistent with an emerging body of federal and state law as well as commercial standards and practices.

The following is an example of how a firm's management can execute Part 11 regulations so as to be compliant as soon as possible.

A.   Put together a task force with members from your Information Technology department, QA (Quality Assurance) personnel and laboratory staff.

B.   Identify all the work that your laboratory or organization does that is subject to FDA inspection under 21 CFR Part 11.

C.   Decide whether to use full electronic records and signatures or hybrid systems (records in electronic and paper format). Give your decision to the FDA. One way of doing this is to send them a report that: "This is to certify that "MyCompany" intends that all electronic signatures executed by our employees, agents, or representatives, located anywhere in the world, are the legally binding equivalent of traditional handwritten signatures".

D.   Make all employees aware of the rules, particularly the accountability of electronic signatures. You should have personnel sign something like this: "I understand that electronic signatures are legally binding and have the same meaning as handwritten signatures".

E.   Train all company and laboratory personnel on other contents and consequences. They need to sign a declaration such as: "I understand the meaning of an electronic signature".

F.   Create an inventory of the equipment used for that work (some firms can use their Y2K program inventory as a starting place).

G.   Put the inventory items into categories of "Part 11" and "not Part 11". See the end of this section for a simple template.

H.   As you go through each system, review Part 11 requirements, your current computer system's functionality, and determine what gaps exist.

I.    Assess the risk of being non-compliant for each one of your systems. "Impact of the system on product quality and deviation" and "nature of non-compliance" are the main criteria.

J.    Formulate an implementation plan for your company and laboratory technical controls. Since systems with the required functions are commercially available, this plan should not span more than 1 or 2 years.

K.   Develop a cost estimate.

L.    Figure out user requirement and functional specifications for computerized systems.

M.   Consider whether or not all signatures done today are actually necessary from a regulatory point of view.

N.   Validate new computer systems. For labs, follow the equipment qualification (EQ) approach with design qualification (DQ), installation qualification (IQ), operational qualification (OQ) and performance qualification (PQ). Formulate and establish a change control procedure.

O. Evaluate your existing systems using the above criteria. Try to upgrade the systems if these criteria cannot be met. Of course, the systems should be replaced if they can't be upgraded.

P. Work out procedures for limited system access to authorized individuals. Password policy should be included here.

Q. Work out procedures for implementing audit trails, to ensure data integrity, and for long term archiving with data retrieval throughout the entire retention period.

R. Secure management support and funding for the project.

Full implementation of the electronic signatures and records regulations will have major consequences. Similar to implementing Good Laboratory Practices at the beginning of the eighties and Validation in the first half of the nineties, e-records and e-signature compliance requirements will also take some time.

Example of Equipment Inventory Categorization for Part 11 Compliance: Equipment Subject to Part 11

| Equipment | Subject to Part 11 |
|---|---|
| Analyses Databases | yes |
| Lab Computer Hard Drives | yes |
| E-mail Server | no |
| Card Key Entry Computer | yes |
| Internet Server | no |
| Laboratory Research Computers | yes |

## PART 11

THE SAGA OF AGENT GXP

An international criminal organization known as "Red Raven" is using parts of the Lax Pharmaceutical Corporation's compound as a front while they hold several people hostage.

These hostages are seriously ill patients who had come to Lax Pharmaceutical almost three months ago to participate in studies of what they thought would be life-saving clinical drug trials.

But there were no actual clinical trials. The pharmaceutical company has been hijacked by the criminals. And they are demanding the release of their murderous comrades from prisons in the U.S. and Europe.

And that's where YOU come in. Role-playing in the point-of-view of "Agent GXP," you are the best secret operative at Pharm Mission Control (the good guys). As Agent GXP, you pose as a new site manager at Lax Pharmaceutical Corporation so as to sneak into the enemy's lair. Your mission is to free the hostages and bring them back to Pharm Mission Control headquarters.

Your agency DOES have clinical trials for the medicines that the dying hostages need. But the longer the innocent victims remain in captivity, the less likely they are to survive.

Pharm Mission Control has prepared you with intelligence for safe passage in a special code: cryptic statements of the FDA Good Clinical Practices regulations. The secret passwords, etc. you need to succeed in the mission are all in a brilliantly cryptic code, which has been based on FDA regulations.

Choosing the correct statements will allow you to escape your enemies and to get safely closer to where the hostages are being held. But you can't always remember which regulation code statements are the right ones!

But be careful! Incorrect choices will result in torture and death for both you and the hostages!

It is truly amazing that a newspaper reporter was able to track down Agent GXP in the middle of this adventure, but his fortitude enables us to bring you exclusive interviews with him scattered throughout the title. These enable you to learn more than the facts and get a <u>perspective</u> on how to think about Part 11.

Chief I. M. Strickter, the professor-like Chief Technical Officer from Pharm Mission Control will try to help you. Joining him will be Minnie Strickter, his overzealous and argumentative research assistant. Studious and nerdy, Minnie is also Chief Strickter's niece.

Each episode presents some related facts, a discussion between the Strickters to help Agent GXP, and some questions that test or build upon what you have just learned.

<u>GLOSSARY</u>

Chief Strickter: Minnie, I think we should make some of Part 11's bureaucratic mumbo-jumbo terms more clear.

**Minnie: Oh, I hate bureaucratese too! I guess we finally agree on something!**

**Attributability** - attributable data is data that can be traced to individuals responsible for observing and recording the data. In an automated system, attributability could be achieved by a computer system designed to identify individuals responsible for any input.

**Audit Trail** - a secure, computer generated, time-stamped electronic record that allows reconstruction of the course of events relating to the creation, modification, and deletion of an electronic record.

**Biometrics** – (in the context of Part 11), each individual's identity can be verified by fingerprints, DNA, or other biologically unique identifier upon issuance of his or her electronic signature. Biometrics can also be used to confirm an electronic signature in the case of a discrepancy.

**Computerized System** - computer hardware, software, and associated documents (e.g., user manual) that create, modify, maintain, archive, retrieve, or transmit in digital form information related to the conduct of a clinical trial.

**Data edit authorization** – only authorized personnel may change data, and both the changes and the identity of those personnel must be recorded in the audit trail.

**Digital Signature** -An electronic signature based upon cryptographic methods of originator authentication, computed by using a set of rules and a set of parameters such that the identity of the signer and the integrity of the data can be verified.

**Electronic Record** – any information in digital form that has been created, modified, archived, or distributed by a computer. Electronic records can be text, pictures, and sound. They are created when they are saved to some durable storage device. While the information is simply in RAM (in the computer's volatile memory) it is not a record.

**Electronic Signature** - a computer data compilation of any symbol or series of symbols, executed, adopted, or authorized by an individual to be the legally binding equivalent of the individual's handwritten signature.

**Electronic Signature Components** – identification codes and passwords are examples of electronic signature components.

**Event Sequencing** – The prescribed order of manufacturing steps that a system operator should follow so as not to result an adulterated or misbranded product.

**Excised Signature** – A signature that has been removed or cut out of the original electronic record.

**Legacy System** – Certain older electronic systems that probably were not in full compliance with Part 11 by August 20, 1997. These systems will have to be modified.

**Operational System Check** – A scrutiny of the computer system's operations to make sure that both the hardware and software are doing what they've been programmed to do, and that users are using the systems in a way that guarantees continuity of compliance.

**Procedural Controls** – The Part 11 controls for record management procedures must be in place regardless of whether actual electronic signature systems are being used. Although the FDA still accepts paper records, firms must be "electronic record" compliant because computers are usually used at some point in the process. Part 11 applies whenever computers are used to create, evaluate, maintain, transmit, and archive data.

**Technology-based Controls** – Part 11 controls for actual hardware and software systems involved in electronic records management.

**Transaction Safeguards** - In order for e-signature software to be Part 11 compliant, it must record an audit trail consisting of the date, time, user, and changes involved in any data entry event. There must be a security system in place to electronically record and report the inbound and outbound transactions of computer network systems, based on the requirement of a complete audit trail of all data.

**Validation** - The documentation that a process or the equipment running that process performs the job it's supposed to perform.

**Minnie: Would you like to know what my favorite example of bureaucratese is?**

Chief Strickter: I don't know. There are so many to choose from.

**Minnie: It's "human readable form." All that means is that it's in a form that a human can read.**

Chief Strickter: I guess they just want to make the point that just because a computer can read something, it doesn't mean a person can also.

**Minnie: Why do you always have to take someone else's side?...**

**Minnie: I got you this time, Uncle. You left out some pretty important terms!**

Chief Strickter: Like what?

**Minnie: Like "validation". Everyone needs to know what validation means.**

Chief Strickter: I didn't even mention it, because I was sure Agent GXP knew it. Validation has been part of regulations for a long time in Parts 211 and 820. But to make you happy, I'll say that it refers to the documentation that a process or the equipment running that process performs the job it's supposed to perform.

# Philadelphia Pharma Times

## Exclusive!!!

Agent GXP gives interview to the Philadelphia Pharma Times while rushing to his first encounter with Red Raven's criminals.

Agent GXP, can you help explain Part 11 in a way that's easy for us to understand?

I'd be glad to.

I like to think of Part 11 as just another part of computer validation. In validation, you certify the accuracy of systems by how they are used. In computer validation, we certify the accuracy of computer systems. Part 11 just ensures that the data from these systems can't be forged. This may be oversimplified, but it's helpful.

That must mean Part 11 covers a lot of ground!

You would be amazed by how much software it covers!

Manufacturing
Research and submission
Regulatory record keeping
Medical devices that are software
Software running a medical device
Software used in a medical device, such as an EKG
Statistical analysis
Content management systems

Not only does it cover a lot of software; it covers a lot of industries, like food, cosmetics, and, of course, medical devices.

Do the companies that work with big pharmaceutical and medical device firms that are Part 11 compliant have to be concerned about Part 11?

First, let me remind you that the FDA regulations cover lots of other companies as well: food, cosmetics, radiation, and so on.

I hate to scare you, but the purpose of Part 11, like other GMPs (Good Manufacturing Practices) is to assure that products are not adulterated. If all a company's shipping records are electronic, what happens if the FDA has to locate a shipment a small supplier made to a bigger company that might be involved in a product recall? This thing could grow....

Does that mean that we can sue Bill Gates if the validation doesn't work?

Computer hardware and software manufacturers often exclude themselves from medical liability. And, again, you validate according to the use, so you don't validate Windows, but rather your use of Windows. With Part 11, you validate the use of the electronic signatures as used by your software.

Of course, if the software works improperly, the company that made it is in hot water. And so are you if you didn't test its use and data in accordance with Part 11.

If an inspector asks me to demonstrate
Part 11 compliance, what can I show him?

- How your electronic signatures work
- Having user names and passwords for
  all important functions
- Event logging
- Integrity of software source code
- Password maintenance
- Security for storage materials
- How your system access was tested

These are just a few examples of important
issues.

Does that mean that someone in the lab or
in production can use check-off forms that
a test was performed?

You have to be careful about that. An
inspector may want to see the data--not
just your conclusion.

Remember that Part 11 covers not just
documents you submit to the FDA; it also
covers any record the FDA requires which
you put in electronic form. If your
machine is producing electronic
information, and you show the FDA a form
with a check mark, it doesn't look too
good.

Is the evidence that I validated the system all I need?

**No way!**

**You need to provide documentation of your requirements and standards for the computer system, just like for anything you validate by paper.**

Are you nervous?

**Just a little. But I have Pharm Mission Control to help me out.**

Now hurry to Episode 1.

## 1. System checks

You are Agent GXP, running back and forth along the uppermost of five platforms, high above large vats of bubbling chemicals and pits of ravenous crocodiles in the gothic, dark lab. Shooters in dark uniforms are chasing and trying to target you. By answering the questions correctly, you escape the shooters and get closer to where the hostages are held.

Overview:

The FDA expects that firms will use file formats that permit the agency to make accurate and complete copies in both human-readable and electronic form of audited electronic records.

The FDA would have little confidence in data from firms that do not hold their employees accountable and responsible for actions taken under their electronic signatures.

The FDA would consider the absence of an audit trail to be highly significant when there are data discrepancies and when individuals deny responsibility for record entries.

The FDA requires operational systems checks to enforce event sequencing.

Any lack of operational system checks to enforce event sequencing would be considered significant if an operator's ability to deviate from the prescribed order of manufacturing steps results in an adulterated or misbranded product.

**Pharm Mission Control Secret Headquarters Laboratory**

Chief Strickter: Agent GXP, one of the most important points is that firms must use file formats that allow the FDA to make copies of audited electronic records.

**Minnie: No, no, the information I have is more pressing. Employees must be held accountable and responsible for anything they do under their electronic signatures.**

Chief Strickter: Minnie, stop cutting me off. It's rude. As I was about to say, audit trails cannot have discrepancies in data, and workers can't deny responsibility for record entries.

**Minnie: He already knows that. But what most people don't know is that operational systems checks have to be done to enforce event sequencing. Now isn't that more important?**

Chief Strickter: Not as important as the fact that the operational system checks have got to weed out any operators who deviate from manufacturing steps--

**Minnie: If it results in an adulterated or misbranded product, that is.**

As always, Chief Strickter ends the communiqué with: Remember, we at Pharm Mission Control are the last hope of freeing the hostages and curing them of their terminal diseases. You must succeed... failure is not an option!

**And as always, Minnie tries to get the last word: Give 'em heck, Agent GXP.**

<u>Question:</u> It is okay for a company to make electronic documents in any file format, whether or not the format allows the FDA to make accurate and complete copies in forms that can be read by computers and people. True or false?
<u>Answer:</u> False. The FDA expects that firms will use file formats that permit the agency to make accurate and complete copies in both human readable and electronic form of audited electronic records.

<u>Question:</u> Which of the following does the FDA require for electronic record keeping systems?
A. system operational checks
B. system authority checks
C. system device checks
D. all of the above
E. none of the above
<u>Answer:</u> D. The answer is all of the above. Don't get inspected until you finish this course!

<u>Question:</u> Which of the following is true regarding questionable product quality and data integrity accompanying the significant absence of a firm's electronic document audit trail?

A. The FDA tolerates data discrepancies or instances of individuals denying responsibility for electronic record entries.
B. The FDA tolerates data discrepancies, but not instances of individuals denying responsibility for electronic record entries.
C. The FDA does not tolerate data discrepancies or instances of individuals denying responsibility for electronic record entries.
Answer: C. The FDA would consider the absence of an audit trail to be highly significant when there are data discrepancies and when individuals deny responsibility for record entries.

## 2. Timetable, legacy systems

Inside the enemy's lab, Agent GXP is stuck in a maze, running up and down, back and forth, turning, and making repeated attempts to escape.

Since the enemy troopers have followed you inside, the only way out is to find the hallway leading to the enemy's main stronghold. This correct hallway will get you closer to the vault in which the hostages are being held. The incorrect hallways will result in your failure and early demise.

Overview:

Firms should have a reasonable timetable for promptly modifying any systems not in compliance (including legacy systems) to make them Part 11 compliant, and should be able to demonstrate progress in implementing their timetable.

The FDA expects that Part 11 requirements for procedural controls will already be in place.

The FDA recognizes that technology-based controls may take longer to install in older systems.

The FDA will consider Part 11 deviations to be more significant if a firm has a history of Part 11 violations or of inadequate or unreliable record keeping.

Until firms attain full compliance with Part 11, FDA investigators will exercise greater vigilance to detect inconsistencies, unauthorized modifications, and poor attributability.

If your company is new to Part 11, you should remember that you are not liable for Part 11 electronic signatures until you have sent a paper letter to the FDA stating that from a certain date on, you are certifying electronic signatures to be binding like handwritten signatures. The FDA does not like to see the failure to implement Part 11. These regulations were promulgated for the benefit of industry. In addition, since Part 11 is so tied up with the concept of computer validation, you may find that you are liable for Part 11 violations without having certified yourself as liable for the proper use of electronic signatures. Part 11 also concerns electronic records!

# Philadelphia Pharma Times

Our readers would like to know how to prepare for FDA Part 11 inspections.

First psyche out what they are likely to look for:
1) Anything that's visible and suspicious
2) Anything crucial to your processes or information
Then do the following:

Make sure you have a plan for handling your legacy systems.
Make sure your systems first meet regular record-keeping requirements, and then show a plan for migration to Part 11 compliance.
Make sure that you can easily deliver to an inspector a print-out of any Part 11 system he wants to inspect.
If your system is not quite up to par, have a corrective action plan prepared.
Have an inventory of all systems and their state of validation.
And never, ever, ever, let your employees leave passwords on Post-Its on their computers or desk drawers!
Set up a special computer and printer for employees to use to help the FDA retrieve the documents desired before the next inspection. Even prepare a password and permissions for the inspector.

**Pharm Mission Control Secret Headquarters Laboratory**

Chief Strickter: Companies have got to get some kind of timetable in place toward compliance.

**Minnie: You always forget the most pressing points, like the fact that firms have to be able to show progress in implementing the timetable.**

Chief Strickter: You never let me finish. Anyway, Agent GXP, procedural controls are expected to already be in place. Although, the FDA understand that technology-based controls could take longer to install in older systems.

Minnie: Talk about older systems! With all due respect to my forgetful uncle, Agent GXP, if you want to succeed, you need to hear the attitude of youth. The FDA frowns on firms with a history of inadequate or unreliable record keeping.

Chief Strickter: This new generation needs to learn a thing or two about respect for the wisdom of experience! Anyway, investigators are going to be more and more vigilant to detect inconsistencies, unauthorized modifications--

Minnie: You didn't mention poor attributability.

Chief Strickter: You didn't let me. That's it, Agent GXP.

As always, Chief Strickter ends the communiqué with: "Remember, we at Pharm Mission Control are the last hope of freeing the hostages and curing them of their terminal diseases. You must succeed... failure is not an option!

And as always, Minnie tries to get the last word: "Give 'em heck, Agent GXP."

Question: Firms should have a reasonable timetable for promptly modifying any systems not in compliance (including legacy systems) to make them Part 11 compliant, and should be able to demonstrate progress in implementing their timetable. True or false?
Answer: True. Firms should have a reasonable timetable for promptly modifying any systems not in compliance (including legacy systems) to make them Part 11 compliant, and should be able to demonstrate progress in implementing their timetable.

Question: FDA will consider Part 11 deviations to be more significant if a firm has a history of Part 11 violations or of inadequate or unreliable record keeping. True or false?
Answer: True. The FDA will consider Part 11 deviations to be more significant if a firm has a history of Part 11 violations or of inadequate or unreliable record keeping.

Question: The FDA recognizes that technology based controls:
A. Must be in place now.
B. Do not necessarily ever have to be in place.
C. May take longer to install in older systems.
Answer: C.

## 3. Electronic records as substitutes for paper records

Inside the enemy's laboratory, you are rushing to tap a crucial touch-screen keypad that will complete the high-tech security identification process at the vault-like door of the criminal's inner sanctum. This is where the hostages are being held. After getting past the fingerprint, retina, and voice pattern checkpoints (Chief Strickter's great gadgets for Part 11 compliance all worked very well), you must get past this final phase of the security check. Enemy security forces are slowly approaching from several directions as you hurry to press the button that will open the vault. Only the correct choice results in your being able to open the vault and enter safely just before the actual attack starts.

Overview:

The FDA will consider regulatory action with respect to Part 11 when the electronic records or electronic signatures are unacceptable substitutes for paper records or handwritten signatures, and that therefore, requirements of the applicable regulations [e.g., good manufacturing practices (GMP) and good laboratory practices (GLP) regulations] are not met.

Firms must establish and maintain procedures to control all documents that are required by 21 CFR 820.40.

Firms must use authority checks to ensure that only authorized individuals can use the system and alter records, as required by 21 CFR 11.10(g).

Any records stored in electronic form, even desktop computers, must be kept secure. Laptops and palm pilots too.

Data storage devices must be kept protected from unauthorized access and modification of their content.

## Pharm Mission Control Secret Headquarters Laboratory

Chief Strickter: Agent GXP, you must understand that FDA will come down hard whenever electronic records or electronic signatures are unacceptable substitutes for paper records or handwritten signatures.

**Minnie: Like that's more important that the fact that companies have to set up and keep procedures to control all of their electronic documents.**

Chief Strickter: Your sarcasm is becoming impertinent, Minnie. I'm going to have a word with your mother. Nevertheless, Agent GXP, firms must use authority checks to make certain that only authorized individuals can use the system and alter records.

Minnie: Uncle, you just don't get it, do you? There's nothing impertinent about trying to give the best information, and I have it; not you! Case in point: any records stored in electronic form, even desktop computers, have to be kept secure--

Chief Strickter: You forgot to mention laptops and Palm pilots. Two can play at your game, Minnie.

Minnie: No fair! You didn't let me finish. I was going to say that, but--

Chief Strickter: And data storage devices have to be kept protected from unauthorized access and modification of their content. There!

Minnie: You win... this time.

As always, Chief Strickter ends the communiqué with: "Remember, we at Pharm Mission Control are the last hope of freeing the hostages and curing them of their terminal diseases. You must succeed... failure is not an option!

And as always, Minnie tries to get the last word: "Give 'em heck, Agent GXP."

# Philadelphia Pharma Times

Could you help our readers clear up confusion about how far use of the computer makes that computer subject to Part 11 compliance. The Part 11 text doesn't seem to cover it enough.

I suggest you take a look at the preface with comments in the Federal Register, volume 62, No. 54, March 20, 1997. It states specifically that Part 11 does not apply to paper records transmitted by fax or electronic means. A computer system that is merely a tool to create a paper document--such as the word processor to create a paper document--does not require validation under Part 11. But if that document is retained in electronic form, the hardware and software needed to produce that document come under Part 11 scrutiny.

I hope that helps your readers breathe more easily!

Question: FDA will consider regulatory action with respect to Part 11 when the electronic records or electronic signatures are unacceptable substitutes for paper records or handwritten signatures, and that therefore, requirements of the applicable regulations (e.g., cGMP and GLP regulations) are not met. True or false?
Answer: True.

Question: There is no FDA requirement to use authority checks to ensure that only authorized individuals can use the system and alter records. True or false?
Answer: True. This is strictly enforced. Firms must use authority checks to ensure that only authorized individuals can use the system and alter records, as required by 21 CFR 11.10(g).

Question: A rewritable CD containing clinical trials data is accidentally left on a table in a Pharm company cafeteria. During an FDA inspection, which of the following would be a reason for the firm's Part 11 violation?
A. The FDA doesn't allow compact disks as coasters during business hours.
B. The storage device was not protected from unauthorized access and modification of the data.
C. Drinking and data just don't mix.
Answer: B.

Question: Which of the following would the FDA consider as reason for a regulatory citation for a violation of the device quality system regulations?
A. Failure to establish and maintain procedures to control all documents that are required by 21 CFR 820.40.
B. Failure to punch in time cards for payroll records of device operators.
C. Failure to provide adequate restroom distance from the cafeteria of device operating employees.
Answer: A.

Question: Which of the following would require proper authority checks to ensure that only authorized individuals can use the system and alter records?
A. Efficacy data of drug tests stored in an office computer.
B. Records of injury to test subjects stored on a floppy disk.
C. Engineering drawings for manufacturing equipment and devices stored in AutoCAD form on a desktop computer.
D. All the above.
Answer: D. For example, any records stored in electronic form, even desktop computers, must be kept secure. Laptops and Palm pilots too.

## 4. Closed systems

You're inside the enemy's human experimentation room. By answering the questions correctly, you hold off the enemies while using the correct secret codes to unshackle the hostages' computer-controlled restraints. Wrong answers will result in capture, torture, and death for you and the hostages.

Overview:

A closed system refers to control over the data itself. In an open system you don't have control over the data. In an open system, you have to be extra cautious about data integrity.

"Controls for closed systems" reference systems to which access is controlled by persons responsible for the content of electronic records on that system.

Closed system controls include measures designed to ensure the integrity of system operations and information stored in the system.

Closed-system controls measure validation, the ability to generate accurate and complete copies of records, archival protection of records, use of appropriate controls over systems documentation, computer-generated audit trails, and time-stamped audit trails.

Another closed system control is a determination that persons who develop, maintain, or use electronic records and signature systems have the education, training, and experience.

**Pharm Mission Control Secret Headquarters Laboratory**

Chief Strickter: Agent GXP, when they mention controls for closed systems, they're talking about systems where access is controlled by persons responsible for the content of electronic records.

**Minnie: No, no, that's not it. Closed system controls include measures designed to ensure the integrity of system operations and information stored in the system.**

Chief Strickter: But that's just what I said. Minnie, if you weren't my niece, I'd--

**Minnie: You'd what?**

Chief Strickter: Agent GXP, never hire family! Anyway, such measures include validation, the ability to generate accurate and complete copies of records, archival protection of records--

**Minnie: And don't forget the use of computer-generated, time-stamped audit trails, use of appropriate controls over systems documentation--**

Chief Strickter: I didn't forget them. And you don't forget that workers who develop, maintain, or use electronic records and signatures have to be trained--

**Minnie jumps in again: To perform their assigned tasks. Gotcha again Uncle!**

Chief Strickter sighs in fatigue.

Then, as always, Chief Strickter ends the communiqué with: "Remember, we at Pharm Mission Control are the last hope of freeing the hostages and curing them of their terminal diseases. You must succeed... failure is not an option!

**And as always, Minnie tries to get the last word: "Give 'em heck, Agent GXP."**

# Philadelphia Pharma Times

Agent GXP, I bet a lot of our readers are wondering whether they can use outside lines to transmit data.

Once again, you can find a discussion of this in the comments section of the Federal Register. A system operated by a third party, such as a commercial online service, would make this an open system. If you use this, you should make use of extra security requirements and it would be a good idea to validate the transmission and security of data.

I'm now going to give you a quotation from a draft guidance document from the FDA that addresses this issue==>

*The Internet can nonetheless be a trustworthy and reliable communications pipeline for electronic records when there are measures in place to ensure the accurate, complete and timely transfer of data and records from source to destination computing systems.*

*Validation of both the source and destination computing systems (i.e., both ends of the Internet communications pipeline) should extend to those measures. We therefore consider it extremely important that those measures are fully documented as part of the*
*system requirements specifications, so they can be validated. Examples of such measures include:*
*• Use of digital signature technology to verify that electronic records have not been altered and that the sender's authenticity is affirmed.*
*• Delivery acknowledgements such as receipts or separate confirmations xecuted apart from the Internet (e.g., via fax or voice telephone lines.)*

Thanks for the scoop! I'll put it as a sidebar in the paper.

Question: Which of the following is the definition of "controls for closed systems," as defined in Part 11?
A. Systems to which access is allowed only by persons in good standing with those responsible for the content of electronic records on that system.
B. Systems to which access is controlled by persons responsible for the content of electronic records on that system.
C. Neither of the above.
Answer: B.

Question: Closed system controls include measures designed to ensure the integrity of system operations and information stored in the system. True or false?

Answer: True.

Question: Which of the following is completely correct in regards to what closed-system controls measure?
A. Validation
B. The ability to generate accurate and complete copies of records
C. Archival protection of records
D. Use of appropriate controls over systems documentation
E. All of the above
Answer: E.

Question: Which item is NOT related to Part 11 closed system controls?
A. Time-stamped audit trails
B. Snail trails
C. Computer-generated audit trails
Answer: B. Computer-generated and time-stamped audit trails are important closed system controls for Part 11 compliance.

Question: A determination must be made by firms that persons who develop, maintain, or use electronic records and signature systems:
A. Have the education, training, and experience to perform their assigned tasks.
B. Be allowed to participate in using electronic records and signature systems at whatever level is comfortable to them.
C. Never let the FDA know when screw-ups occur.
D. All of the above.
Answer: A. This determination that persons who develop, maintain, or use electronic records and signature systems have the education, training, and experience is another closed system control.

## 5. Electronic signatures

You are still in the enemy's human experimentation room. By answering the questions correctly, you activate the correct psychological trigger statements needed to deprogram the hostages' brainwashed minds. With wrong answers, you all get fried by the enemy's booby-trap: Ceiling-mounted, flesh-broiling laser guns.

Overview:

Electronic signatures executed to electronic records must be linked to their respective records so that signatures cannot be excised, copied, or otherwise transferred to falsify an electronic record by ordinary means.

Handwritten signatures (just like electronic signatures) executed to electronic records, must also be linked to their respective records so that signatures cannot be excised, copied, or otherwise transferred to falsify an electronic record by ordinary means.
Each electronic signature must be unique to one individual.

An electronic signature issued to one individual must not be reused by, or reassigned to, anyone else.

Any organization should identify an individual's identity before it establishes, assigns, certifies, or otherwise sanctions that individual's electronic signature.

**Pharm Mission Control Secret Headquarters Laboratory**

Chief Strickter: Now, Minnie... please be quiet until I've explained the secret codes to Agent GXP.

Minnie: Sure, Uncle. (To herself, "Yeah, right!)

Chief Strickter: Electronic and handwritten signatures have to be linked to their respective electronic records--

**Minnie: So that signatures can't be excised, copied, or otherwise transferred to falsify an electronic record.**

Chief Strickter: Minnie!

**Minnie: And every electronic signature's got to be unique to a single person--**

Chief Strickter: Minnie!

**Minnie: And it can't be reused by, or reassigned to, anyone else.**

Chief Strickter: Minnie, I'm working on your performance review, remember?

**Minnie: Okay, okay! Go ahead!**

Chief Strickter: That's more like it. Agent GXP, before an organization establishes, assigns, certifies, or otherwise sanctions someone's electronic signature--

**Minnie: The organization has to verify the individual's identity.**

Chief Strickter: That's it! I'm writing you up, Minnie. Family or not!

As always, Chief Strickter ends the communiqué with:
"Remember, we at Pharm Mission Control are the last hope of
freeing the hostages and curing them of their terminal diseases.
You must succeed... failure is not an option!

**And as always, Minnie tries to get the last word: "Give 'em
heck, Agent GXP."**

Question: Electronic signatures executed to electronic records
must be linked to their respective records so that signatures
cannot be excised, copied, or otherwise transferred to falsify an
electronic record by ordinary means. True or false?
Answer: True.

Question: Handwritten signatures executed to electronic records
do not have to be linked to their respective records so that
signatures cannot be excised, copied, or otherwise transferred to
falsify an electronic record by ordinary means. True or false?
Answer: False. You're on the right track! Handwritten
signatures (just like electronic signatures) executed to electronic
records, must also be linked to their respective records so that
signatures cannot be excised, copied, or otherwise transferred to
falsify an electronic record by ordinary means.

Question: Which of the following is not a cause for a Part 11
violation citation?
A. The CEO of a pharmaceutical company's electronic
signature is the same as the company president's.
B. The lab manager shares an electronic signature with her
husband.
C. Each electronic signature in the company is unique to one
individual.
Answer: C.

Question: Before an organization establishes, assigns, certifies, or otherwise sanctions a individual's electronic signature, the organization must verify the identity of the individual. True or false?
Answer: True.

Question: Which of the following is true about an electronic signature? An electronic signature...
A. Issued to two individuals can be used by either of them.
B. Issued to one individual must not be reused by another person, but it can be reassigned to someone else.
C. Issued to one individual must not be reused by, or reassigned to, anyone else.
Answer: C.

## 6. Signatures: uniqueness and biometrics

You are in the interior distribution area of the criminals' facility. By answering the questions correctly, you open a fortified closet door with the secret combination so as to shelter the group from the onslaught of more enemy force attackers. Wrong answers will end your mission, your health, and your life.

Overview:

Electronic signatures not based on biometrics must employ at least two distinct identification components such as an identification code and password.

When an individual executes a series of signings during a single period of controlled system access, the first signing must be executed using all electronic signature components and the subsequent signings must be executed using at least one component designed to be used only by that individual.

When an individual executes one or more signings not performed during a single period of controlled system access, each signing must be executed using all of the electronic signature components.

Electronic signatures not based on biometrics are also required to be used only by their genuine owners and administered and executed to ensure that attempted use of an individual's electronic signature by anyone else requires the collaboration of two or more individuals.

The required collaboration of two or more individuals in order to use of an individual's electronic signature by anyone else is designed to make it more difficult for anyone to forge an electronic signature.

**Pharm Mission Control Secret Headquarters Laboratory**

Chief Strickter: Minnie, why don't I let you just go first so you can get it out of your system?

**Minnie: Now you're talking. Agent GXP, when electronic signatures are not based on biometrics they must--**

Chief Strickter: Use at least two different identification components such as an identification code and password.

**Minnie: Uncle! I thought you said I could go first?!**

Chief Strickter: Also when someone executes a series of signings in a single period of controlled system access, the first signing has to be executed using all electronic signature components...

**Minnie: Uncle!**

Chief Strickter: ...and the subsequent signings need to be executed using at least one component designed to be used only by that individual.

**Minnie: Uncle, no!**

Chief Strickter: Furthermore, when a person executes one or more signings not performed during a single period of controlled system access--

**Minnie: Each signing must be executed using all of the electronic signature components. There! I got it in, finally. Uncle, what's wrong with you?**

Chief Strickter: What? Can't handle a taste of your own medicine?

**Minnie: Medicine, schmedicine! Agent GXP, electronic signatures not based on biometrics are also required to be used only by their genuine owners--**

Chief Strickter: Plus they've got to be administered and executed to ensure that attempted use of someone's electronic signature by anyone else--

**Minnie: Agent GXP, this type of situation requires the collaboration of two or more individuals. Uncle, I'll tell him! That was MY research!**

Chief Strickter: Your research is MY research. You work for me and don't forget it!

**Minnie: I'm gonna let my mom deal with you, later. We've got to go, Agent GXP. But remember, the reason for theses rules is that--**

Chief Strickter: This would make it more difficult for anyone to forge an electronic signature.

As always, Chief Strickter ends the communiqué with: "Remember, we at Pharm Mission Control are the last hope of freeing the hostages and curing them of their terminal diseases. You must succeed... failure is not an option!

**And as always, Minnie tries to get the last word: "Give 'em heck, Agent GXP."**

Question: Electronic signatures not based on biometrics must employ at least two distinct identification components such as:
A. A cheek cell DNA identifier and a urine test.
B. A retina scan and a fingerprint
C. An identification code and password.
Answer: C.

Question: When an individual executes a series of signings during a single period of controlled system access, the first signing must be executed using all electronic signature components and the subsequent signings must be executed using at least one component designed to be used only by that individual. True or false?
Answer: True.

Question: When an individual executes one or more signings not performed during a single period of controlled system access, each signing must be executed using:
A. All of the electronic signature components.
B. Most of the electronic signature components.
C. At least one of the electronic signature components.
Answer: A.

Question: Electronic signatures not based on biometrics are required to be administered and executed to ensure that attempted use of an individual's electronic signature by anyone else requires the collaboration of two or more individuals. True or false?
Answer: True.

Question: The required collaboration of two or more individuals in order to use an individual's electronic signature by anyone else is designed to:
Add red tape to an already complicated process.
Make sure violators can share the expense of a citation, or that they can even share a jail cell.
Make it more difficult for anyone to forge an electronic signature.
Answer: C. Firms should do anything possible to make it more difficult for anyone to forge an electronic signature.

## 7. Signatures: codes and biometrics

You are inside the bowels of the enemy laboratory. By answering the questions correctly, you successfully get through the maze of hallways and reach the interior monorail tram that leads to the exterior road-vehicle parking lot. Wrong answers result in your being detained, gassed, and then tortured.

Overview:

Electronic signatures based upon biometrics must be designed to ensure that such signatures cannot be used by anyone other than the genuine owners.

Electronic signatures based upon use of identification codes in combination with passwords must employ controls to ensure security and integrity.

Electronic signature controls must include specific provisions, all of which are listed in Part 11.

The uniqueness of each combined identification code and password must be maintained in such a way that no two individuals have the same combination of identification code and password.

Persons using identification codes and/or passwords must ensure that they are periodically recalled or revised.

**Pharm Mission Control Secret Headquarters Laboratory**

Chief Strickter: Agent GXP, electronic signatures based upon biometrics have to be designed to ensure that such signatures cannot be used by anyone other than the genuine owners.

**Minnie: Biometrics! You just rattle stuff off like everyone knows what that means. Do YOU even know what "biometrics" means?**

Chief Strickter: Yes, I do, as a matter of fact. In this case it means that fingerprints or DNA samples are used to establish the person's identity before authorizing their individual e-signature.

**Minnie: Show off! Listen, Agent GXP, electronic signatures based on the use of identification codes in combination with passwords--**

Chief Strickter: Have to employ control to ensure security and integrity.

**Minnie: Can I get a word in edgewise? The controls must include specific provisions, all of which are listed in Part 11.**

Chief Strickter: I can be just as rude as you young people of today! Agent, GXP, the uniqueness of each combined identification code and password have got to be maintained in such a way--

**Minnie: That no two people have the same combination of identification code and password. Also--**

Chief Strickter: Persons using identification codes and/or passwords have to be sure that they are periodically recalled or revised.

**Minnie: Hmmph!**

As always, Chief Strickter ends the communiqué with: "Remember, we at Pharm Mission Control are the last hope of freeing the hostages and curing them of their terminal diseases. You must succeed... failure is not an option!

**And as always, Minnie tries to get the last word: "Give 'em heck, Agent GXP."**

**Question:** Electronic signatures based upon biometrics must be designed to ensure that such signatures...
A. Cannot be used by anyone other than the genuine owners.
B. Cannot be used by anyone other than the genuine owners and the highest authorized official of the firm.
C. Cannot be used by anyone other than the genuine owners and the security staff of the third-party software firm hired to manage the electronic records.
**Answer:** A.

**Question:** Electronic signatures based upon use of identification codes in combination with passwords are secure enough, and there is no requirement to employ any control to ensure further security and integrity. True or false?
**Answer:** False. The opposite is true: electronic signatures based upon use of identification codes in combination with passwords must employ control to ensure security and integrity.

**Question:** Which of the following is true about electronic signature controls?
A. Any e-signature software will do, according to Part 11.
B. A company can decide what Part 11 provisions must be included.
C. The controls must include the specific provisions listed in Part 11.
**Answer:** C.

**Question:** The uniqueness of each combined identification code and password must be maintained in such a way that no two individuals have the same combination of identification code and password. True or false?
**Answer:** True.

## 8. Code safeguards

You are now in the interior section of the enemy lab's tram area. By answering the questions correctly, you get the hostages to the correct monorail tram and successfully get them to the parking lot outside. With wrong answers, you and the hostages are reduced to crimson carnage by trams full of enemy troopers.

Overview:

Loss management procedures must be followed to de-authorize lost, stolen, missing, or otherwise potentially compromised tokens, cards, and other devices that bear or generate identification codes or password information.

Explicit transaction safeguards are required to prevent unauthorized use of the electronic signature, even when using passwords and/or identification codes.

Transaction safeguards must be used to prevent unauthorized use of passwords and/or identification codes.

Devices that bear or generate identification codes or password information, such as tokens or cards, must be tested initially and periodically to ensure that they function correctly, and they cannot be allowed to be altered in an unauthorized manner.

**Pharm Mission Control Secret Headquarters Laboratory**

**Minnie: Okay, Uncle, let's be civilized about this. You give one part of the code, and I'll give the next. We'll take turns.**

Chief Strickter: Absolutely not. You don't know how! I'm going to brief you myself this time, Agent GXP. Listen, loss management procedures have to be followed to de-authorize lost, stolen, missing, or otherwise potentially compromised tokens, cards, and other devices--

**Minnie: That bear or generate identification codes or password information. Uncle, I SAID, let's take turns! Anyway, Agent GXP, transaction safeguards have to be used to not let unauthorized use of passwords and/or identification codes happen...**

Chief Strickter: Okay, my turn...

**Minnie: ...And transaction safeguards have to be used to locate and report any attempt to misuse the codes.**

Chief Strickter: I SAID, it's my turn now!

**Minnie: Devices that bear or generate identification codes or password information--**

Chief Strickter: Such as tokens or cards, have to be tested initially and periodically--

**Minnie: To be sure that they function correctly--**

Chief Strickter: And that they have not been altered in an unauthorized manner.

As always, Chief Strickter ends the communiqué with: "Remember, we at Pharm Mission Control are the last hope of freeing the hostages and curing them of their terminal diseases. You must succeed... failure is not an option!

**And as always, Minnie tries to get the last word: "Give 'em heck, Agent GXP."**

Question: Loss management procedures must be followed to de-authorize lost, stolen, missing, or otherwise potentially compromised tokens, cards, and other devices that bear or generate identification codes or password information. True or false?
Answer: True.

Question: No additional transaction safeguards are required if you use passwords and/or identification codes to prevent unauthorized use of the electronic signature. True or false?
Answer: False.

Question: Transaction safeguards must be used to detect and report:
A. Stinginess with sharing passwords and/or identification codes.
B. Any attempt to misuse passwords and/or identification codes.
C. Improper password and/or identification code etiquette.
Answer: B.

Question: Devices that bear or generate identification codes or password information, such as tokens or cards, must be tested initially and periodically to ensure that:
A. They are the correct color.
B. They have the correct odor.
C. They have not been altered in an unauthorized manner.
Answer: C.

## 9. Audit trails in the lab

On the highway at night, you are rushing away from the enemy's compound. A herd of criminals leap from a speeding semi-truck and overtake you. They wrestle the hostages away from you and dash away into the night, although you manage to avoid capture. By answering the questions correctly, you locate the hostages' whereabouts. With wrong answers, the hostages will be taken back to the torture chambers.

Overview:

The FDA expects firms to establish, maintain and update controls in the laboratory electronic record keeping system, which is used for maintaining chromatography and audit trails.

Since without an electronically-recorded audit trail, personnel can change data without it being detected, the recording of an audit trail is virtually the only way to maintain integrity of data with respect to changes.

The FDA makes it clear that all of the data derived from all tests must be complete, and they require firms to include 100% complete data derived from all tests necessary to assure compliance with established specifications and standards.

All process values must be recorded, from beginning to end.

FDA inspectors may take your paper SOPs and make sure you are carrying out what you say you are.

This is the way an audit trail might look:

| Name | Time | Record | Old Value | New Value | Action |
|------|------|--------|-----------|-----------|--------|
| John Doe | 12:00:00 01/01/2001 | SOP 23.1 | must | should | Modify |
| John Doe | 12:00:02 01/01/2001 | Weight 1 | 67 g | 68 g | Modify |

| John Doe | 12:00:04 01/01/2001 | SOP 24 | adjust | | Delete |
|----------|---------------------|--------|--------|--|--------|

## Pharm Mission Control Secret Headquarters Laboratory

Chief Strickter: A main point in the secret code, Agent GXP, is that the FDA has issued warnings for deficient controls in the laboratory electronic record keeping system--

**Minnie: You forgot to say "such as those used for maintaining chromatography and audit trails".**

Chief Strickter: Once again! You just can't let me--

**Minnie: Agent GXP, the recording of an audit trail is kind of the only way to maintain integrity of data with respect to changes.**

Chief Strickter: Minnie, I wish you'd maintain some kind of integrity of etiquette.

**Minnie: Without an electronically-recorded audit trail, personnel can change data without it being detected.**

Chief Strickter: You're not going to let me finish one code point, are you?

**Minnie: Agent GXP, all process values have to be recorded, from beginning to end. And the FDA points out that---**

Chief Strickter: That every bit of the data derived from all tests have to be complete. There! I finally got a word in!

As always, Chief Strickter ends the communiqué with: "Remember, we at Pharm Mission Control are the last hope of freeing the hostages and curing them of their terminal diseases. You must succeed... failure is not an option!

**And as always, Minnie tries to get the last word: "Give 'em heck, Agent GXP."**

Question: The FDA does not inspect such trivial items as deficient controls in the laboratory electronic record keeping system, which is used for maintaining chromatography and audit trails. True or false?
Answer: False.

Question: If an electronic records system does not generate an audit trail, which of the following is true?
There is no way to determine if values have been changed on batch production records.
There is no way to determine if the production values have been recorded.
There is no way to determine who entered production value data.
Answer: A.

Question: Part 11 requirements don't apply to drafts, only completed documents.
Answer: False. The FDA is concerned that people might call batch records and other records "drafts" and delete them.

Question: The audit trail feature of a good electronic records system:
Can be the only evidence that data has been entered.
Can be the first line of defense against bad data.

Can be the only evidence that an electronic record has been altered.
Answer: C.

Question: Even if things worked out well in the end, the FDA would consider it a violation for a system operator to only record a later, conforming data value without recording an earlier non-conforming value. True or false?
Answer: True. All process values must be recorded, from beginning to end.

Question: As long as firms makes an effort to maintain good laboratory records, the FDA:
A. Doesn't require them to include 100% complete data derived from all tests necessary to assure compliance with established specifications and standards.
B. Requires them to include 100% complete data derived from all tests necessary to assure compliance with established specifications and standards.
C. Firm managers are free to choose their own level of commitment to data completeness.
Answer: B.

## 10. Lack of data integrity

Under the thick cloak of night, the criminals have hijacked a farm and are using it as their new lair. Agent GXP must find out which one. You use a satellite-tracking equipment rig, but it's not locking on the correct frequency. Can you successfully recalibrate it... or not? By answering the questions correctly, you recalibrate the satellite tracker. With wrong answers, you and the hostages become toast....

Overview:

If there is any missing data in an electronic records process, the FDA requires that the firm conduct an investigation to determine the cause of the missing data.

The FDA considers it a violation if no corrective measures are implemented to prevent the recurrence of an event such as an instance of missing data. Citations are issued against firms that don't have corrective measures in place or that don't execute such procedures.

The FDA sends warning letters to companies that fail to maintain the integrity and adequacy of the laboratory's computer systems used by the Quality Control Unit in the analysis and processing of test data.

With any lack of a secure system to prevent unauthorized entry in restricted data systems, data edit authorization rights could become available to all unauthorized users, not only the system administrator.

Any failure to implement appropriate system controls to assure that only authorized changes can be made is considered a violation.

**Pharm Mission Control Secret Headquarters Laboratory**

Chief Strickter: Agent GXP, firms have been cited for not conducting investigations of missing data.

**Minnie: But that's not as important as that fact that citations are issued against firms that don't have corrective measures in place or that don't execute such procedures.**

Chief Strickter: Minnie, what you think is the most important thing isn't always so pressing! Agent GXP, integrity and adequacy has to be maintained in laboratory computer systems used by the Quality Control Unit to analyze and process test data.

**Minnie: Uncle, isn't this important? If a there's lack of a secure system to prevent unauthorized entry in restricted data systems--**

Chief Strickter: I know, I know... data edit authorization rights could be available to all unauthorized users, besides the system administrator. Yes, that's important, Minnie.

**Minnie: I told you! And another violation would come from any failure to implement appropriate system controls to assure that only authorized changes can be made.**

As always, Chief Strickter ends the communiqué with: "Remember, we at Pharm Mission Control are the last hope of freeing the hostages and curing them of their terminal diseases. You must succeed... failure is not an option!"

**And as always, Minnie tries to get the last word: "Give 'em heck, Agent GXP."**

Question: If there is any missing data in an electronic records process, the FDA requires that the firm:
Report it and move on to other, more important things.
Conduct an investigation to determine the cause of the missing data.
Answer: B. Firms have been cited for not conducting such investigations.

Question: The FDA considers it a violation if no corrective measures are implemented to prevent the recurrence of an event such as an instance of missing data. True or false?
Answer: True. Citations are issued against firms that don't have corrective measures in place or that don't execute such procedures.

Question: The FDA sends warning letters to companies that fail to maintain the integrity and adequacy of:
A. The laboratory's computer systems used by the Quality Control Unit in the analysis and processing of test data.
B. The receptionist's switchboard computer.
C. The secret video game computer that the CEO hides under his desk.
Answer: A.

Question: Greg Thomas, the system administrator leaves his computer on when he goes out to lunch for an hour or so. Is this a violation of Part 11 requirements?
A. No, silly! The FDA wouldn't be so petty.
B. Maybe... if his lunches extend beyond 60 minutes.
C. Yes.
Answer: C. With this lack of a secure system to prevent unauthorized entry in restricted data systems, data edit authorization rights were available to all unauthorized users, not only the system administrator.

Question: When the FDA inspected one firm, they found that there was an option on the High Performance Liquid Chromatography (HPLC) that allows analysts to delete results after they are processed. Did they issue a warning letter?
A. No
B. Yes
C. Only if the company put FDA officials in a bad mood.

Answer: B. All analysis data must be retained for FDA inspection. It cannot be deleted.

## 11. Electronic documentation

It's daybreak, and you're inside a farm silo. While masquerading as a "drifter" farm hand, you try to use your hand-held computer to analyze clues to the victims' whereabouts. By answering the questions correctly, you pinpoint the enemy's moving lair. Wrong answers will get you connected to an electronic milking machine....

Overview:

Firms' electronic records procedures require the documentation of calculation or entry errors, under the Part 11 mandate that security measures must be in place to prevent unauthorized access of the software.

Unacceptable electronic records deficiencies include no audit trails, and data that can be copied or changed at will, with no documentation of the copying or changes.

Part 11 expressly requires that firms train all users of the electronic records systems and provide documentation to indicate that analysts are trained in the electronic records software and its applications.

Part 11 requires the automatic creation of back-up files for laboratory UV spectrophotometer and other test results, since original data could get lost and the tests would have to be performed again to determine final disposition of the processes.

Part 11 requires that records show when study data is received and when it is entered into the database via date and time stamping of data receipt and data entry.

Since Part 11 demands an audit trail of any and all changes made to the database, if a company can't show verifiable records for a particular data entry step in a test process, the FDA requires the firm to generate data queries or clarifications and then send them to the site to verify missing information or to clarify discrepancies.

It is vital that employees accord their electronic signatures the same legal weight and solemnity as their traditional handwritten signatures. Part 11's written and unambiguous policies were created because employees may be more likely to make errors, mistakenly assuming that they'll be held to a lower level of accountability than they would in executing traditional handwritten signatures.

### Pharm Mission Control Secret Headquarters Laboratory

Chief Strickter: Agent GXP, security measures have to be in place to not allow unauthorized access of the software.

**Minnie: That's not specific enough, Uncle. This kind of system would also have problems like: no audit trails, and data that can be copied or changed at will--**

Chief Strickter: With no documentation of the copying or changes. Minnie, I was getting to that!

**Minnie: Yeah, right! When were you gonna get to the part about how firms have got to train all users of the electronic**

records systems... even clerical personnel, not just analysts and systems administrators?

Chief Strickter: I would get to it if you'd find some way to be silent long enough for my larynx to vibrate. Nevertheless, Agent GXP, backup files have to be automatically created, since original data could get lost and the tests would have to be performed again to determine final disposition of the processes.

**Minnie: So you said a whole sentence, Uncle. Are you happy now?**

Chief Strickter: The hilarity is overwhelming?

**Minnie: See, while you're being sarcastic you could be saying that date and time stamping of data receipt and data entry is required.**

Chief Strickter: The written and unambiguous policies dissuade employees from making errors--

**Minnie: Mistakenly assuming that they'll be held to a lower level of accountability than they would in executing traditional handwritten signatures. Uncle, gotcha again!**

As always, Chief Strickter ends the communiqué with: "Remember, we at Pharm Mission Control are the last hope of freeing the hostages and curing them of their terminal diseases. You must succeed... failure is not an option!

**And as always, Minnie tries to get the last word: "Give 'em heck, Agent GXP."**

Question: Firms' electronic records procedures do not have to require the documentation of calculation or entry errors. True or false?

Answer: False. This falls under the Part 11 mandate that security measures must be in place to prevent unauthorized access of the software. A system such as this would also suffer the following deficiencies: no audit trails, and data that can be copied or changed at will, with no documentation of the copying or changes.

Question: When it comes to firms providing documentation to indicate that analysts are trained in the electronic records software and its applications, Part 11:

A. Strongly suggests it.

B. Darn near requests it.

C. Absolutely demands it.

Answer: C. Part 11 expressly requires that firms train all users of the electronic records systems.

Question: In a case where a firm satisfied every other Part 11 requirement, but didn't automatically create a back-up file for laboratory UV spectrophotometer test results for some tests, the FDA would:

Issue a citation or warning.

Allow for partial compliance.

Not even consider the absence of such back-up files as significant.

Answer: A. Part 11 requires that such files be automatically created, since original data could get lost and the tests would have to be performed again to determine final disposition of the processes.

Question: There is no Part 11 requirement that records show when study data is received and when it is entered into the database. True or false?

Answer: False. Part 11 specifically requires date and time stamping of data receipt and data entry.

Question: If a company can't show verifiable records for a particular data entry step in a test process, the FDA requires the firm to:
Generate data queries or clarifications and then send them to the site to verify missing information or to clarify discrepancies.
Discard all data and start over.
Answer: A. At stake here is Part 11's demands for an audit trail of any and all changes made to the database.

Question: It is not vital that employees accord their electronic signatures the same legal weight and solemnity as their traditional handwritten signatures. True or false?
Answer: False. Without Part 11's written and unambiguous policies, employees may be more likely to make errors, mistakenly assuming that they'll be held to a lower level of accountability than they would in executing traditional handwritten signatures.

## 12. Software

It's daytime outside of a farmhouse. You have to take shelter from a violent tornado. You point your electronic locator at the cluster of farm buildings, but the twister confuses your equipment. When the storm ends you get a "blip" on your screen that indicates the presence of the hostages. But which building? By answering the questions correctly, you locate the correct structure. With wrong answers, you're forced to wear a cow suit before the enemies throw you into a pen of mating-hungry bulls!

Overview:

The FDA doesn't require any specific brands of e-sign software, as long as the system satisfies the necessary features at issue in Part 11.

Part 11 regulations state that it is imperative for software systems to be subject to rigorous procedures that include periodic challenges and evaluation.

There must be Standard Operating Procedures for software error handling, including software testing simulating worst-case conditions.

Even spreadsheet and other calculation programs must be validated, beyond the Part 11 demands on the actual laboratory processes, since these other software programs are a part of the data testing process.

It is necessary to evaluate the impact of software changes on other parts of the testing process program, since software changes could inadvertently impact the integrity and/or the security of the test data.

There must be documentation to ensure that the system is operated as intended by the vendor and performed according to the firm's user requirement specifications. This falls under the Part 11 requirement that comprehensive initial and periodic testing-- as well as training-- be conducted as Standard Operating Procedure.

**Pharm Mission Control Secret Headquarters Laboratory**

Chief Strickter: Agent GXP, no specific brand of software is required, just that system satisfies the necessary Part 11 features.

**Minnie: And the software systems have to be subject to rigorous procedures made up of things like periodic challenges and evaluation.**

Chief Strickter: Boy, you're being nice, for a change, Minnie. Agent GXP, any software programs that are involved in a part of the data testing process must also be validated.

**Minnie: Firms have to be careful about source code.**

Chief Strickter: I'd like to tell him about this. The menu has to be consistent with the source code, the source code has to be consistent througout the company, and...

**Minnie: Firms have to be careful about changing software, since software changes could--**

Chief Strickter: Inadvertently impact the test data's integrity and/or security.

**Minnie: See what I mean? Now you're cutting in on me! Agent GXP, you know that there's got to be Standard Operating Procedure about initial and periodic testing--**

Chief Strickter: And training. Can't stress that too much.

**Minnie: Uncle, you ARE too much!**

As always, Chief Strickter ends the communiqué with: "Remember, we at Pharm Mission Control are the last hope of freeing the hostages and curing them of their terminal diseases. You must succeed... failure is not an option!

**And as always, Minnie tries to get the last word: "Give 'em heck, Agent GXP."**

Question: Which of the following is true about computer software programs that operate all of a firm's laboratory equipment during analysis processes?
Any e-sign software can be used to satisfy Part 11 regulations.
The FDA requires that a specific brand of e-sign software be used, exclusively.
The FDA demands that e-sign software been qualified and/or validated.
Answer: C. The FDA doesn't require any specific brands of software, as long as the system satisfies the necessary features at issue in Part 11.

Question: There must be Standard Operating Procedures for software error handling, including software testing simulating worst case conditions. True or false?
Answer: True. E-sign regulations state that it is imperative for software systems to be subject to rigorous procedures that include periodic challenges and evaluation.

Question: Even spreadsheet and other calculation programs must be validated, beyond the e-sign demands on the actual laboratory processes. True or false?
Answer: True. Since these other software programs are a part of the data testing process, they too must be validated.

Question: It is not necessary to evaluate the impact of software changes on other parts of the testing process program. True or false?

Answer: False. This evaluation is imperative, since software changes could inadvertently impact the integrity and/or the security of the test data.

Question: Which of the following would be a citable violation?
A. There is no documentation to ensure that the system was the most expensive that money could buy.
B. There is no documentation to ensure that the system is operated as intended by the vendor and performed according to the firm's user requirement specifications.
C. There is no documentation to ensure that other similar firms are using the system.
Answer: B. This falls under the Part 11 requirement that comprehensive initial and periodic testing-- as well as training-- be conducted as Standard Operating Procedure.

## 13. Back-ups, record copies, security

At the farmhouse, you attempt to get information out of a reticent enemy agent who poses as a "simple farmer." By answering the questions correctly, you scare the living daylights out of the enemy agent, he gives you the information, and you successfully exit the gates. With wrong answers, the enemy agent ties you upside down on a tractor wheel near the chicken pen and glues chicken feed to your eyelids!

Overview:

Back-up tapes for test processes must be stored in a locked onsite compartment, which only authorized system administrators can access, since Part 11 makes it clear that no unauthorized personnel can have access to data, since it could be changed or destroyed without accountability.

It is a serious matter if a company's system cannot generate accurate and complete copies of records in electronic form onsite, since it is vital for the FDA to be able to audit electronic production records by reviewing electronic copies of a firm's electronic records while inspecting a site.

Employees cannot post their user names and computer passwords in an unsecure place; this lack of security for user name and password will result in a warning letter or a citation.

A firm's electronic records systems cannot allow personnel who have lost their "authorized" status to maintain contact with, or access to, sensitive critical and Data Management System functions.

There must be a security system in place to electronically record and report the inbound and outbound transactions of the laboratory's network system, per the requirement of a complete audit trail of all laboratory test data.

**Pharm Mission Control Secret Headquarters Laboratory**

Chief Strickter: Agent GXP, no unauthorized personnel can have access to electronic data, since it could be changed or destroyed without accountability.

**Minnie: There you go again with the lightweight stuff. Here's a heavy one, Agent GXP: The FDA's got to be able to audit electronic production records.**

Chief Strickter: By reviewing electronic copies of a firm's electronic records while inspecting a site.

**Minnie: And I'm rude?**

Chief Strickter: I'm learning "the younger way of doing things," as you call it. So, Agent GXP, a lack of security for user names and passwords will result in a warning letter or a citation.

**Minnie: (Cough. Ahem!) No compliant system lets people who have lost their "authorized" status--**

Chief Strickter: Maintain contact or access to sensitive critical and limited Data Management System functions.

**Minnie: (Cough. Ahem!) And those ever-important audit trails--**

Chief Strickter: Complete... complete audit trails of all laboratory test data. That's what's important.

**Minnie: I agree.**

Chief Strickter: Agree? I didn't think you knew how.

As always, Chief Strickter ends the communiqué with: "Remember, we at Pharm Mission Control are the last hope of freeing the hostages and curing them of their terminal diseases. You must succeed... failure is not an option!

**And as always, Minnie tries to get the last word: "Give 'em heck, Agent GXP."**

# 𝕻𝖍𝖎𝖑𝖆𝖉𝖊𝖑𝖕𝖍𝖎𝖆 𝕻𝖍𝖆𝖗𝖒𝖆 𝕿𝖎𝖒𝖊𝖘

What happens when companies need to update their computer systems, transfer data to current formats, etc.?

That's a big problem.

As always, you have to make sure your conversion process is validated. You have to have a plan for data migration that ensures no loss of data.

You may have to archive old hardware to make the transition. What if you have data in the old 5-inch floppy form? Once you have copied it, you can dispose of the old data storage form. Be careful with material needed for GLP inspections: you may need to reproduce the whole system.

The good news is that if you have data on a CD that can't be rewritten, that CD doesn't require an audit trail.

Question: So as not to violate Part 11, back-up tapes for test processes can be stored in which valid location?
A. Offsite in an employee's home.
B. A locked onsite compartment, which only authorized system administrators can access.
C. The old, unused refrigerator in the hall outside of the lab cafeteria.
Answer: B. Part 11 makes it clear that no unauthorized personnel can have access to data, since it could be changed or destroyed without accountability.

Question: It is a serious matter if a company's system cannot generate accurate and complete copies of records in electronic form onsite. True or false?

Answer: True. It is vital for the FDA to be able to audit electronic production records by reviewing electronic copies of a firm's electronic records while inspecting a site.

Question: A company anxious to be Part 11 Compliant puts away the originals of magnetic tape backups every 30 days and archives them for years in a locked storage facility.
This is state of the art practice. True or false?
Answer: False. It's good except for one thing: the tape needs to be maintained, checked, and recycled into newer tapes as a protection against deterioration from aging.

Question: John, the system administrator, decides to make a text file back up of the audit log database records from his older but secure computer system before importing the information into his new Part 11 compliant database. Which statement is most correct?
A. He should do it to make sure the system has all the information.
B. He should keep using the old system.
C. He should only export the text file if the whole export process is secure.
Answer: C. A text file is usually not secure. The conversion from one secure system to another via an insecure system is problematic.

Question: Sarah Jenkins and Thomas Meekins had terminated their employment with XYZ laboratories in 1998 and 1999, respectively. Yet they still had access to critical and limited Data Management System functions on June 6, 2000. How would this be viewed by the FDA in light of Part 11?
A. Bravo! This saves the wasted time and money involved in modifying the system to terminate their access.

B. Ho-hum. Who has time for such petty details involving people who no longer work there?

C. Cripes! Is the management of this company out of their minds? Warning letters are in the mail now!

Answer: C. There is nothing secure about a system that allows personnel who have lost their "authorized" status to maintain contact-- much less access-- to sensitive critical and limited Data Management System functions.

Question: There should be a security system in place to electronically record and report the inbound and outbound transactions of the laboratory's network system. True or false?

Answer: True. This is another situation involving the requirement of a complete audit trail of all laboratory test data.

Question: Tony Mitchell posts his user name and computer password on the bulletin board in the company break room. What is most accurate?

A. This is rude.

B. This is stupid.

C. This is stupid and citable.

Answer: C. These items must be kept in a secure place so that no one else has access to them.

## 14. Software and account lock-out

It's night, inside the wine cellar under a farmhouse. You search for the hostages, but you realize that you're in the wrong building. You activate your high-tech equipment to locate the correct structure where the hostages have been hidden. By answering the questions correctly, you triangulate the coordinates of the right edifice and safely get out of the wrong one. With wrong answers, you're thrown from a high silo ledge onto a series of pitchforks tongs rigged by the enemy!

Overview:

The FDA would issue a citation if a firm's system allowed an analyst to bypass the Windows environment of the e-sign software and access all programs, including the DOS prompt, autoexec.bat, and config.sys files through the task bar. This would be a compromise to the security and data integrity issues.

The audit trail switch of a firm's electronic records cannot be intentionally disabled, since the FDA demands that the software allows every data event to be recorded, including modifications and/or deletions.

An excellent feature for Part 11 compliance is one that allows the system to lock out intruders who can't readily provide the correct security authorizations.

Account lock-out on an individual basis gives more of an assurance that only the authorized personnel will have access to the critical and sensitive parts of the system.

In order for e-sign software to be Part 11 compliant, it must record an audit trail consisting of the date, time, user, and changes involved in any data entry event.

**Pharm Mission Control Secret Headquarters Laboratory**

Chief Strickter: Agent GXP, security and data integrity issues cannot be compromised--

**Minnie: Not only that, but, the software has to let every data event be recorded, including modifications and/or deletions.**

Chief Strickter: You're starting again! Let me finish my points, will you? Agent GXP, a system that locks out intruders who can't readily provide the correct security authorizations is a good one.

**Minnie: But I know why!**

Chief Strickter: I do too!

**Minnie: It's because account lock-out on an individual basis further assures that only the authorized personnel can access the critical parts of the system.**

Chief Strickter: And the sensitive parts.

**Minnie: Okay, those too.**

Chief Strickter: And software has got to record an audit trail that includes the date, time, user, and changes--

**Minnie: Don't forget that this involves ANY data entry event, Agent GXP.**

As always, Chief Strickter ends the communiqué with: "Remember, we at Pharm Mission Control are the last hope of freeing the hostages and curing them of their terminal diseases. You must succeed... failure is not an option!

**And as always, Minnie tries to get the last word: "Give 'em heck, Agent GXP."**

Question: The FDA would issue a citation if a firm's system allowed an analyst to bypass the Windows environment of the e-sign software and access all programs, including the DOS

prompt, autoexec.bat, and config.sys files through the task bar. True or false?
Answer: True. This would be a compromise to the security and data integrity issues.

Question: It would be a bad idea to use a software program that included a user definable parameter on # of failed attempts until the account becomes locked. True or false?
Answer: False. This is an excellent feature for Part 11 compliance. It allows the system to lock out intruders who can't readily provide the correct security authorizations.

Question: Account locking should ideally be set up to alert the administrator if too many attempts are made from a certain computer. True or false?
Answer: True. External security provided by your firewall is not all you need to worry about.

Question: Which of the following would result in a Part 11 violation?
A. The audit trail switch can be intentionally disabled thus preventing the act of recording analytical data that was modified or edited.
B. The audit trail switch can jam and remain on even if someone tried to turn it off.
C. There is no switch that allows the audit trail function to be turned off.
Answer: A. The FDA demands that the software allows every data event to be recorded, including modifications and/or deletions.

Question: In choosing a software that is Part-11 compliant, which of the following best indicates the data field that must recorded by the software by necessity?

A. Date
B. Time
C. User making the change
D. Actual changes
E. All of the above
Answer: E. In order for the software to be compliant, it must record an audit trail consisting of the date, time, user, and changes involved in any data entry event.

## 15. Part 11 and the FDA

That night outside of the farm's tornado shelter, you try to enter the criminals' locked and guarded secret stronghold. You are trying to get to where the victims are being held. By answering the questions correctly, you get past the guards and enter the structure. With wrong answers, you're buried in a soggy fertilizer pit... head first.

Overview:

The FDA realized that software development, as well as implementation, takes time. So, although 21 CFR Part 11 regulations have been in place since August 1997, the FDA had not strictly enforced them for years, in order to give manufacturers time to bring their systems and processes into compliance. But during the past years, the agency has become much more diligent about enforcing Part 11 by issuing inspection observation documents and, in some cases, warning letters.

The FDA has the power to terminate a firm's operations for non-compliance.

Biologics licenses, product licenses, new drug applications, and handwritten electronic signatures are all subject to electronic records regulations.

Personal e-mail is not subject to the regulations, unless it somehow becomes part of the lab-testing data process.

The paperless system Part 11 seeks to regulate will yield benefits for both users and the FDA, including: increased speed of information exchange, improved ability to integrate, trend, and search data, a reduction in errors, and a reduction in costs related to data storage. These benefits far outweigh the cumbersome process of learning and executing Part 11 compliance.

### Pharm Mission Control Secret Headquarters Laboratory

Chief Strickter: Agent GXP, the FDA understands that software development takes time. Implementation too.

**Minnie: But that's not to say that the FDA hasn't begun to enforce Part 11 regulations. They can do a lot of things to punish a non-compliant company.**

Chief Strickter: Like, terminating its operations.

**Minnie: Here's one you didn't think of, Uncle? Computer games and personal e-mail are not subjected to the regulations--**

Chief Strickter: I thought of them, all right. But if they become part of the lab-testing data process, then the regulations do apply.

**Minnie: That's a long shot! I bet some employees are gonna think that all these electronic records statutes are too cumbersome to be worth it.**

Chief Strickter: Ah! But they'd be wrong. The reduction in costs and the increase in speed outweigh the difficulty.

As always, Chief Strickter ends the communiqué with: "Remember, we at Pharm Mission Control are the last hope of freeing the hostages and curing them of their terminal diseases. You must succeed... failure is not an option!

**And as always, Minnie tries to get the last word: "Give 'em heck, Agent GXP."**

# Philadelphia Pharma Times

Exclusive!!!

The Philadelphia Pharma Times grabbed hold of Agent GXP in between life-threatening adventures to tell us about Part 11 and e-mail. Click ahead for more.

What advice can you give us about handling e-mail? Does it need to be Part 11 compliant?

**If you don't think about this issue, you could get yourself into more trouble than the crocodile-filled waters I escaped from before!**

If you use e-mail to send alerts about your equipment and manufacturing or to communicate official reports and decisions, they would need to become Part 11 compliant, and that's not easy, because they are probably backed up differently from other systems, and many e-mails are deleted. My advice is to try to keep e-mail out of situations requiring Part 11 compliance.

Question: Which of the following are not subject to electronic records regulations?
A. Biologics and product licenses
B. New drug applications
C. Personal e-mail on company computer
Answer: C. Personal e-mails are not subjected to the regulations, unless they somehow become part of the lab-testing data process.

Question: 21 CFR Part 11 regulations have been in place since August 1997, but the FDA had not strictly enforced them for years, in order to give manufacturers time to bring their systems and processes into compliance. True or false?
Answer: True. The FDA realized that software development, as well as implementation, takes time.

Question: Which of the following is true?
A. The FDA can cry and scream all they want, but they can't do anything detrimental to non-compliant firms.
B. The FDA has the power to actually come in and shut down operations that are not in compliance.
C. The FDA can only give firms a "slap on the wrist" for non-compliance.

<u>Answer:</u> B. The agency can terminate a firm's operations for non-compliance.

<u>Question:</u> According to the FDA, the paperless system Part 11 seeks to regulate will yield benefits for both users and the agency, including:
A. Increased speed of information exchange.
B. Improved ability to integrate, trend and search data.
C. A reduction in errors.
D. A reduction in costs related to data storage.
E. All of the above.
<u>Answer:</u> E. These benefits far outweigh the cumbersome process of learning and executing Part 11 compliance.

## 16. Accountability of employees and its parameters

You are inside the farm's tornado shelter on the next day. If you make the right moves, you can regain possession of the hostages. By answering the questions correctly, you burst into the tornado shelter and unlatch the hostages. With wrong answers, you and the hostages are locked inside the shelter with a canister of activated nerve gas.

Overview:
Part 11 requires firms to implement "written policies that hold individuals accountable and responsible for actions initiated under their electronic signatures, in order to determine record and signature falsification."

Employees should be made to sign a paragraph like: "I understand that electronic signatures are legally binding and have the same meaning as handwritten signatures". There should be documented evidence that employees are trained on Part 11 and on the meaning of electronic signatures.

An electronic records system is not considered a closed system if it allows access via e-mail through the Internet.

The name, date and time of an electronic signature do not have to be displayed on every page of the signed document. The electronic signature information may appear in only one place in the document just like when you're using a conventional paper document. However, the information must be linked to the document and must be readable in electronic and hard copy.

The FDA will still accept paper documents after 2002.

Part 11's requirements for "meta data" (information about information) do not require the manufacturer to provide the FDA with unlimited access to all data, just those records required under predicate rules and their associated audit trails.

**Pharm Mission Control Secret Headquarters Laboratory**

Chief Strickter: Agent GXP, not only should there be employee training on e-signatures, but the training must be documented.

**Minnie: Yes, yes. But, once again, you miss the vital issues here. Internet access would make the system an open one.**

Chief Strickter: Because of the number of relay station servers involved. I know, I know.

**Minnie: Really? I thought that was part of MY research.**

Chief Strickter: Hey, I make sure Web sites use encryption when I use my credit card over the Internet.

**Minnie: Hmmm. You know, maybe you're not as behind the times as I thought. So, Agent GXP, e-signature information only has to show up in one place in the document--**

Chief Strickter: Just like when you're using a conventional paper document.

**Minnie: Let me finish this one, please? Agent GXP, the e-signature information still has to be linked to the document and it has to be readable in electronic and hard copy.**

Chief Strickter: When were you going to mention that, after the year 2002, the FDA will still be accepting paper documents?

**Minnie: When were you going to mention that only those records required under predicate rules and their associated audit trails have to be made available without limit?**

Chief Strickter: When you assist me in doing my job, instead of trying to do it for me!

As always, Chief Strickter ends the communiqué with: "Remember, we at Pharm Mission Control are the last hope of freeing the hostages and curing them of their terminal diseases. You must succeed... failure is not an option!

**And as always, Minnie tries to get the last word: "Give 'em heck, Agent GXP."**

# Philadelphia Pharma Times

To the Editor,

On the subject of adminstrative controls, I would like to write you about the importance of involving appropriate personnel in Part 11 procedures. If the Vice President of Medical Affairs signs off on an electronic report from the lab, that may not be good enough. Just because you have e-signatures doesn't mean that you can bypass the usual chain of command and control.

Sincerely,
Agent GXP
Philadelphia, Pennsylvania

The editors of the Philadelphia Pharma Times are very pleased to introduce our new column, "Dear Agent GXP". He will begin with a topic that is relevant to the current episode on employee accountability.

Dear Agent GXP,

Employee accountability can only be established through training. Do the training systems need to be Part 11 compliant?

Sincerely,

Perplexed in Philadelphia

**Dear Perplexed,**

I will answer not only your specific question but show you how to think through a question that may not be specifically addressed in the regulations.

First, is it an area over which the FDA has authority? The answer is yes. Let's proceed to the next question.

Second, do you keep your records in electronic form?
If the answer is no, then you don't have to be concerned about Part 11--but you do need to be concerned about maintaining paper records on thousands of employees in a manner that the FDA can easily audit.

Do you have a Learning Management System to run your training? That needs to be Part 11 compliant. However, since the only parts the FDA is concerned about are student scores and tracking, those are the parts that need to be compliant. If they are secured against one person in the company manipulating them and require collusion to access, they should be adequately compliant. You do need to validate it....

A problem can come from the in-between situations. For example, let's say that your secretary keeps a record of attendance and scores at training sessions on a disc in her file cabinet but keeps paper records of the sign-in sheets. (This is a hybrid system, containing both paper and electronic records, and is very common at FDA-inspected companies.) You might not think of telling her that a potential Part 11 violation is going on.

Therefore, the third question to ask yourself is, "Is it possible for someone to alter the data without collusion and without an audit trail?" If the answer is yes, you may have a Part 11 problem.

Question: How can a firm implement the required "written policies that hold individuals accountable and responsible for actions initiated under their electronic signatures, in order to determine record and signature falsification?"
A. There is no concrete way to implement the referenced written policies.
B. Let each employee sign a paragraph like: "I understand that electronic signatures are legally binding and have the same meaning as handwritten signatures."
C. Let each employee decide how and when they will give oral assent to being held accountable.
Answer: B. There should be documented evidence that employees are trained on part 11 and on the meaning of electronic signatures.

Question: If an electronic records system maintains security controls to restrict external access by unauthorized personnel in a system allowing access via e-mail through the Internet, is it considered a closed system?
A. Yes
B. No
C. Who cares, as long as unauthorized personnel are restricted?

Answer: B. This constitutes an open system since Internet access usually involves a number of relay station servers. That's why encryption is utilized when using credit cards to place orders via Internet.

Question: The name, date, and time of an electronic signature should be displayed on every page of the signed document. True or false?
Answer: False. The electronic signature information may appear in only one place in the document just like when you're using a conventional paper document. However, the information must be linked to the document and must be readable in electronic and hard copy.

Question: Part 11's requirements for "meta data" (information about information) require the manufacturer to provide the FDA with unlimited access to:
A. All electronic data within a computerized system.
B. All vending machines and coffeemakers in the cafeteria.
C. Specified data
Answer: C. Only those records required under predicate rules and their associated audit trails must be made available without limit.

## 17. Audit trail issues

It's daytime on the highway. Because the criminal troopers have intercepted the Pharm Mission Control transmissions, they have learned your escape route. They spring up out of nowhere to attack the escaping hostages led by you, Agent GXP. By answering the questions correctly, you and the hostages survive the ambush to flee. With wrong answers, you and the hostages become road kill... until ravenous buzzards circle, dive, and scavenge the flesh from your bones!

Overview:

There is not yet a standard across all agencies for submission of e-records, but further technological developments may soon provide for such a standard.

According to GLP regulations, you must not delete raw data. But you can delete electronic raw data from your hard disk after you've copied them accurately and completely to a permanent storage device. The copy process must be robust and validated. There must also be an audit trail about date and time of this procedure.

Records in electronic form must be archived in electronic form. A paper print-out is not a substitute for an electronic record.

E-sign software should be designed so that the operator cannot switch off the audit trail.
Since computer generated audit trail is a key requirement, e-sign software without this feature must be upgraded to compliant status. Also, an implementation plan must be developed with a time schedule on when the audit trail will be available.

**Pharm Mission Control Secret Headquarters Laboratory**

Chief Strickter: Agent GXP, there isn't a standard across all agencies yet--

**Minnie: But don't let that fool you! Further technological developments could cause for such a standard to be adopted. Soon.**

Chief Strickter: Here's one that Minnie didn't know about: raw data can be deleted from the hard disk--

**Minnie: But only if the copy process is robust and validated. What, Uncle, you think I'm behind you?**

Chief Strickter: Bet you didn't know that there has be an audit trail about date and time... even for this deletion!

**Minnie: I knew that! How about this? You're not allowed to archive the paper print-out of an electronic record.**

Chief Strickter: Because records in electronic form have to be archived in electronic form.

**Minnie: A paper print-out is not a substitute for an electronic record.**

Chief Strickter: I don't know which one of us won that round, but I'm sure you didn't know that e-sign software shouldn't be designed in a way that allows an operator to switch off the audit trail.

**Minnie: Yes I did! In fact, because computer generated audit trail is a major requirement, non-compliant firms need to find out when the vendor can add on or upgrade the e-sign software.**

Chief Strickter: Minnie, that's not enough. This non-compliant company has to develop an implementation plan stating when the audit trail feature will be available.

**Minnie: With an acceptable timetable. I know, I know!**

As always, Chief Strickter ends the communiqué with: "Remember, we at Pharm Mission Control are the last hope of freeing the hostages and curing them of their terminal diseases. You must succeed... failure is not an option!

**And as always, Minnie tries to get the last word: "Give 'em heck, Agent GXP."**

# Philadelphia Pharma Times

Agent GXP, do you have any hints for us about buying software for Part 11?

**Pharm Mission Control won't let me endorse any particular product, but I can tell you this: Before you buy "Part 11 Compliant Software System" ask the vendor whether the product produces audit trails not just on people but also on the software installed on your system, because software modifications can lead not only to the need to revalidate, but also to changes in the data. Of course, make sure you have a data back-up before you change the software.**

While we're getting ready for some dangerous answers on audit trails, let me ask you something I always wondered about: What time do you use for a time stamp?

**That's a good question, and since I'm in a rush, I'll give you just the basics: Whatever your choice is, it should be**

consistent and written down as an SOP. The best solution would be to use the time of your database server. One problem could be a local time stamp that isn't posted to your central server. Ask about this when you set up your Part 11 compliant software.

Question: Is there a standard across all agencies for submission of e-records?
A. Yes, of course!
B. There never will be a standard, silly!
C. No, not at the moment .
Answer: C. Although there isn't a standard across all agencies yet, further technological developments may soon provide for such a standard.

Question: According to GLP regulations you must not delete raw data, but can you delete electronic raw data from your hard disk after you've copied them accurately and completely to a permanent storage device?
A. Yes
B. No
C. Just don't get caught!
Answer: A. You can delete the raw data from the hard disk, but only if the copy process is robust and validated. Furthermore, there must be an audit trail about date and time.

Question: If you have an electronic record and want to archive it, can you make a print-out of that record, archive the paper, and delete the record?
A. Yes
B. No
C. Don't let the right hand know what the left hand is doing.

Answer: B. You can't archive the paper print-out of an electronic record. Records in electronic form must be archived in electronic form. A paper print-out is not a substitute for an electronic record.

## 18. Topics related to system administration

On the next day, outside of a sleazy lakeside motel, you try to fend off enemy agents that have located your hiding place for the rescued hostages. By answering the questions correctly, you keep the criminal shooters at bay. With wrong answers, you and the hostages are bullet-riddled... into human Swiss cheese!

Overview:

An operator should not be able to sign an audit trail. If somebody could sign an audit trail, that person could also change the content of the audit trail.

Part 11 does not require a back up power supply for automated equipment. However, if a power failure could result in the loss of required records or data, a back-up power supply could assure compliance in the event of a power failure.

Before FDA inspectors' arrival at a firm to audit electronic records, or during the audit, the firm must set inspectors up with a User Account on the network in the company being inspected, since it's a closed system by requirement.

The system administrator should not be allowed to know the operator's password. In fact, after entering the system for the first time, an operator should change the password. If the operator forgets the password, the system administrator must reset the password and the user defines a new one.

The exact definition of an electronic record is: any information in digital form that has been created, modified, archived or distributed by a computer. Electronic records can be text, pictures, and sound. They are created when they're saved to some durable storage device. While the information is simply in RAM (in the computer's volatile memory), it is not a record.

## Pharm Mission Control Secret Headquarters Laboratory

Chief Strickter: Agent GXP, a firm can't let an operator sign an audit trail. And I bet "Smarty-Pants Minnie" here doesn't know why.

**Minnie: "Smarty-Pants Minnie" DOES know. Anybody who could sign an audit trail could also change the audit trail's content.**

Chief Strickter: Bravo! But not that impressive. How about this one: There's no requirement for a back-up power supply--

**Minnie: But, but, but if a power failure could result in the loss of required records or data, a back-up power supply could make for compliance in the event of a power failure.**

Chief Strickter: Bravo again. But I bet you don't get this one: a company needs to set up user accounts for anybody who enters the system--

**Minnie: Duh! It's a CLOSED system.**

Chief Strickter: This includes internal auditors and external inspectors.

**Minnie:** I'll stump you with this one for sure! After entering the system for the first time, an operator needs to change the password.

**Chief Strickter:** Hah! If the operator forgets the password, the system administrator has to reset the password and the user will define a new one.

**Minnie: You've been reading my notes at night... I know it! Here's one: electronic records can be text, pictures, and sound. But when are they considered created?**

**Chief Strickter:** Minnie, you underestimate me! They're created when they're saved to any type of durable storage device.

**Minnie: You're not fighting fair... I can't prove it, but I'm sure of it! Anyway, Agent GXP, while the information is simply in RAM it is not a record.**

**Chief Strickter:** And are you going to explain what RAM is?

**Minnie: Sure. Random Access Memory... the volatile memory that's deleted when you turn off the computer.**

As always, Chief Strickter ends the communiqué with: "Remember, we at Pharm Mission Control are the last hope of freeing the hostages and curing them of their terminal diseases. You must succeed... failure is not an option!"

**And as always, Minnie tries to get the last word: "Give 'em heck, Agent GXP."**

<u>Question:</u> Which of the following is true?
A. Every operator must sign an audit trail.

B. No operator signature is required for an audit trail.

C. The e-sign requirements are a pain in the neck.

Answer: B. An operator should not be able to sign an audit trail. If somebody could sign an audit trail, that person could also change the content of the audit trail.

Question: Part 11 requires a back up power supply for automated equipment supply. True or false?

Answer: False. However, if a power failure could result in the loss of required records or data, a back-up power supply could assure compliance in the event of a power failure.

Question: Before FDA inspectors' arrival at a firm to audit electronic records, or during the audit, the firm must set inspectors up with a User Account on the network in the company being inspected. True or false?

Answer: True. In the required case of a closed system, it is recommended that the company set up user accounts for anybody who enters the system. This includes internal auditors and external inspectors.

Question: The system administrator should be allowed to know the operator's password. True or false?

Answer: False. After entering the system for the first time, an operator should change the password. If the operator forgets the password, the system administrator must reset the password and the user defines a new one.

Question: What is the exact definition of an electronic record?

A. Any information in digital form that has been created, modified, archived or distributed by a computer.

B. Any 45, 33-1/3, or 78 rpm vinyl phonograph disk.

C. Digital readouts of statistics involving unusual sports achievement.

Answer: A. Electronic records can be text, pictures, and sound. They are created when they're saved to some durable storage device. While the information is simply in RAM (in the computer's volatile memory) it is not a record.

## 19. Exclusions from Part 11

It's night time, and you're on the rooftop of the sleazy motel with the hostages. As the Pharm Mission Control helicopter finally shows up and lets down a rope ladder for you and the victims to climb up, the enemy troopers are approaching fast! By answering the questions correctly, you and the hostages successfully climb up and into the helicopter. With wrong answers, you and the hostages fall from the rooftop.

Overview:

Part 11 applies regardless of whether the electronic record was created in a pharmaceutical industry lab or in a contract lab.

Part 11 regulations apply to manufacturing controls of drugs that are already on the market. However, data that have been generated before August 20, 1997 in support for that new drug application don't have to comply with part 11.

Site access systems (e.g. swipe cards, people departure recorders) are not subject to Part 11 unless, for some unusual reason, they became part of an FDA submission.

If lots or batches were rejected during manufacturing, the instrument records must be retained, since analysis of data to ID nonconforming product and problems is required. This analysis can't be performed if the rejected-lot data is not retained. If records are deleted after analysis, the FDA might not be able to determine if you performed the mandated analysis.

Data that have been generated before August 20, 1997 and have to be submitted to the FDA are exempt from Part 11 compliance, since Part 11 is not retroactive.

**Pharm Mission Control Secret Headquarters Laboratory**

Chief Strickter: Agent GXP, Part 11 applies whether the electronic record was created in a pharmaceutical industry lab or in a contract lab.

**Minnie: So what? This is what the field agent needs the most: manufacturing control of drugs that are already on the market are subject to Part 11 regulations.**

Chief Strickter: But data that have been generated before August 20, 1997 in support for a new drug application don't have to comply. And Part 11 isn't retroactive.

**Minnie: Know-it-all! Anyway, Agent GXP, site access information wouldn't usually be subject to Part 11.**

Chief Strickter: Here's one to stump you, Minnie: a firm can't delete records after analysis. Otherwise--

**Minnie: Otherwise, the FDA might not be able to determine if the mandated procedures were performed. Gotcha again!**

As always, Chief Strickter ends the communiqué with: "Remember, we at Pharm Mission Control are the last hope of freeing the hostages and curing them of their terminal diseases. You must succeed... failure is not an option!

**And as always, Minnie tries to get the last word: "Give 'em heck, Agent GXP."**

Question: Part 11 applies only to pharmaceutical industry laboratories, but not to contract labs. True or false?
Answer: False. It doesn't matter whether the electronic record was created in a pharmaceutical industry lab or in a contract lab.

Question: Part 11 applies only for new drug applications and not for drugs that are already on the market. True or false?
Answer: False. Manufacturing control of drugs that are already on the market is subject to Part 11 regulations. However, data that have been generated before August 20, 1997 in support for that new drug application don't have to comply with part 11.

Question: Site access systems (e.g. swipe cards, people departure) are subject to Part 11. True or false?
Answer: False. This information would be normally only be subject to Part 11 if for some unusual reason it became part of an FDA submission.

Question: If lots or batches were rejected during manufacturing, the instrument records:
A. Must be retained.
B. Can be deleted.
C. Shouldn't even have been saved.
Answer: A. Analysis of data to ID nonconforming product and problems is required. This analysis can't be performed if the rejected-lot data is not retained. If records are deleted after analysis, the FDA might not be able to determine if you performed the mandated analysis.

Question: Data that have been generated before August 20, 1997 and have to be submitted to the FDA:
A. Must comply with part 11.
B. Are exempt from Part 11 compliance.
C. Are outdated and should be disregarded.
Answer: B. Part 11 is not retroactive.

## 20. Computers in a Part 11 environment

It's night time, outside of the Pharm Mission Control complex. The criminals have hit your rescue chopper with a hand-held missile launcher beside their vehicle on the ground. If the pilot can just land the disabled helicopter inside the perimeter of the Pharm Mission Control compound, then ground support agents can provide them with the cover of counter fire. By answering the questions correctly, you safely land upon the heavily-guarded grounds of Pharm Mission Control. With wrong answers, you and the hostages are shot down.

Overview:

If a system can store instrument control parameters on a floppy, on a PC card, or in internal memory, Part 11 could apply, at least in theory.

Although the FDA still accepts paper records, firms must be "electronic record" compliant because computers are usually used at some point in the process. Part 11 applies whenever computers are used to create, evaluate, maintain, transmit, and archive data.

Part 11 requirements for electronic records state that, when you turn off the computer, remove all intermediate power supplies, and switch it on again, if the data are still there, they are stored in a durable storage device. Therefore, they must be compliant.

## Pharm Mission Control Secret Headquarters Laboratory

Chief Strickter: Agent GXP, listen up! Part 11 could apply if a system can store instrument control parameters on a floppy disk, on a PC card--

**Minnie: Or in internal memory. And it applies whenever computers are used to create, evaluate, maintain--**

Chief Strickter: Transmit and archive data.

**Minnie: All phases, Agent GXP. All phases.**

Chief Strickter: So Minnie, trick question: how could a chromatography laboratory get around Part 11 regulations?

**Minnie: It would have to go back to a strip chart recorder, since most modern integrators can do some kind of data reprocessing.**

Chief Strickter: Can't get anything by you, huh? And what's the specific reason?

**Minnie: Any type of electronic record system that can store information in a durable storage device has to be Part 11 compliant. Want more?**

Chief Strickter: Let's just call a truce.

**Minnie: Okay. Truce.**

As always, Chief Strickter ends the communiqué with: "Remember, we at Pharm Mission Control are the last hope of freeing the hostages and curing them of their terminal diseases. You must succeed... failure is not an option!

**And as always, Minnie tries to get the last word: "Give 'em heck, Agent GXP."**

Question: Which of the following is true of a system which can store instrument control parameters on a floppy disc?
Part 11 could apply.
Part 11 could not possibly apply.
The FDA could care less about some simple floppy disc.
Answer: A. If a system can store instrument control parameters on a floppy, on a PC card, or in internal memory, Part 11 could apply, at least in theory.

Question: Part 11 requirements for electronic records say that, when you turn off the computer, remove all intermediate power supplies, and switch it on again, if the data are still in there, they are stored in...
A. A durable storage device
B. Cyberspace
C. Outer space
Answer: A. Part 11 requirements for electronic records say that when you turn off the computer, remove all intermediate power supplies, and switch it on again, if the data are still there, they are stored in a durable storage device. Therefore, this data must be handled in a manner that is compliant with Part 11 regulations.

Question: What is wrong with this picture?

A. The key is left unattended in the lock.
B. The green on light shows the computer is working and noone is watching it.
C. The CD-ROM cover can be easily opened and someone can insert a CD into the server.
D. The server is not bolted down so that noone can access the hardware except the system administrator.
Answer: A. This is a warning letter waiting to be delivered. Did you ever see this happen?

Congratulations!

You as Agent GXP have successfully ended Red Raven's reign of terror at the Lax Pharmaceutical Corporation's compound.

You have rescued the hostages and have brought them safely back to Pharm Mission Control headquarters, where they will participate in clinical trials for the medicines they so desperately need.

The regulations follow:

**Minnie: Uncle, I have trouble understanding what "predicate" means in that Compliance Policy Guide. I**

**always thought it was something with grammar, like "subject" and "predicate."**

Chief Strickter: Minnie, that's not such a bad way to think about it. Just like the subject carries more weight than the predicate, Part 11 is a more fundamental rule than predicate rules like Part 211 or 820.

Title 21 Code of Federal Regulations (21 CFR Part 11)
Electronic Records; Electronic Signatures
Final Rule Published in the Federal Register
WAIS Document Retrieval [Federal Register: March 20, 1997 (Volume 62, Number 54)]
[Rules and Regulations]
[Page 13429-13466]
From the Federal Register Online via GPO Access [wais.access.gpo.gov]
[DOCID:fr20mr97-25]
[[Page 13429]]
_____ Part II
Department of Health and Human Services
_____
Food and Drug Administration
_____
21 CFR Part 11
Electronic Records; Electronic Signatures; Final Rule
Electronic Submissions; Establishment of Public Docket; Notice
DEPARTMENT OF HEALTH AND HUMAN SERVICES
Food and Drug Administration
21 CFR Part 11
[Docket No. 92N-0251]
RIN 0910-AA29
Electronic Records; Electronic Signatures
AGENCY: Food and Drug Administration, HHS.
ACTION: Final rule.
-----------------------------------------------------------------------
SUMMARY: The Food and Drug Administration (FDA) is issuing regulations
that provide criteria for acceptance by FDA, under certain
circumstances, of electronic records, electronic signatures, and
handwritten signatures executed to electronic records as equivalent to
paper records and handwritten signatures executed on paper. These
regulations, which apply to all FDA program areas, are intended to
permit the widest possible use of electronic technology, compatible
with FDA's responsibility to promote and protect public health. The use
of electronic records as well as their submission to FDA is voluntary.
Elsewhere in this issue of the Federal Register, FDA is publishing a
document providing information concerning submissions that the agency
is prepared to accept electronically .
DATES: Effective August 20, 1997. Submit written comments on the
information collection provisions of this final rule by May 19, 1997.
ADDRESSES: Submit written comments on the information collection
provisions of this final rule to the Dockets Management Branch (HFA-
305), Food and Drug Administration, 12420 Parklawn Dr., rm. 1-23,
Rockville, MD 20857.
The final rule is also available electronically via Internet:
http://www.fda.gov.

FOR FURTHER INFORMATION CONTACT:
Paul J. Motise, Center for Drug Evaluation and Research (HFD-325),
Food and Drug Administration, 7520 Standish Pl., Rockville, MD 20855,
301-594-1089. E-mail address via Internet: Motise@CDER.FDA.GOV, [[Note 5/21/2001: Current address is
pmotise@ora.fda.gov]] or
Tom M. Chin, Division of Compliance Policy (HFC-230), Food and Drug
Administration, 5600 Fishers Lane, Rockville, MD 20857, 301-827-0410.
E-mail address via Internet: TChin@FDAEM.SSW.DHHS.GOV [[Note 5/21/2001: Current address is
tchin@ora.fda.gov]]

SUPPLEMENTARY INFORMATION:
I. Background
In 1991, members of the pharmaceutical industry met with the agency
to determine how they could accommodate paperless record systems under
the current good manufacturing practice (CGMP) regulations in parts 210
and 211 (21 CFR parts 210 and 211). FDA created a Task Force on
Electronic Identification/Signatures to develop a uniform approach by
which the agency could accept electronic signatures and records in all
program areas. In a February 24, 1992, report, a task force subgroup,
the Electronic Identification/Signature Working Group, recommended
publication of an advance notice of proposed rulemaking (ANPRM) to
obtain public comment on the issues involved.
In the Federal Register of July 21, 1992 (57 FR 32185), FDA
published the ANPRM, which stated that the agency was considering the
use of electronic identification/signatures, and requested comments on
a number of related topics and concerns. FDA received 53 comments on
the ANPRM. In the Federal Register of August 31, 1994 (59 FR 45160),
the agency published a proposed rule that incorporated many of the
comments to the ANPRM, and requested that comments on the proposed
regulation be submitted by November 29, 1994. A complete discussion of
the options considered by FDA and other background information on the
agency's policy on electronic records and electronic signatures can be
found in the ANPRM and the proposed rule.
FDA received 49 comments on the proposed rule. The commenters
represented a broad spectrum of interested parties: Human and
veterinary pharmaceutical companies as well as biological products,
medical device, and food interest groups, including 11 trade
associations, 25 manufacturers, and 1 Federal agency.
II. Highlights of the Final Rule
The final rule provides criteria under which FDA will consider
electronic records to be equivalent to paper records, and electronic
signatures equivalent to traditional handwritten signatures. Part 11
(21 CFR part 11) applies to any paper records required by statute or
agency regulations and supersedes any existing paper record
requirements by providing that electronic records may be used in lieu
of paper records. Electronic signatures which meet the requirements of
the rule will be considered to be equivalent to full handwritten
signatures, initials, and other general signings required by agency
regulations.
Section 11.2 provides that records may be maintained in electronic
form and electronic signatures may be used in lieu of traditional
signatures. Records and signatures submitted to the agency may be
presented in an electronic form provided the requirements of part 11
are met and the records have been identified in a public docket as the
type of submission the agency accepts in an electronic form. Unless
records are identified in this docket as appropriate for electronic
submission, only paper records will be regarded as official
submissions.
Section 11.3 defines terms used in part 11, including the terms:
Biometrics, closed system, open system, digital signature, electronic
record, electronic signature, and handwritten signature.

Section 11.10 describes controls for closed systems, systems to which access is controlled by persons responsible for the content of electronic records on that system. These controls include measures designed to ensure the integrity of system operations and information stored in the system. Such measures include: (1) Validation; (2) the ability to generate accurate and complete copies of records; (3) archival protection of records; (4) use of computer-generated, time-stamped audit trails; (5) use of appropriate controls over systems documentation; and (6) a determination that persons who develop, maintain, or use electronic records and signature systems have the education, training, and experience to perform their assigned tasks. Section 11.10 also addresses the security of closed systems and requires that: (1) System access be limited to authorized individuals; (2) operational system checks be used to enforce permitted sequencing of steps and events as appropriate; (3) authority checks be used to ensure that only authorized individuals can use the system, electronically sign a record, access the operation or computer system input or output device, alter a record, or perform operations; (4) device (e.g., terminal) checks be used to determine the validity of the source of data input or operation instruction; and (5) written policies be established and adhered to holding individuals accountable and responsible for actions initiated under their electronic signatures, so as to deter record and signature falsification.

Section 11.30 sets forth controls for open systems, including the controls required for closed systems in Sec. 11.10 and additional measures such as document encryption and use of appropriate digital signature standards

[[Page 13431]]

to ensure record authenticity, integrity, and confidentiality.

Section 11.50 requires signature manifestations to contain information associated with the signing of electronic records. This information must include the printed name of the signer, the date and time when the signature was executed, and the meaning (such as review, approval, responsibility, and authorship) associated with the signature. In addition, this information is subject to the same controls as for electronic records and must be included in any human readable forms of the electronic record (such as electronic display or printout).

Under Sec. 11.70, electronic signatures and handwritten signatures executed to electronic records must be linked to their respective records so that signatures cannot be excised, copied, or otherwise transferred to falsify an electronic record by ordinary means.

Under the general requirements for electronic signatures, at Sec. 11.100, each electronic signature must be unique to one individual and must not be reused by, or reassigned to, anyone else. Before an organization establishes, assigns, certifies, or otherwise sanctions an individual's electronic signature, the organization shall verify the identity of the individual.

Section 11.200 provides that electronic signatures not based on biometrics must employ at least two distinct identification components such as an identification code and password. In addition, when an individual executes a series of signings during a single period of controlled system access, the first signing must be executed using all electronic signature components and the subsequent signings must be executed using at least one component designed to be used only by that individual. When an individual executes one or more signings not performed during a single period of controlled system access, each signing must be executed using all of the electronic signature components.

Electronic signatures not based on biometrics are also required to be used only by their genuine owners and administered and executed to

- 101 -

ensure that attempted use of an individual's electronic signature by anyone else requires the collaboration of two or more individuals. This would make it more difficult for anyone to forge an electronic signature. Electronic signatures based upon biometrics must be designed to ensure that such signatures cannot be used by anyone other than the genuine owners.

Under Sec. 11.300, electronic signatures based upon use of identification codes in combination with passwords must employ controls to ensure security and integrity. The controls must include the following provisions: (1) The uniqueness of each combined identification code and password must be maintained in such a way that no two individuals have the same combination of identification code and password; (2) persons using identification codes and/or passwords must ensure that they are periodically recalled or revised; (3) loss management procedures must be followed to deauthorize lost, stolen, missing, or otherwise potentially compromised tokens, cards, and other devices that bear or generate identification codes or password information; (4) transaction safeguards must be used to prevent unauthorized use of passwords and/or identification codes, and to detect and report any attempt to misuse such codes; (5) devices that bear or generate identification codes or password information, such as tokens or cards, must be tested initially and periodically to ensure that they function properly and have not been altered in an unauthorized manner.

III. Comments on the Proposed Rule

A. General Comments

1. Many comments expressed general support for the proposed rule. Noting that the proposal's regulatory approach incorporated several suggestions submitted by industry in comments on the ANPRM, a number of comments stated that the proposal is a good example of agency and industry cooperation in resolving technical issues.

Several comments also noted that both industry and the agency can realize significant benefits by using electronic records and electronic signatures, such as increasing the speed of information exchange, cost savings from the reduced need for storage space, reduced errors, data integration/trending, product improvement, manufacturing process streamlining, improved process control, reduced vulnerability of electronic signatures to fraud and abuse, and job creation in industries involved in electronic record and electronic signature technologies.

One comment noted that, when part 11 controls are satisfied, electronic signatures and electronic records have advantages over paper systems, advantages that include: (1) Having automated databases that enable more advanced searches of information, thus obviating the need for manual searches of paper records; (2) permitting information to be viewed from multiple perspectives; (3) permitting determination of trends, patterns, and behaviors; and (4) avoiding initial and subsequent document misfiling that may result from human error. There were several comments on the general scope and effect of proposed part 11. These comments noted that the final regulations will be viewed as a standard by other Government agencies, and may strongly influence the direction of electronic record and electronic signature technologies. One comment said that FDA's position on electronic signatures/electronic records is one of the most pressing issues for the pharmaceutical industry and has a significant impact on the industry's future competitiveness. Another comment said that the rule constitutes an important milestone along the Nation's information superhighway.

FDA believes that the extensive industry input and collaboration that went into formulating the final rule is representative of a productive partnership that will facilitate the use of advanced technologies. The agency acknowledges the potential benefits to be gained by electronic record/electronic signature systems. The agency expects that the magnitude of these benefits should significantly outweigh the costs of making these systems, through compliance with part 11, reliable, trustworthy, and compatible with FDA's responsibility to promote and protect public health. The agency is aware of the potential impact of the rule, especially regarding the need to accommodate and encourage new technologies while maintaining the agency's ability to carry out its mandate to protect public health. The agency is also aware that other Federal agencies share the same concerns and are addressing the same issues as FDA; the agency has held informal discussions with other Federal agencies and participated in several interagency groups on electronic records/electronic signatures and information technology issues. FDA looks forward to exchanging information and experience with other agencies for mutual benefit and to promote a consistent Federal policy on electronic records and signatures. The agency also notes that benefits, such as the ones listed by the comments, will help to offset any system modification costs that persons may incur to achieve compliance with part 11.

B. Regulations Versus Guidelines

2. Several comments addressed whether the agency's policy on electronic signatures and electronic records should be issued as a regulation

[[Page 13432]]

or recommended in a guideline. Most comments supported a regulation, citing the need for a practical and workable approach for criteria to ensure that records can be stored in electronic form and are reliable, trustworthy, secure, accurate, confidential, and authentic. One comment specifically supported a single regulation covering all FDA-regulated products to ensure consistent requirements across all product lines. Two comments asserted that the agency should only issue guidelines or ``make the regulations voluntary.'' One of these comments said that by issuing regulations, the agency is shifting from creating tools to enhance communication (technological quality) to creating tools for enforcement (compliance quality).

The agency remains convinced, as expressed in the preamble to the proposed rule (59 FR 45160 at 45165), that a policy statement, inspection guide, or other guidance would be an inappropriate means for enunciating a comprehensive policy on electronic signatures and records. FDA has concluded that regulations are necessary to establish uniform, enforceable, baseline standards for accepting electronic signatures and records. The agency believes, however, that supplemental guidance documents would be useful to address controls in greater detail than would be appropriate for regulations. Accordingly, the agency anticipates issuing supplemental guidance as needed and will afford all interested parties the opportunity to comment on the guidance documents.

The need for regulations is underscored by several opinions expressed in the comments. For example, one comment asserted that it should be acceptable for supervisors to remove the signatures of their subordinates from signed records and replace them with their own signatures. Although the agency does not object to the use of a supervisor's signature to endorse or confirm a subordinate's actions, removal of an original signature is an action the agency views as falsification. Several comments also argued that an electronic signature should consist of only a password, that passwords need not be unique, that it is acceptable for people to use passwords associated with their personal lives (like the names of their children or their pets), and that passwords need only be changed every 2 years. FDA believes that such procedures would greatly increase the possibility that a password could be compromised and the chance that any resulting impersonation and/or falsification would continue for a long time. Therefore, an enforceable regulation describing the acceptable characteristics of an electronic signature appears necessary.

C. Flexibility and Specificity

3. Several comments addressed the flexibility and specificity of the proposed rule. The comments contended that agency acceptance of electronic records systems should not be based on any particular technology, but rather on the adequacy of the system controls under which they are created and managed. Some comments claimed that the proposed rule was overly prescriptive and that it should not specify the mechanisms to be used, but rather only require owners/users to design appropriate safeguards and validate them to reasonably ensure electronic signature integrity and authenticity. One comment commended the agency for giving industry the freedom to choose from a variety of electronic signature technologies, while another urged that the final rule be more specific in detailing software requirements for electronic records and electronic notebooks in research and testing laboratories. The agency believes that the provisions of the final rule afford firms considerable flexibility while providing a baseline level of confidence that records maintained in accordance with the rule will be of high integrity. For example, the regulation permits a wide variety of existing and emerging electronic signature technologies, from use of identification codes in conjunction with manually entered passwords to more sophisticated biometric systems that may necessitate additional hardware and software. While requiring electronic signatures to be linked to their respective electronic records, the final rule affords flexibility in achieving that link through use of any appropriate means, including use of digital signatures and secure relational database references. The final rule accepts a wide variety of electronic record technologies, including those based on optical storage devices. In addition, as discussed in comment 40 of this document, the final rule does not establish numerical standards for levels of security or validation, thus offering firms flexibility in determining what levels are appropriate for their situations. Furthermore, while requiring operational checks, authority checks, and periodic testing of identifying devices, persons have the flexibility of conducting those controls by any suitable method. When the final rule calls for a certain control, such as periodic testing of identification tokens, persons have the option of determining the frequency.

D. Controls for Electronic Systems Compared with Paper Systems

4. Two comments stated that any controls that do not apply to paper-based document systems and handwritten signatures should not apply to electronic record and signature systems unless those controls are needed to address an identified unique risk associated with electronic record systems. One comment expressed concern that FDA was establishing a much higher standard for electronic signatures than necessary.

In attempting to establish minimum criteria to make electronic signatures and electronic records trustworthy and reliable and compatible with FDA's responsibility to promote and protect public health (e.g., by hastening the availability of new safe and effective medical products and ensuring the safety of foods), the agency has attempted to draw analogies to handwritten signatures and paper records wherever possible. In doing so, FDA has found that the analogy does not always hold because of the differences between paper and electronic systems. The agency believes some of those differences necessitate controls that will be unique to electronic technology and that must be addressed on their own merits and not evaluated on the basis of their equivalence to controls governing paper documents.

The agency found that some of the comments served to illustrate the differences between paper and electronic record technologies and the need to address controls that may not generally be found in paper record systems. For example, several comments pointed out that electronic records built upon information databases, unlike paper records, are actually transient views or representations of information that is dispersed in various parts of the database. (The agency notes that the databases themselves may be geographically dispersed but linked by networks.) The same software that generates representations of database information on a screen can also misrepresent that information, depending upon how the software is written (e.g., how a query is prepared). In addition, database elements can easily be changed at any time to misrepresent information, without evidence that a change was made, and in a manner that destroys the original information. Finally, more people have potential access to electronic record

[[Page 13433]]

systems than may have access to paper records.

Therefore, controls are needed to ensure that representations of database information have been generated in a manner that does not distort data or hide noncompliant or otherwise bad information, and that database elements themselves have not been altered so as to distort truth or falsify a record. Such controls include: (1) Using time-stamped audit trails of information written to the database, where such audit trails are executed objectively and automatically rather than by the person entering the information, and (2) limiting access to the database search software. Absent effective controls, it is very easy to falsify electronic records to render them indistinguishable from original, true records.

The traditional paper record, in comparison, is generally a durable unitized representation that is fixed in time and space. Information is recorded directly in a manner that does not require an intermediate means of interpretation. When an incorrect entry is made, the customary method of correcting FDA-related records is to cross out the original entry in a manner that does not obscure the prior data. Although paper records may be falsified, it is relatively difficult (in comparison to falsification of electronic records) to do so in a nondetectable manner. In the case of paper records that have been falsified, a body of evidence exists that can help prove that the records had been changed; comparable methods to detect falsification of electronic records have yet to be fully developed.

In addition, there are significant technological differences between traditional handwritten signatures (recorded on paper) and electronic signatures that also require controls unique to electronic technologies. For example, the traditional handwritten signature cannot be readily compromised by being ``loaned'' or ``lost,'' whereas an electronic signature based on a password in combination with an identification code can be compromised by being ``loaned'' or ``lost.'' By contrast, if one person attempts to write the handwritten signature of another person, the falsification would be difficult to execute and a long-standing body of investigational techniques would be available to detect the falsification. On the other hand, many electronic signatures are relatively easy to falsify and methods of falsification almost impossible to detect.

Accordingly, although the agency has attempted to keep controls for electronic record and electronic signatures analogous to traditional paper systems, it finds it necessary to establish certain controls specifically for electronic systems.

E. FDA Certification of Electronic Signature Systems

5. One comment requested FDA certification of what it described as a low-cost, biometric-based electronic signature system, one which uses dynamic signature verification with a parameter code recorded on

magnetic stripe cards.

The agency does not anticipate the need to certify individual electronic signature products. Use of any electronic signature system that complies with the provisions of part 11 would form the basis for agency acceptance of the system regardless of what particular technology or brand is used. This approach is consistent with FDA's policy in a variety of program areas. The agency, for example, does not certify manufacturing equipment used to make drugs, medical devices, or food.

F. Biometric Electronic Signatures

6. One comment addressed the agency's statement in the proposed rule (59 FR 45160 at 45168) that the owner of a biometric/behavioral link could not lose or give it away. The comment stated that it was possible for an owner to ``lend'' the link for a file to be opened, as a collaborative fraudulent gesture, or to unwittingly assist a fraudulent colleague in an ``emergency,'' a situation, the comment said, that was not unknown in the computer industry.

The agency acknowledges that such fraudulent activity is possible and that people determined to falsify records may find a means to do so despite whatever technology or preventive measures are in place. The controls in part 11 are intended to deter such actions, make it difficult to execute falsification by mishap or casual misdeed, and to help detect such alterations when they occur (see Sec. 11.10 (introductory paragraph and especially Secs. 11.10(j) and 11.200(b)).

G. Personnel Integrity

7. A few comments addressed the role of individual honesty and trust in ensuring that electronic records are reliable, trustworthy, and authentic. One comment noted that firms must rely in large measure upon the integrity of their employees. Another said that subpart C of part 11, Electronic Signatures, appears to have been written with the belief that pharmaceutical manufacturers have an incentive to falsify electronic signatures. One comment expressed concern about possible signature falsification when an employee leaves a company to work elsewhere and the employee uses the electronic signature illegally.

The agency agrees that the integrity of any electronic signature/ electronic record system depends heavily upon the honesty of employees and that most persons are not motivated to falsify records. However, the agency's experience with various types of records and signature falsification demonstrates that some people do falsify information under certain circumstances. Among those circumstances are situations in which falsifications can be executed with ease and have little likelihood of detection. Part 11 is intended to minimize the opportunities for readily executing falsifications and to maximize the chances of detecting falsifications.

Concerning signature falsification by former employees, the agency would expect that upon the departure of an employee, the assigned electronic signature would be ``retired'' to prevent the former employee from falsely using the signature.

H. Security of Industry Electronic Records Submitted to FDA

8. Several comments expressed concern about the security and confidentiality of electronic records submitted to FDA. One suggested that submissions be limited to such read-only formats as CD-ROM with raw data for statistical manipulation provided separately on floppy diskette. One comment suggested that in light of the proposed rule, the agency should review its own internal security procedures. Another addressed electronic records that may be disclosed under the Freedom of Information Act and expressed concern regarding agency deletion of trade secrets. One comment anticipated FDA's use of open systems to access industry records (such as medical device production and control records) and suggested that such access should be restricted to closed systems.

The agency is well aware of its legal obligation to maintain the confidentiality of trade secret information in its possession, and is committed to meet that obligation regardless of the form (paper or electronic) a record takes. The procedures used to ensure confidentiality are consistent with the provisions of part 11. FDA is also examining other controls, such as use of digital signatures, to ensure submission integrity. To permit legitimate changes to be made, the agency does not believe that it is necessary to restrict submissions to those maintained in
[[Page 13434]]
read-only formats in all cases; each agency receiving unit retains the flexibility to determine whatever format is most suitable. Those intending to submit material are expected to consult with the appropriate agency receiving unit to determine the acceptable formats. Although FDA access to electronic records on open systems maintained by firms is not anticipated in the near future, the agency believes it would be inappropriate to rule out such a procedure. Such access can be a valuable inspection tool and can enhance efficiencies by reducing the time investigators may need to be on site. The agency believes it is important to develop appropriate procedures and security measures in cooperation with industry to ensure that such access does not jeopardize data confidentiality or integrity.
I. Effective Date/Grandfathering
9. Several comments addressed the proposed effective date of the final rule, 90 days after publication in the Federal Register, and suggested potential exemptions (grandfathering) for systems now in use. Two comments requested an expedited effective date for the final rule. One comment requested an effective date at least 18 months after publication of the final rule to permit firms to modify and validate their systems. One comment expressed concern about how the rule, in general, will affect current systems, and suggested that the agency permit firms to continue to use existing electronic record systems that otherwise conform to good manufacturing or laboratory practices until these firms make major modifications to those systems or until 5 years have elapsed, whichever comes first. Several other comments requested grandfathering for specific sections of the proposed rule.
The agency has carefully considered the comments and suggestions regarding the final rule's effective date and has concluded that the effective date should be 5 months after date of publication in the Federal Register. The agency wishes to accommodate firms that are prepared now to comply with part 11 or will be prepared soon, so as to encourage and foster new technologies in a manner that ensures that electronic record and electronic signature systems are reliable, trustworthy, and compatible with FDA's responsibility to promote and protect public health. The agency believes that firms that have consulted with FDA before adopting new electronic record and electronic signature technologies (especially technologies that may impact on the ability of the agency to conduct its work effectively) will need to make few, if any, changes to systems used to maintain records required by FDA.
The agency believes that the provisions of part 11 represent minimal standards and that a general exemption for existing systems that do not meet these provisions would be inappropriate and not in the public interest because such systems are likely to generate electronic records and electronic signatures that are unreliable, untrustworthy, and not compatible with FDA's responsibility to promote and protect public health. Such an exemption might, for example, mean that a firm could: (1) Deny FDA inspectional access to electronic record systems, (2) permit unauthorized access to those systems, (3) permit individuals to share identification codes and passwords, (4) permit systems to go unvalidated, and (5) permit records to be falsified in many ways and in

a manner that goes undetected.

The agency emphasizes that these regulations do not require, but rather permit, the use of electronic records and signatures. Firms not confident that their electronic systems meet the minimal requirements of these regulations are free to continue to use traditional signatures and paper documents to meet recordkeeping requirements.

J. Comments by Electronic Mail (e-mail) and Electronic Distribution of FDA Documents

10. One comment specifically noted that the agency has accepted comments by e-mail and that this provides an additional avenue for public participation in the rulemaking process. Another comment encouraged FDA to expand the use of electronic media to provide information by such open systems as bulletin boards.

The agency intends to explore further the possibility of continuing to accept public comments by e-mail and other electronic means. For this current experiment, the agency received only one comment by e-mail. The comment that addressed this issue was, itself, transmitted in a letter. The agency recognizes the benefits of distributing information electronically, has expanded that activity, and intends to continue that expansion. Although only one e-mail comment was received, the agency does not attribute that low number to a lack of ability to send e-mail because the agency received e-mail from 198 persons who requested the text of the proposed rule, including requests from people outside the United States.

K. Submissions by Facsimile (Fax)

11. One comment said that part 11 should include a provision for FDA acceptance of submissions by fax, such as import form FDA 2877. The comment noted that the U.S. Customs Service accepts fax signatures on its documents, and claimed that FDA's insistence on hard copies of form FDA 2877 is an impediment to imports.

The agency advises that part 11 permits the unit that handles import form FDA 2877 to accept that record in electronic form when it is prepared logistically to do so. As noted in the discussion on Sec. 11.1(b) in comment 21 of this document, the agency recognizes that faxes can be in paper or electronic form, based on the capabilities of the sender and recipient.

L. Blood Bank Issues

12. Two comments addressed blood bank issues in the context of electronic records and electronic signatures and said the agency should clarify that part 11 would permit electronic crossmatching by a central blood center for individual hospitals. One comment stated that remote blood center and transfusion facilities should be permitted to rely on electronically communicated information, such as authorization for labeling/issuing units of blood, and that the electronic signature of the supervisor in the central testing facility releasing the product for labeling and issuance should be sufficient because the proposed rule guards against security and integrity problems.

One comment questioned whether, under part 11, electronic signatures would meet the signature requirements for the release of units of blood, and if there would be instances where a full signature would be required instead of a technician's identification. Another comment asserted that it is important to clarify how the term ``batch'' will be interpreted under part 11, and suggested that the term used in relation to blood products refers to a series of units of blood having undergone common manufacturing processes and recorded on the same computerized document. The comment contrasted this to FDA's current view that each unit of blood be considered a batch.

The agency advises that part 11 permits release records now in paper form to be in electronic form and traditional handwritten signatures to be electronic signatures. Under part 11, the name of the technician must appear in the record display or printout to clearly identify the technician. The appearance of the technician's identification code

[[Page 13435]]

alone would not be sufficient. The agency also advises that the definition of a ``batch'' for blood or other products is not affected by part 11, which addresses the trustworthiness and reliability of electronic records and electronic signatures, regardless of how a batch, which is the subject of those records and signatures, is defined.

M. Regulatory Flexibility Analysis

13. One comment said that, because part 11 will significantly impact a substantial number of small businesses, even though the impact would be beneficial, FDA is required to perform a regulatory flexibility analysis and should publish such an analysis in the Federal Register before a final rule is issued.

The comment states that the legislative history of the Regulatory Flexibility Act is clear that, ``significant economic impact,'' as it appears at 5 U.S.C. 605(b) is neutral with respect to whether such impact is beneficial or adverse.

Contrary to the comment's assertion, the legislative history is not dispositive of this matter. It is well established that the task of statutory construction must begin with the actual language of the statute. (See Bailey v. United States, 116 S. Ct. 595, 597 (1996).) A statutory term must not be construed in isolation; a provision that may seem ambiguous in isolation is often clarified by the remainder of the statute. (See Dept. Of Revenue of Oregon v. ACF Industries, 114 S. Ct. 843, 850 (1994).) Moreover, it is a fundamental canon of statutory construction that identical terms within the same statute must bear the same meaning. (See Reno v. Koray, 115 S. Ct. 2021, 2026 (1995).) In addition to appearing in 5 U.S.C. 605(b), the term ``significant economic impact'' appears elsewhere in the statute. The legislation is premised upon the congressional finding that alternative regulatory approaches may be available which ``minimize the significant economic impact'' of rules (5 U.S.C. 601 note). In addition, an initial regulatory flexibility analysis must describe significant regulatory alternatives that ``minimize any significant economic impact'' (5 U.S.C. 603(c)). Similarly, a final regulatory flexibility analysis must include a description of the steps the agency has taken to ``minimize any significant economic impact'' (5 U.S.C. 604(a)(5)). The term appeared as one of the elements of a final regulatory flexibility analysis, as originally enacted in 1980. (See Pub. L. No. 96-354, 3(a), 94 Stat. 1164, 1167 (1980) (formerly codified at 5 U.S.C. 604(a)(3)).) In addition, when Congress amended the elements of a final regulatory flexibility analysis in 1996, it re-enacted the term, as set forth above. (See Pub. L. 104-121, 241(b), 110 Stat. 857, 865 (1996) (codified at 5 U.S.C.604(a)(5)).)

Unless the purpose of the statute was intended to increase the economic burden of regulations by minimizing positive or beneficial effects, ``significant economic impact'' cannot include such effects. Because it is beyond dispute that the purpose of the statute is not increasing economic burdens, the plain meaning of ``significant economic impact'' is clear and necessarily excludes beneficial or positive effects of regulations. Even where there are some limited contrary indications in the statute's legislative history, it is inappropriate to resort to legislative history to cloud a statutory text that is clear on its face. (See Ratzlaff v. United States, 114 S. Ct. 655, 662 (1994).) Therefore, the agency concludes that a final regulatory flexibility analysis is not required for this regulation or any regulation for which there is no significant adverse economic impact on small entities. Notwithstanding these conclusions, FDA has nonetheless considered the impact of the rule on small entities. (See section XVI. of this document.)

N. Terminology

14. One comment addressed the agency's use of the word ``ensure'' throughout the rule and argued that the agency should use the word ``assure'' rather than ``ensure'' because ``ensure'' means ``to guarantee or make certain'' whereas ``assure'' means ``to make confident.'' The comment added that ``assure'' is also more consistent with terminology in other regulations.

The agency wishes to emphasize that it does not intend the word ``ensure'' to represent a guarantee. The agency prefers to use the word ``ensure'' because it means to make certain.

O. General Comments Regarding the Prescription Drug Marketing Act of 1987 (PDMA)

15. Three comments addressed the use of handwritten signatures that are recorded electronically (SRE's) under part 11 and PDMA. One firm described its delivery information acquisition device and noted its use of time stamps to record when signatures are executed. The comments requested clarification that SRE's would be acceptable under the PDMA regulations. One comment assumed that subpart C of part 11 (Electronic Signatures) would not apply to SRE's, noting that it was not practical under PDMA (given the large number of physicians who may be eligible to receive drug product samples) to use such alternatives as identification codes combined with passwords.

The agency advises that part 11 applies to handwritten signatures recorded electronically and that such signatures and their corresponding electronic records will be acceptable for purposes of meeting PDMA's requirements when the provisions of part 11 are met. Although subpart C of part 11 does not apply to handwritten signatures recorded electronically, the agency advises that controls related to electronic records (subpart B), and the general provisions of subpart A, do apply to electronic records in the context of PDMA. The agency emphasizes, however, that part 11 does not restrict PDMA signings to SRE's, and that organizations retain the option of using electronic signatures in conformance with part 11. Furthermore, the agency believes that the number of people in a given population or organization should not be viewed as an insurmountable obstacle to use of electronic signatures. The agency is aware, for example, of efforts by the American Society of Testing and Materials to develop standards for electronic medical records in which digital signatures could theoretically be used on a large scale.

P. Comments on the Unique Nature of Passwords

16. Several comments noted, both generally and with regard to Secs. 11.100(a), 11.200(a), and 11.300, that the password in an electronic signature that is composed of a combination of password and identification code is not, and need not be, unique. Two comments added that passwords may be known to system security administrators who assist people who forget passwords and requested that the rule acknowledge that passwords need not be unique. One comment said that the rule should describe how uniqueness is to be determined.

The agency acknowledges that when an electronic signature consists of a combined identification code and password, the password need not be unique. It is possible that two persons in the same organization may have the same password. However, the agency believes that where good password practices are implemented, such coincidence would be highly unlikely. As discussed in section XIII. of this document in the context of comments on proposed Sec. 11.300, records are less trustworthy and reliable if it is relatively easy for someone to deduce or execute, by chance, a person's electronic

[[Page 13436]]

signature where the identification code of the signature is not
confidential and the password is easily guessed.

The agency does not believe that revising proposed Sec. 11.100(a)
is necessary because what must remain unique is the electronic
signature, which, in the case addressed by the comments, consists not
of the password alone, but rather the password in combination with an
identification code. If the combination is unique, then the electronic
signature is unique.

The agency does not believe that it is necessary to describe in the
regulations the various ways of determining uniqueness or achieving
compliance with the requirement. Organizations thereby maintain
implementation flexibility.

The agency believes that most system administrators or security
managers would not need to know passwords to help people who have
forgotten their own. This is because most administrators or managers
have global computer account privileges to resolve such problems.

IV. Scope (Sec. 11.1)

17. One comment suggested adding a new paragraph to proposed
Sec. 11.1 that would exempt computer record maintenance software
installed before the effective date of the final rule, and that would
exempt electronic records maintained before that date. The comment
argued that such exemptions were needed for economic and constitutional
reasons because making changes to existing systems would be costly and
because the imposition of additional requirements after the fact could
be regarded as an ex post facto rule. The comment said firms have been
using electronic systems that have demonstrated reliability and
security for many years before the agency's publication of the ANPRM,
and that the absence of FDA's objections in inspectional form FDA 483
was evidence of the agency's acceptance of the system.

As discussed in section III.I. of this document, the agency is
opposed to ``grandfathering'' existing systems because such exemptions
may perpetuate environments that provide opportunities for record
falsification and impair FDA's ability to protect and promote public
health. However, the agency wishes to avoid any confusion regarding the
application of the provisions of part 11 to systems and electronic
records in place before the rule's effective date. Important
distinctions need to be made relative to an electronic record's
creation, modification, and maintenance because various portions of
part 11 address matters relating to these actions. Those provisions
apply depending upon when a given electronic record is created,
modified, or maintained.

Electronic records created before the effective date of this rule
are not covered by part 11 provisions that relate to aspects of the
record's creation, such as the signing of the electronic record. Those
records would not, therefore, need to be altered retroactively.

Regarding records that were first created before the effective date,
part 11 provisions relating to modification of records, such as audit
trails for record changes and the requirement that original entries not
be obscured, would apply only to those modifications made on or after
the rule's effective date, not to modifications made earlier. Likewise,
maintenance provisions of part 11, such as measures to ensure that
electronic records can be retrieved throughout their retention periods,
apply to electronic records that are being maintained on or after the
rule's effective date. The hardware and software, as well as
operational procedures used on or after the rule's effective date, to
create, modify, or maintain electronic records must comply with the
provisions of part 11.

The agency does not agree with any suggestion that FDA endorsement
or acceptance of an electronic record system can be inferred from the
absence of objections in an inspection report. Before this rulemaking,
FDA did not have established criteria by which it could determine the

reliability and trustworthiness of electronic records and electronic signatures and could not sanction electronic alternatives when regulations called for signatures. A primary reason for issuing part 11 is to develop and codify such criteria. FDA will assess the acceptability of electronic records and electronic signatures created prior to the effective date of part 11 on a case-by-case basis.

18. One comment suggested that proposed Sec. 11.1 exempt production of medical devices and in vitro diagnostic products on the grounds that the subject was already adequately addressed in the medical device CGMP regulations currently in effect in Sec. 820.195 (21 CFR 820.195), and that additional regulations would be confusing and would limit compliance.

The agency believes that part 11 complements, and is supportive of, the medical device CGMP regulations and the new medical device quality system regulation, as well as other regulations, and that compliance with one does not confound compliance with others. Before publication of the ANPRM, the agency determined that existing regulations, including the medical device CGMP regulations, did not adequately address electronic records and electronic signatures. That determination was reinforced in the comments to the ANPRM, which focused on the need to identify what makes electronic records reliable, trustworthy, and compatible with FDA's responsibility to promote and protect public health. For example, the provision cited by the comment, Sec. 820.195, states ``When automated data processing is used for manufacturing or quality assurance purposes, adequate checks shall be designed and implemented to prevent inaccurate data output, input, and programming errors.'' This section does not address the many issues addressed by part 11, such as electronic signatures, record falsification, or FDA access to electronic records. The relationship between the quality system regulation and part 11 is discussed at various points in the preamble to the quality system regulation.

19. One comment asserted that for purposes of PDMA, the scope of proposed part 11 should be limited to require only those controls for assessing signatures in paper-based systems because physicians' handwritten signatures are executed to electronic records. The comment further asserted that, because drug manufacturers' representatives carry computers into physicians' offices (where the physicians then sign sample requests and receipts), only closed system controls should be needed.

The agency believes that, for purposes of PDMA, controls needed for electronic records bearing handwritten signatures are no different from controls needed for the same kinds of records and signatures used elsewhere, and that proposed Sec. 11.1 need not make any such distinction.

In addition, the agency disagrees with the implication that all PDMA electronic records are, in fact, handled within closed systems. The classification of a system as open or closed in a particular situation depends on what is done in that situation. For example, the agency agrees that a closed system exists where a drug producer's representative (the person responsible for the content of the electronic record) has control over access to the electronic record system by virtue of possessing the portable computer and controlling who may use the computer to sign electronic records. However, should the firm's representative transfer copies of those records to a public online service that stores them for the drug firm's

[[Page 13437]]

subsequent retrieval, the agency considers such transfer and storage to be within an open system because access to the system holding the records is controlled by the online service, which is not responsible for the record's content. Activities in the first example would be subject to closed system controls and activities in the second example would be subject to open system controls.

20. One comment urged that proposed Sec. 11.1 contain a clear statement of what precedence certain provisions of part 11 have over other regulations.

The agency believes that such statements are found in Sec. 11.1(c): Where electronic signatures and their associated records meet the requirements of this part, the agency will consider the electronic signatures to be equivalent to full handwritten signatures, initials, and other general signings as required under agency regulations unless specifically excepted by regulations * * *.

and Sec. 11.1(d) (``Electronic records that meet the requirements of this part may be used in lieu of paper records, in accordance with Sec. 11.2, unless paper records are specifically required."). These provisions clearly address the precedence of part 11 and the equivalence of electronic records and electronic signatures.

To further clarify the scope of the rule, FDA has revised Sec. 11.1 to apply to electronic records submitted to the agency under requirements of the Federal Food, Drug, and Cosmetic Act (the act) and the Public Health Service Act (the PHS Act). This clarifies the point that submissions required by these statutes, but not specifically mentioned in the Code of Federal Regulations (CFR), are subject to part 11.

21. Proposed Sec. 11.1(b) stated that the regulations would apply to records in electronic form that are created, modified, maintained, or transmitted, under any records requirements set forth in Chapter I of Title 21. One comment suggested that the word ``transmitted" be deleted from proposed Sec. 11.1(b) because the wording would inappropriately apply to paper documents that are transmitted by fax. The comment noted that if the records are in machine readable form before or after transmission, they would still be covered by the revised wording.

The agency does not intend part 11 to apply to paper records even if such records are transmitted or received by fax. The agency notes that the records transmitted by fax may be in electronic form at the sender, the recipient, or both. Part 11 would apply whenever the record is in electronic form. To remedy the problem noted by the comment, the agency has added a sentence to Sec. 11.1(b) stating that part 11 does not apply to paper records that are, or have been, transmitted by electronic means.

22. One comment asked whether paper records created by computer would be subject to proposed part 11. The comment cited, as an example, the situation in which a computer system collects toxicology data that are printed out and maintained as ``raw data."

Part 11 is intended to apply to systems that create and maintain electronic records under FDA's requirements in Chapter I of Title 21, even though some of those electronic records may be printed on paper at certain times. The key to determining part 11 applicability, under Sec. 11.1(b), is the nature of the system used to create, modify, and maintain records, as well as the nature of the records themselves.

Part 11 is not intended to apply to computer systems that are merely incidental to the creation of paper records that are subsequently maintained in traditional paper-based systems. In such cases, the computer systems would function essentially like manual typewriters or pens and any signatures would be traditional handwritten signatures. Record storage and retrieval would be of the traditional ``file cabinet" variety. More importantly, overall reliability, trustworthiness, and FDA's ability to access the records would derive primarily from well-established and generally accepted procedures and controls for paper records. For example, if a person were to use word processing software to generate a paper submission to FDA, part 11 would not apply to the computer system used to generate the submission, even though, technically speaking, an electronic record was initially created and then printed on paper.

When records intended to meet regulatory requirements are in electronic form, part 11 would apply to all the relevant aspects of managing those records (including their creation, signing, modification, storage, access, and retrieval). Thus, the software and hardware used to create records that are retained in electronic form for purposes of meeting the regulations would be subject to part 11. Regarding the comment about ``raw data,'' the agency notes that specific requirements in existing regulations may affect the particular records at issue, regardless of the form such records take. For example, ``raw data,'' in the context of the good laboratory practices regulations (21 CFR part 58), include computer printouts from automated instruments as well as the same data recorded on magnetic media. In addition, regulations that cover data acquisition systems generally include requirements intended to ensure the trustworthiness and reliability of the collected data.

23. Several comments on proposed Sec. 11.1(b) suggested that the phrase ``or archived and retrieved'' be added to paragraph (b) to reflect more accurately a record's lifecycle.

The agency intended that record archiving and retrieval would be part of record maintenance, and therefore already covered by Sec. 11.1(b). However, for added clarity, the agency has revised Sec. 11.1(b) to add ``archived and retrieved.''

24. One comment suggested that, in describing what electronic records are within the scope of part 11, proposed Sec. 11.1(b) should be revised by substituting ``processed'' for ``modified'' and ``communicated'' for ``transmitted'' because ``communicated'' reflects the fact that the information was dispatched and also received. The comment also suggested substituting ``retained'' for ``maintained,'' or adding the word ``retained,'' because ``maintain'' does not necessarily convey the retention requirement.

The agency disagrees. The word ``modified'' better describes the agency's intent regarding changes to a record; the word ``processed'' does not necessarily infer a change to a record. FDA believes ``transmitted'' is preferable to ``communicated'' because ``communicated'' might infer that controls to ensure integrity and authenticity hinge on whether the intended recipient actually received the record. Also, as discussed in comment 22 of this document, the agency intends for the term ``maintain'' to include records retention.

25. Two comments suggested that proposed Sec. 11.1(b) explicitly state that part 11 supersedes all references to handwritten signatures in 21 CFR parts 211 through 226 that pertain to a drug, and in 21 CFR parts 600 through 680 that pertain to biological products for human use. The comments stated that the revision should clarify coverage and permit blood centers and transfusion services to take full advantage of electronic systems that provide process controls.

The agency does not agree that the revision is necessary because, under Sec. 11.1(b) and (c), part 11 permits electronic records or submissions under all FDA regulations in Chapter I of Title 21 unless specifically excepted by future regulations.

26. Several comments expressed concern that the proposed rule had inappropriately been expanded in scope

[[Page 13438]]

from the ANPRM to address electronic records as well as electronic signatures. One comment argued that the scope of part 11 should be restricted only to those records that are currently required to be signed, witnessed, or initialed, and that the agency should not require electronic records to contain electronic signatures where the corresponding paper records are not required to be signed.

- 114 -

The agency disagrees with the assertion that part 11 should address only electronic signatures and not electronic records for several reasons. First, based on comments on the ANPRM, the agency is convinced that the reliability and trustworthiness of electronic signatures depend in large measure on the reliability and trustworthiness of the underlying electronic records. Second, the agency has concluded that electronic records, like paper records, need to be trustworthy, reliable, and compatible with FDA's responsibility to promote and protect public health regardless of whether they are signed. In addition, records falsification is an issue with respect to both signed and unsigned records. Therefore, the agency concludes that although the ANPRM focused primarily on electronic signatures, expansion of the subject to electronic records in the proposed rule was fully justified.

The agency stresses that part 11 does not require that any given electronic record be signed at all. The requirement that any record bear a signature is contained in the regulation that mandates the basic record itself. Where records are signed, however, by virtue of meeting a signature requirement or otherwise, part 11 addresses controls and procedures intended to help ensure the reliability and trustworthiness of those signatures.

27. Three comments asked if there were any regulations, including CGMP regulations, that might be excepted from part 11 and requested that the agency identify such regulations.

FDA, at this time, has not identified any current regulations that are specifically excepted from part 11. However, the agency believes it is prudent to provide for such exceptions should they become necessary in the future. It is possible that, as the agency's experience with part 11 increases, certain records may need to be limited to paper if there are problems with the electronic versions of such records.

28. One comment requested clarification of the meaning of the term ``general signings'' in proposed Sec. 11.1(c), and said that the distinction between ``full handwritten'' signatures and ``initials'' is unnecessary because handwritten includes initials in all common definitions of handwritten signature. The comment also suggested changing the term ``equivalent'' to ``at least equivalent'' because electronic signatures are not precise equivalents of handwritten signatures and computer-based signatures have the potential of being more secure.

The agency advises that current regulations that require records to be signed express those requirements in different ways depending upon the agency's intent and expectations. Some regulations expressly state that records must be signed using ``full handwritten'' signatures, whereas other regulations state that records must be ``signed or initialed;'' still other regulations implicitly call for some kind of signing by virtue of requiring record approvals or endorsements. This last broad category is addressed by the term ``general signings'' in Sec. 11.1(c).

Where the language is explicit in the regulations, the means of meeting the requirement are correspondingly precise. Therefore, where a regulation states that a signature must be recorded as ``full handwritten,'' the use of initials is not an acceptable substitute. Furthermore, under part 11, for an electronic signature to be acceptable in place of any of these signings, the agency only needs to consider them as equivalent; electronic signatures need not be superior to those other signings to be acceptable.

29. Several comments requested clarification of which FDA records are required to be in paper form, and urged the agency to allow and promote the use of electronic records in all cases. One comment suggested that proposed Sec. 11.1(d) be revised to read, in part, ``* * * unless the use of electronic records is specifically prohibited.''

The agency intends to permit the use of electronic records required

- 115 -

to be maintained but not submitted to the agency (as noted in Sec. 11.2(a)) provided that the requirements of part 11 are met and paper records are not specifically required. The agency also wishes to encourage electronic submissions, but is limited by logistic and resource constraints. The agency is unaware of ``maintenance records'' that are currently explicitly required to be in paper form (explicit mention of paper is generally unnecessary because, at the time most regulations were prepared, only paper-based technologies were in use) but is providing for that possibility in the future. For purposes of part 11, the agency will not consider that a regulation requires ``maintenance'' records to be in paper form where the regulation is silent on the form the record must take. FDA believes that the comments' suggested wording does not offer sufficient advantages to adopt the change.

However, to enable FDA to accept as many electronic submissions as possible, the agency is amending Sec. 11.1(b) to include those submissions that the act and the PHS Act specifically require, even though such submissions may not be identified in agency regulations. An example of such records is premarket submissions for Class I and Class II medical devices, required by section 510(k) of the act (21 U.S.C. 360(k)).

30. Several comments addressed various aspects of the proposed requirement under Sec. 11.1(e) regarding FDA inspection of electronic record systems. Several comments objected to the proposal as being too broad and going beyond the agency's legal inspectional authority. One comment stated that access inferred by such inspection may include proprietary financial and sales data to which FDA is not entitled. Another comment suggested adding the word ``authorized'' before ``inspection.'' Some comments suggested revising proposed Sec. 11.1(e) to limit FDA inspection only to the electronic records and electronic signatures themselves, thus excluding inspection of hardware and software used to manage those records and signatures. Other comments interpreted proposed Sec. 11.1(e) as requiring them to keep supplanted or retired hardware and software to enable FDA inspection of those outdated systems.

The agency advises that FDA inspections under part 11 are subject to the same legal limitations as FDA inspections under other regulations. The agency does not believe it is necessary to restate that limitation by use of the suggested wording. However, within those limitations, it may be necessary to inspect hardware and software used to generate and maintain electronic records to determine if the provisions of part 11 are being met. Inspection of resulting records alone would be insufficient. For example, the agency may need to observe the use and maintenance of tokens or devices that contain or generate identification information. Likewise, to assess the adequacy of systems validation, it is generally necessary to inspect hardware that is being used to determine, among other things, if it matches the system documentation description of such hardware. The agency has concluded that hardware and software used to generate and maintain electronic records and signatures are ``pertinent

[[Page 13439]]

equipment'' within the meaning of section 704 of the act (21 U.S.C. 374).

The agency does not expect persons to maintain obsolete and supplanted computer systems for the sole purpose of enabling FDA inspection. However, the agency does expect firms to maintain and have available for inspection documentation relevant to those systems, in terms of compliance with part 11, for as long as the electronic records are required by other relevant regulations. Persons should also be mindful of the need to keep appropriate computer systems that are capable of reading electronic records for as long as those records must be retained. In some instances, this may mean retention of otherwise outdated and supplanted systems, especially where the old records cannot be converted to a form readable by the newer systems. In most cases, however, FDA believes that where electronic records are accurately and completely transcribed from one system to another, it would not be necessary to maintain older systems.

31. One comment requested that proposed part 11 be revised to give examples of electronic records subject to FDA inspection, including pharmaceutical and medical device production records, in order to reduce the need for questions.

The agency does not believe that it is necessary to include examples of records it might inspect because the addition of such examples might raise questions about the agency's intent to inspect other records that were not identified.

32. One comment said that the regulation should state that certain security related information, such as private keys attendant to cryptographic implementation, is not intended to be subject to inspection, although procedures related to keeping such keys confidential can be subject to inspection.

The agency would not routinely seek to inspect especially sensitive information, such as passwords or private keys, attendant to security systems. However, the agency reserves the right to conduct such inspections, consistent with statutory limitations, to enforce the provisions of the act and related statutes. It may be necessary, for example, in investigating cases of suspected fraud, to access and determine passwords and private keys, in the same manner as the agency may obtain specimens of handwritten signatures (``exemplars"). Should there be any reservations about such inspections, persons may, of course, change their passwords and private keys after FDA inspection.

33. One comment asked how persons were expected to meet the proposed requirement, under Sec. 11.1(e), that computer systems be readily available for inspection when such systems include geographically dispersed networks. Another comment said FDA investigators should not be permitted to access industry computer systems as part of inspections because investigators would be untrained users.

The agency intends to inspect those parts of electronic record or signature systems that have a bearing on the trustworthiness and reliability of electronic records and electronic signatures under part 11. For geographically dispersed systems, inspection at a given location would extend to operations, procedures, and controls at that location, along with interaction of that local system with the wider network. The agency would inspect other locations of the network in a separate but coordinated manner, much the same way the agency currently conducts inspections of firms that have multiple facilities in different parts of the country and outside of the United States.

FDA does not believe it is reasonable to rule out computer system access as part of an inspection of electronic record or signature systems. Historically, FDA investigators observe the actions of establishment employees, and (with the cooperation of establishment management) sometimes request that those employees perform some of their assigned tasks to determine the degree of compliance with established requirements. However, there may be times when FDA investigators need to access a system directly. The agency is aware that such access will generally require the cooperation of and, to some degree, instruction by the firms being inspected. As new, complex technologies emerge, FDA will need to develop and implement new inspectional methods in the context of those technologies.

V. Implementation (Sec. 11.2)

34. Proposed Sec. 11.2(a) stated that for ``records required by chapter I of this title to be maintained, but not submitted to the

agency, persons may use electronic records/signatures in lieu of paper records/conventional signatures, in whole or in part, * * *."

Two comments requested clarification of the term ``conventional signatures." One comment suggested that the term ``traditional signatures" be used instead. Another suggested rewording in order to clarify the slash in the phrase ``records/signatures."

The agency advises that the term ``conventional signature" means handwritten signature. The agency agrees that the term ``traditional signature" is preferable, and has revised Sec. 11.2(a) and (b) accordingly. The agency has also clarified proposed Sec. 11.2(a) by replacing the slash with the word ``or."

35. One comment asked if the term ``persons" in proposed Sec. 11.2(b) would include devices because computer systems frequently apply digital time stamps on records automatically, without direct human intervention.

The agency advises that the term ``persons" excludes devices. The agency does not consider the application of a time stamp to be the application of a signature.

36. Proposed Sec. 11.2(b)(2) provides conditions under which electronic records or signatures could be submitted to the agency in lieu of paper. One condition is that a document, or part of a document, must be identified in a public docket as being the type of submission the agency will accept in electronic form. Two comments addressed the nature of the submissions to the public docket. One comment asked that the agency provide specifics, such as the mechanism for updating the docket and the frequency of such updates. One comment suggested making the docket available to the public by electronic means. Another comment suggested that acceptance procedures be uniform among agency units and that electronic mail be used to hold consultations with the agency. One comment encouraged the agency units receiving the submissions to work closely with regulated industry to ensure that no segment of industry is unduly burdened and that agency guidance is widely accepted.

The agency intends to develop efficient electronic records acceptance procedures that afford receiving units sufficient flexibility to deal with submissions according to their capabilities. Although agencywide uniformity is a laudable objective, to attain such flexibility it may be necessary to accommodate some differences among receiving units. The agency considers of primary importance, however, that all part 11 submissions be trustworthy, reliable, and in keeping with FDA regulatory activity. The agency expects to work closely with industry to help ensure that the mechanics and logistics of accepting electronic submissions do not pose any undue burdens. However, the agency expects persons to consult with the

[[Page 13440]]

intended receiving units on the technical aspects of the submission, such as media, method of transmission, file format, archiving needs, and technical protocols. Such consultations will ensure that submissions are compatible with the receiving units' capabilities. The agency has revised proposed Sec. 11.2(b)(2) to clarify this expectation.

Regarding the public docket, the agency is not at this time establishing a fixed schedule for updating what types of documents are acceptable for submission because the agency expects the docket to change and grow at a rate that cannot be predicted. The agency may, however, establish a schedule for updating the docket in the future. The agency agrees that making the docket available electronically is advisable and will explore this option. Elsewhere in this issue of the Federal Register, FDA is providing further information on this docket.

VI. Definitions (Sec. 11.3)

37. One comment questioned the incorporation in proposed Sec. 11.3(a) of definitions under section 201 of the act (21 U.S.C.

321), noting that other FDA regulations (such as 21 CFR parts 807 and 820) lack such incorporation, and suggested that it be deleted.

The agency has retained the incorporation by reference to definitions under section 201 of the act because those definitions are applicable to part 11.

38. One comment suggested adding the following definition for the term ``digital signature:'' ``data appended to, or a cryptographic transformation of, a data unit that allows a recipient of the data unit to prove the source and integrity of the data unit and protect against forgery, e.g., by the recipient.''

The agency agrees that the term digital signature should be defined and has added new Sec. 11.3(b)(5) to provide a definition for digital signature that is consistent with the Federal Information Processing Standard 186, issued May 19, 1995, and effective December 1, 1995, by the U.S. Department of Commerce, National Institute of Standards and Technology (NIST). Generally, a digital signature is ``an electronic signature based upon cryptographic methods of originator authentication, computed by using a set of rules and a set of parameters such that the identity of the signer and the integrity of the data can be verified.'' FDA advises that the set of rules and parameters is established in each digital signature standard.

39. Several comments suggested various modifications of the proposed definition of biometric/behavioral links, and suggested revisions that would exclude typing a password or identification code which, the comments noted, is a repeatable action. The comments suggested that actions be unique and measurable to meet the intent of a biometric method.

The agency agrees that the proposed definition of biometric/ behavioral links should be revised to clarify the agency's intent that repetitive actions alone, such as typing an identification code and password, are not considered to be biometric in nature. Because comments also indicated that it would be preferable to simplify the term, the agency is changing the term ``biometric/behavioral link'' to ``biometrics.'' Accordingly, Sec. 11.3(b)(3) defines the term ``biometrics'' to mean ``a method of verifying an individual's identity based on measurement of the individual's physical feature(s) or repeatable action(s) where those features and/or actions are both unique to that individual and measurable.''

40. One comment said that the agency should identify what biometric methods are acceptable to verify a person's identity and what validation acceptance criteria the agency has used to determine that biometric technologies are superior to other methods, such as use of identification codes and passwords.

The agency believes that there is a wide variety of acceptable technologies, regardless of whether they are based on biometrics, and regardless of the particular type of biometric mechanism that may be used. Under part 11, electronic signatures that employ at least two distinct identification components such as identification codes and passwords, and electronic signatures based on biometrics are equally acceptable substitutes for traditional handwritten signatures. Furthermore, all electronic record systems are subject to the same requirements of subpart B of part 11 regardless of the electronic signature technology being used. These provisions include requirements for validation.

Regarding the comment's suggestion that FDA apply quantitative acceptance criteria, the agency is not seeking to set specific numerical standards or statistical performance criteria in determining the threshold of acceptability for any type of technology. If such standards were to be set for biometrics-based electronic signatures, similar numerical performance and reliability requirements would have to be applied to other technologies as well. The agency advises, however, that the differences between system controls for biometrics-based electronic signatures and other electronic signatures are a result of the premise that biometrics-based electronic signatures, by their nature, are less prone to be compromised than other methods such as identification codes and passwords. Should it become evident that additional controls are warranted for biometrics-based electronic signatures, the agency will propose to revise part 11 accordingly.

41. Proposed Sec. 11.3(b)(4) defined a closed system as an environment in which there is communication among multiple persons, and where system access is restricted to people who are part of the organization that operates the system.

Many comments requested clarification of the term ``organization'' and stated that the rule should account for persons who, though not strictly employees of the operating organization, are nonetheless obligated to it in some manner, or who would otherwise be granted system access by the operating organization. As examples of such persons, the comments cited outside contractors, suppliers, temporary employees, and consultants. The comments suggested a variety of alternative wording, including a change of emphasis from organizational membership to organizational control over system access. One comment requested clarification of whether the rule intends to address specific disciplines within a company.

Based on the comments, the agency has revised the proposed definition of closed system to state ``an environment in which system access is controlled by persons who are responsible for the content of electronic records that are on the system.'' The agency agrees that the most important factor in classifying a system as closed or open is whether the persons responsible for the content of the electronic records control access to the system containing those records. A system is closed if access is controlled by persons responsible for the content of the records. If those persons do not control such access, then the system is open because the records may be read, modified, or compromised by others to the possible detriment of the persons responsible for record content. Hence, those responsible for the records would need to take appropriate additional measures in an open system to protect those records from being read, modified, destroyed, or otherwise compromised by unauthorized and potentially unknown parties. The agency does not believe it is necessary to codify the basis or criteria for authorizing system access, such as existence of a fiduciary

[[Page 13441]]

responsibility or contractual relationship. By being silent on such criteria, the rule affords maximum flexibility to organizations by permitting them to determine those criteria for themselves.

42. Concerning the proposed definition of closed system, one comment suggested adding the words ``or devices'' after ``persons'' because communications may involve nonhuman entities.

The agency does not believe it is necessary to adopt the suggested revision because the primary intent of the regulation is to address communication among humans, not devices.

43. One comment suggested defining a closed system in terms of functional characteristics that include physical access control, having professionally written and approved procedures with employees and supervisors trained to follow them, conducting investigations when abnormalities may have occurred, and being under legal obligation to the organization responsible for operating the system.

The agency agrees that the functional characteristics cited by the comment are appropriate for a closed system, but has decided that it is unnecessary to include them in the definition. The functional characteristics themselves, however, such as physical access controls, are expressed as requirements elsewhere in part 11.

44. Two comments said that the agency should regard as closed a system in which dial-in access via public phone lines is permitted, but where access is authorized by, and under the control of, the organization that operates the system.

The agency advises that dial-in access over public phone lines could be considered part of a closed system where access to the system that holds the electronic records is under the control of the persons responsible for the content of those records. The agency cautions, however, that, where an organization's electronic records are stored on systems operated by third parties, such as commercial online services, access would be under control of the third parties and the agency would regard such a system as being open. The agency also cautions that, by permitting access to its systems by public phone lines, organizations lose the added security that results from restricting physical access to computer terminal and other input devices. In such cases, the agency believes firms would be prudent to implement additional security measures above and beyond those controls that the organization would use if the access device was within its facility and commensurate with the potential consequences of such unauthorized access. Such additional controls might include, for example, use of input device checks, caller identification checks (phone caller identification), call backs, and security cards.

45. Proposed Sec. 11.3(b)(5) defined electronic record as a document or writing comprised of any combination of text, graphic representation, data, audio information, or video information, that is created, modified, maintained, or transmitted in digital form by a computer or related system. Many comments suggested revising the proposed definition to reflect more accurately the nature of electronic records and how they differ from paper records. Some comments suggested distinguishing between machine readable records and paper records created by machine. Some comments noted that the term ``document or writing'' is inappropriate for electronic records because electronic records could be any combination of pieces of information assembled (sometimes on a transient basis) from many noncontiguous places, and because the term does not accurately describe such electronic information as raw data or voice mail. Two comments suggested that the agency adopt definitions of electronic record that were established, respectively, by the United Nations Commission on International Trade Law (UNCITRAL) Working Group on Electronic Data Interchange, and the American National Standards Institute/Institute of Electrical and Electronic Engineers Software Engineering (ANSI/IEEE) Standard (729-1983).

The agency agrees with the suggested revisions and has revised the definition of ``electronic record'' to emphasize this unique nature and to clarify that the agency does not regard a paper record to be an electronic record simply because it was created by a computer system. The agency has removed ``document or writing'' from this definition and elsewhere in part 11 for the sake of clarity, simplicity, and consistency.

However, the agency believes it is preferable to adapt or modify the words ``document'' and ``writing'' to electronic technologies rather than discard them entirely from the lexicon of computer technology. The agency is aware that the terms ``document'' and ``electronic document'' are used in contexts that clearly do not intend to describe paper. Therefore, the agency considers the terms ``electronic record'' and ``electronic document'' to be generally synonymous and may use the terms ``writing,'' ``electronic document,'' or ``document'' in other publications to describe records in electronic form. The agency believes that such usage is a prudent conservation of language and is consistent with the use of other terms and expressions that have roots in older technologies, but have nonetheless been adapted to newer technologies. Such terms include telephone ``dialing,'' internal combustion engine ``horse power,'' electric light luminance expressed as ``foot candles,'' and (more relevant to computer technology) execution of a ``carriage return.''

Accordingly, the agency has revised the definition of electronic record to mean ``any combination of text, graphics, data, audio, pictorial, or other information representation in digital form that is created, modified, maintained, archived, retrieved, or distributed by a computer system.''

46. Proposed Sec. 11.3(b)(6) defined an electronic signature as the entry in the form of a magnetic impulse or other form of computer data compilation of any symbol or series of symbols, executed, adopted or authorized by a person to be the legally binding equivalent of the person's handwritten signature. One comment supported the definition as proposed, noting its consistency with dictionary definitions (Random House Dictionary of the English Language, Unabridged Ed. 1983, and American Heritage Dictionary, 1982). Several other comments, however, suggested revisions. One comment suggested replacing ``electronic signature'' with ``computer based signature,'' ``authentication,'' or ``computer based authentication'' because ``electronic signature'' is imprecise and lacks clear and recognized meaning in the information security and legal professions. The comment suggested a definition closer to the UNCITRAL draft definition:

(1) [a] method used to identify the originator of the data message and to indicate the originator's approval of the information contained therein; and (2) that method is as reliable as was appropriate for the purpose for which the data message was generated or communicated, in the light of all circumstances, including any agreement between the originator and the addressee of the data message.

One comment suggested replacing ``electronic signature'' with ``electronic identification'' or ``electronic authorization'' because the terms include many types of technologies that are not easily distinguishable and because the preamble to the proposed rule gave a rationale for using ``electronic signature'' that was too ``esoteric for practical consideration.''

[[Page 13442]]

The agency disagrees that ``electronic signature'' as proposed should be replaced with other terms and definitions. As noted in the preamble to the proposed rule, the agency believes that it is vital to retain the word ``signature'' to maintain the equivalence and significance of various electronic technologies with the traditional handwritten signature. By not using the word ``signature,'' people may treat the electronic alternatives as less important, less binding, and less in need of controls to prevent falsification. The agency also believes that use of the word signature provides a logical bridge between paper and electronic technologies that facilitates the general transition from paper to electronic environments. The term helps people comply with current FDA regulations that specifically call for signatures. Nor does the agency agree that this reasoning is beyond the reach of practical consideration.

The agency declines to accept the suggested UNCITRAL definition because it is too narrow in context in that there is not always a specified message addressee for electronic records required by FDA regulations (e.g., a batch production record does not have a specific ``addressee'').

47. Concerning the proposed definition of ``electronic signature,'' other comments suggested deletion of the term ``magnetic impulse'' to render the term media neutral and thus allow for such alternatives as an optical disk. Comments also suggested that the term ``entry'' was unclear and recommended its deletion. Two comments suggested revisions

that would classify symbols as an electronic signature only when they are committed to permanent storage because not every computer entry is a signature and processing to permanent storage must occur to indicate completion of processing.

The agency advises that the proposal did not limit electronic signature recordings to ``magnetic impulse'' because the proposed definition added, ``or other form of computer data * * *.'' However, in keeping with the agency's intent to accept a broad range of technologies, the terms ``magnetic impulse'' and ``entry'' have been removed from the proposed definition. The agency believes that recording of computer data to ``permanent'' storage is not a necessary or warranted qualifier because it is not relevant to the concept of equivalence to a handwritten signature. In addition, use of the qualifier regarding permanent storage could impede detection of falsified records if, for example, the signed falsified record was deleted after a predetermined period (thus, technically not recorded to ``permanent'' storage). An individual could disavow a signature because the record had ceased to exist.

For consistency with the proposed definition of handwritten signature, and to clarify that electronic signatures are those of individual human beings, and not those of organizations (as included in the act's definition of ``person''), FDA is changing ``person'' to ``individual'' in the final rule.

Accordingly, Sec. 11.3(b)(7) defines electronic signature as a computer data compilation of any symbol or series of symbols executed, adopted, or authorized by an individual to be the legally binding equivalent of the individual's handwritten signature.

48. Proposed Sec. 11.3(b)(7) (redesignated Sec. 11.3(b)(8) in the final rule) defined ``handwritten signature'' as the name of an individual, handwritten in script by that individual, executed or adopted with the present intention to authenticate a writing in a permanent form. The act of signing with a writing or marking instrument such as a pen or stylus is preserved. The proposed definition also stated that the scripted name, while conventionally applied to paper, may also be applied to other devices which capture the written name. Many comments addressed this proposed definition. Two comments suggested that it be deleted on the grounds it is redundant and that, when handwritten signatures are recorded electronically, the result fits the definition of electronic signature.

The agency disagrees that the definition of handwritten signature should be deleted. In stating the criteria under which electronic signatures may be used in place of traditional handwritten signatures, the agency believes it is necessary to define handwritten signature. In addition, the agency believes that it is necessary to distinguish handwritten signatures from electronic signatures because, with handwritten signatures, the traditional act of signing one's name is preserved. Although the handwritten signature recorded electronically and electronic signatures, as defined in part 11, may both ultimately result in magnetic impulses or other forms of computerized symbol representations, the means of achieving those recordings and, more importantly, the controls needed to ensure their reliability and trustworthiness are quite different. In addition, the agency believes that a definition for handwritten signature is warranted to accommodate persons who wish to implement record systems that are combinations of paper and electronic technologies.

49. Several comments suggested replacing the reference to ``scripted name'' in the proposed definition of handwritten signature with ``legal mark'' so as to accommodate individuals who are physically unable to write their names in script. The comments asserted that the term ``legal mark'' would bring the definition to closer agreement with generally recognized legal interpretations of signature.

The agency agrees and has added the term ``legal mark'' to the definition of handwritten signature.

50. One comment recommended that the regulation state that, when the handwritten signature is not the result of the act of signing with a writing or marking instrument, but is applied to another device that captures the written name, a system should verify that the owner of the signature has authorized the use of the handwritten signature.

The agency declines to accept this comment because, if the act of signing or marking is not preserved, the type of signature would not be considered a handwritten signature. The comment appears to be referring to instances in which one person authorizes someone else to use his or her stamp or device. The agency views this as inappropriate when the signed record does not clearly show that the stamp owner did not actually execute the signature. As discussed elsewhere in this preamble, the agency believes that where one person authorizes another to sign a document on his or her behalf, the second person must sign his or her own name (not the name of the first person) along with some notation that, in doing so, he or she is acting in the capacity, or on behalf, of the first person.

51. One comment suggested that where handwritten signatures are captured by devices, there should be a register of manually written signatures to enable comparison for authenticity and the register also include the typed names of individuals.

The agency agrees that the practice of establishing a signature register has merit, but does not believe that it is necessary, in light of other part 11 controls. As noted elsewhere in this preamble (in the discussion of proposed Sec. 11.50), the agency agrees that human readable displays of electronic records must display the name of the signer.

52. Several comments suggested various editorial changes to the proposed definition of handwritten signature including: (1) Changing the word ``also'' in the last sentence to ``alternatively,'' (2) clarifying the
[[Page 13443]]
difference between the words ``individual'' and ``person,'' (3) deleting the words ``in a permanent form,'' and (4) changing ``preserved'' to ``permitted.'' One comment asserted that the last sentence of the proposed definition was unnecessary.

The agency has revised the definition of handwritten signature to clarify its intent and to keep the regulation as flexible as possible. The agency believes that the last sentence of the proposed definition is needed to address devices that capture handwritten signatures. The agency is not adopting the suggestion that the word ``preserved'' be changed to ``permitted'' because ``preserved'' more accurately states the agency's intent and is a qualifier to help distinguish handwritten signatures from others. The agency advises that the word ``individual'' is used, rather than ``person,'' because the act's definition of person extends beyond individual human beings to companies and partnerships. The agency has retained the term ``permanent'' to discourage the use of pencils, but recognizes that ``permanent'' does not mean eternal.

53. One comment asked whether a signature that is first handwritten and then captured electronically (e.g., by scanning) is an electronic signature or a handwritten signature, and asked how a handwritten signature captured electronically (e.g., by using a stylus-sensing pad device) that is affixed to a paper copy of an electronic record would be classified.

FDA advises that when the act of signing with a stylus, for example, is preserved, even when applied to an electronic device, the result is a handwritten signature. The subsequent printout of the signature on paper would not change the classification of the original method used to execute the signature.

54. One comment asserted that a handwritten signature recorded electronically should be considered to be an electronic signature, based on the medium used to capture the signature. The comment argued that the word signature should be limited to paper technology.

The agency disagrees and believes it is important to classify a signature as handwritten based upon the preserved action of signing with a stylus or other writing instrument.

55. One comment asked if the definition of handwritten signature encompasses handwritten initials.

The agency advises that, as revised, the definition of handwritten signature includes handwritten initials if the initials constitute the legal mark executed or adopted with the present intention to authenticate a writing in a permanent form, and where the method of recording such initials involves the act of writing with a pen or stylus.

56. Proposed Sec. 11.3(b)(8) (redesignated as Sec. 11.3(b)(9) in the final rule) defined an open system as an environment in which there is electronic communication among multiple persons, where system access extends to people who are not part of the organization that operates the system.

Several comments suggested that, for simplicity, the agency define ``open system'' as any system that does not meet the definition of a closed system. One comment suggested that the definition be deleted on the grounds it is redundant, and that it is the responsibility of individual firms to take appropriate steps to ensure the validity and security of applications and information, regardless of whether systems are open or closed. Other comments suggested definitions of ``open system'' that were opposite to what they suggested for a closed system. The agency has revised the definition of open system to mean ``an environment in which system access is not controlled by persons who are responsible for the content of electronic records that are on the system.'' The agency believes that, for clarity, the definition should stand on its own rather than as any system that is not closed. The agency rejects the suggestion that the term need not be defined at all because FDA believes that controls for open systems merit distinct provisions in part 11 and defining the term is basic to understanding which requirements apply to a given system. The agency agrees that companies have the responsibility to take steps to ensure the validity and security of their applications and information. However, FDA finds it necessary to establish part 11 as minimal requirements to help ensure that those steps are, in fact, acceptable.

VII. Electronic Records--Controls for Closed Systems (Sec. 11.10)

The introductory paragraph of proposed Sec. 11.10 states that:
Closed systems used to create, modify, maintain, or transmit electronic records shall employ procedures and controls designed to ensure the authenticity, integrity, and confidentiality of electronic records, and to ensure that the signer cannot readily repudiate the signed record as not genuine. * * *
The rest of the section lists specific procedures and controls.

57. One comment expressed full support for the list of proposed controls, calling them generally appropriate and stated that the agency is correctly accommodating the fluid nature of various electronic record and electronic signature technologies. Another comment, however, suggested that controls should not be implemented at the time electronic records are first created, but rather only after a document is accepted by a company.

The agency disagrees with this suggestion. To ignore such controls at a stage before official acceptance risks compromising the record. For example, if ``preacceptance'' records are signed by technical personnel, it is vital to ensure the integrity of their electronic signatures to prevent record alteration. The need for such integrity is no less important at preacceptance stages than at later stages when managers officially accept the records. The possibility exists that some might seek to disavow, or avoid FDA examination of, pertinent records by declaring they had not been formally ``accepted.'' In addition, FDA routinely can and does inspect evolving paper documents (e.g., standard operating procedures and validation protocols) even though they have yet to receive a firm's final acceptance.

58. One comment said proposed Sec. 11.10 contained insufficient requirements for firms to conduct periodic inspection and monitoring of their own systems and procedures to ensure compliance with the regulations. The comment also called for a clear identification of the personnel in a firm who would be responsible for system implementation, operation, change control, and monitoring.

The agency does not believe it is necessary at this time to codify a self-auditing requirement, as suggested by the comment. Rather, the agency intends to afford organizations flexibility in establishing their own internal mechanisms to ensure compliance with part 11. Self-audits, however, may be considered as a general control, within the context of the introductory paragraph of Sec. 11.10. The agency encourages firms to conduct such audits periodically as part of an overall approach to ensure compliance with FDA regulations generally. Likewise, the agency does not believe it is necessary or practical to codify which individuals in an organization should be responsible for compliance with various provisions of part 11. However, ultimate responsibility for part 11 will generally rest with persons responsible for electronic record content, just as responsibility for compliance with paper record requirements generally lies with those responsible for the record's content.

[[Page 13444]]

59. Several comments interpreted proposed Sec. 11.10 as applying all procedures and controls to closed systems and suggested revising it to permit firms to apply only those procedures and controls they deem necessary for their own operations, because some requirements are excessive in some cases.

The agency advises that, where a given procedure or control is not intended to apply in all cases, the language of the rule so indicates. Specifically, use of operational checks (Sec. 11.10(f)) and device checks (Sec. 11.10(h)) is not required in all cases. The remaining requirements do apply in all cases and are, in the agency's opinion, the minimum needed to ensure the trustworthiness and reliability of electronic record systems. In addition, certain controls that firms deem adequate for their routine internal operations might nonetheless leave records vulnerable to manipulation and, thus, may be incompatible with FDA's responsibility to protect public health. The suggested revision would effectively permit firms to implement various controls selectively and possibly shield records from FDA, employ unqualified personnel, or permit employees to evade responsibility for fraudulent use of their electronic signatures.

The agency believes that the controls in Sec. 11.10 are vital, and notes that almost all of them were suggested by comments on the ANPRM. The agency believes the wording of the regulation nonetheless permits firms maximum flexibility in how to meet those requirements.

60. Two comments suggested that the word ``confidentiality'' in the introductory paragraph of proposed Sec. 11.10 be deleted because it is unnecessary and inappropriate. The comments stated that firms should determine if certain records need to be confidential, and that as long as records could not be altered or deleted without appropriate authority, it would not matter whether they could read the records.

The agency agrees that not all records required by FDA need to be kept confidential within a closed system and has revised the reference in the introductory paragraph of Sec. 11.10 to state ``* * * and, when appropriate, the confidentiality of electronic records." The agency believes, however that the need for retaining the confidentiality of certain records is not diminished because viewers cannot change them. It may be prudent for persons to carefully assess the need for record confidentiality. (See, e.g., 21 CFR 1002.42, Confidentiality of records furnished by dealers and distributors, with respect to certain radiological health products.) In addition, FDA's obligation to retain the confidentiality of information it receives in some submissions hinges on the degree to which the submitter maintains confidentiality, even within its own organization. (See, e.g., 21 CFR 720.8(b) with respect to cosmetic ingredient information in voluntary filings of cosmetic product ingredient and cosmetic raw material composition statements.)

61. One comment asked if the procedures and controls required by proposed Sec. 11.10 were to be built into software or if they could exist in written form.

The agency expects that, by their nature, some procedures and controls, such as use of time-stamped audit trails and operational checks, will be built into hardware and software. Others, such as validation and determination of personnel qualifications, may be implemented in any appropriate manner regardless of whether the mechanisms are driven by, or are external to, software or hardware. To clarify this intent, the agency has revised the introductory paragraph of proposed Sec. 11.10 to read, in part, ``Persons who use closed systems to create, modify * * *.'' Likewise, for clarity and consistency, the agency is introducing the same phrase, ``persons who use * * *'' in Secs. 11.30 and 11.300.

62. One comment contended that the distinction between open and closed systems should not be predominant because a $100,000 transaction in a closed system should not have fewer controls than a $1 transaction in an open system.

The agency believes that, within part 11, firms have the flexibility they need to adjust the extent and stringency of controls based on any factors they choose, including the economic value of the transaction. The agency does not believe it is necessary to modify part 11 at this time so as to add economic criteria.

63. One comment suggested that the reference to repudiation in the introductory paragraph of Sec. 11.10 should be deleted because repudiation can occur at any time in legal proceedings. Another comment, noting that the proposed rule appeared to address only nonrepudiation of a signer, said the rule should address nonrepudiation of record ``genuineness'' or extend to nonrepudiation of submission, delivery, and receipt. The comment stated that some firms provide nonrepudiation services that can prevent someone from successfully claiming that a record has been altered.

In response to the first comment, the agency does not agree that the reference to repudiation should be deleted because reducing the likelihood that someone can readily repudiate an electronic signature as not his or her own, or that the signed record had been altered, is vital to the agency's basic acceptance of electronic signatures. The agency is aware that the need to deter such repudiation has been addressed in many forums and publications that discuss electronic signatures. Absent adequate controls, FDA believes some people would be more likely to repudiate an electronically-signed record because of the relative ease with which electronic records may be altered and the ease with which one individual could impersonate another. The agency notes, however, that the rule does not call for nonrepudiation as an absolute guarantee, but requires that the signer cannot ``readily'' repudiate the signature.

In response to the second comment, the agency agrees that it is also important to establish nonrepudiation of submission, delivery, and

receipt of electronic records, but advises that, for purposes of
Sec. 11.10, the agency's intent is to limit nonrepudiation to the
genuineness of the signer's record. In other words, an individual
should not be able to readily say that: (1) He or she did not, in fact,
sign the record; (2) a given electronic record containing the
individual's signature was not, in fact, the record that the person
signed; or (3) the originally signed electronic record had been altered
after having been signed.

64. Proposed Sec. 11.10(a) states that controls for closed systems
are to include the validation of systems to ensure accuracy,
reliability, consistent intended performance, and the ability to
conclusively discern invalid or altered records.

Many comments objected to this proposed requirement because the
word ``conclusively'' inferred an unreasonably high and unattainable
standard, one which is not applied to paper records.

The agency intends to apply the same validation concepts and
standards to electronic record and electronic signature systems as it
does to paper systems. As such, FDA does not intend the word
``conclusively'' to suggest an unattainable absolute and has,
therefore, deleted the word from the final rule.

65. One comment suggested qualifying the proposed validation
requirement in Sec. 11.10(a) to state that validation be performed
``where

[[Page 13445]]

necessary'' and argued that validation of commercially available
software is not necessary because such software has already been
thoroughly validated. The comment acknowledged that validation may be
required for application programs written by manufacturers and others
for special needs.

The agency disagrees with the comment's claim that all commercial
software has been validated. The agency believes that commercial
availability is no guarantee that software has undergone ``thorough
validation'' and is unaware of any regulatory entity that has
jurisdiction over general purpose software producers. The agency notes
that, in general, commercial software packages are accompanied not by
statements of suitability or compliance with established standards, but
rather by disclaimers as to their fitness for use. The agency is aware
of the complex and sometimes controversial issues in validating
commercial software. However, the need to validate such software is not
diminished by the fact that it was not written by those who will use
the software.

In the future, the agency may provide guidance on validation of
commercial software used in electronic record systems. FDA has
addressed the matter of software validation in general in such
documents as the ``Draft Guideline for the Validation of Blood
Establishment Computer Systems,'' which is available from the
Manufacturers Assistance and Communications Staff, Center for Biologics
Evaluation and Research (HFM-42), Food and Drug Administration, 1401
Rockville Pike, Rockville, MD 20852-1448, 301-594-2000. This guideline
is also available by sending e-mail to the following Internet address:
CBER__INFO@A1.CBER.FDA.GOV). For the purposes of part 11, however, the
agency believes it is vital to retain the validation requirement.

66. One comment requested an explanation of what was meant by the
phrase ``consistent intended'' in proposed Sec. 11.10(a) and why
``consistent performance'' was not used instead. The comment suggested
that the rule should distinguish consistent intended performance from
well-recognized service ``availability.''

The agency advises that the phrase ``consistent intended
performance'' relates to the general principle of validation that
planned and expected performance is based upon predetermined design
specifications (hence, ``intended''). This concept is in accord with

- 128 -

the agency's 1987 "Guideline on General Principles of Process Validation," which is available from the Division of Manufacturing and Product Quality, Center for Drug Evaluation and Research (HFD-320), Food and Drug Administration, 7520 Standish Pl., Rockville, MD 20855, 301-594-0093). This guideline defines validation as establishing documented evidence that provides a high degree of assurance that a specific process will consistently produce a product meeting its predetermined specifications and quality attributes. The agency believes that the comment's concepts are accommodated by this definition to the extent that system "availability" may be one of the predetermined specifications or quality attributes.

67. One comment said the rule should indicate whether validation of systems does, or should, require any certification or accreditation. The agency believes that although certification or accreditation may be a part of validation of some systems, such certification or accreditation is not necessary in all cases, outside of the context of any such approvals within an organization itself. Therefore, part 11 is silent on the matter.

68. One comment said the rule should clarify whether system validation should be capable of discerning the absence of electronic records, in light of agency concerns about falsification. The comment added that the agency's concerns regarding invalid or altered records can be mitigated by use of cryptographically enhanced methods, including secure time and date stamping.

The agency does not believe that it is necessary at this time to include an explicit requirement that systems be capable of detecting the absence of records. The agency advises that the requirement in Sec. 11.10(e) for audit trails of operator actions would cover those actions intended to delete records. Thus, the agency would expect firms to document such deletions, and would expect the audit trail mechanisms to be included in the validation of the electronic records system.

69. Proposed Sec. 11.10(b) states that controls for closed systems must include the ability to generate true copies of records in both human readable and electronic form suitable for inspection, review, and copying by the agency, and that if there were any questions regarding the ability of the agency to perform such review and copying, persons should contact the agency.

Several comments objected to the requirement for "true" copies of electronic records. The comments asserted that information in an original record (as may be contained in a database) may be presented in a copy in a different format that may be more usable. The comments concluded that, to generate precise "true" copies of electronic records, firms may have to retain the hardware and software that had been used to create those records in the first place (even when such hardware and software had been replaced by newer systems). The comments pointed out that firms may have to provide FDA with the application logic for "true" copies, and that this may violate copyright provisions. One comment illustrated the difference between "true" copies and other equally reliable, but not exact, copies of electronic records by noting that pages from FDA's paper publications (such as the CFR and the Compliance Policy Guidance Manual) look quite different from electronic copies posted to FDA's bulletin board. The comments suggested different wording that would effectively require accurate and complete copies, but not necessarily "true" copies.

The agency agrees that providing exact copies of electronic records in the strictest meaning of the word "true" may not always be feasible. The agency nonetheless believes it is vital that copies of electronic records provided to FDA be accurate and complete. Accordingly, in Sec. 11.10(b), "true" has been replaced with "accurate and complete." The agency expects that this revision should obviate the potential problems noted in the comments. The revision should also reduce the costs of providing copies by making clear that firms need not maintain obsolete equipment in order to make copies that are ``true" with respect to format and computer system.

70. Many comments objected to the proposed requirement that systems be capable of generating electronic copies of electronic records for FDA inspection and copying, although they generally agreed that it was appropriate to provide FDA with readable paper copies. Alternative wording was suggested that would make providing electronic copies optional, such that persons could provide FDA with nothing but paper copies if they so wished. The comments argued that providing FDA with electronic copies was unnecessary, unjustified, not practical considering the different types of computer systems that may be in use, and would unfairly limit firms in their selection of hardware and software if they could only use systems that matched FDA's capabilities (capabilities which, it was argued, would not be uniform throughout the United States). One comment suggested that the rule specify

[[Page 13446]]

a particular format, such as ASCII, for electronic copies to FDA.

The agency disagrees with the assertion that FDA need only be provided with paper copies of electronic records. To operate effectively, the agency must function on the same technological plane as the industries it regulates. Just as firms realize efficiencies and benefits in the use of electronic records, FDA should be able to conduct audits efficiently and thoroughly using the same technology. For example, where firms perform computerized trend analyses of electronic records to improve their processes, FDA should be able to use computerized methods to audit electronic records (on site and off, as necessary) to detect trends, inconsistencies, and potential problem areas. If FDA is restricted to reviewing only paper copies of those records, the results would severely impede its operations. Inspections would take longer to complete, resulting in delays in approvals of new medical products, and expenditure of additional resources both by FDA (in performing the inspections and transcribing paper records to electronic format) and by the inspected firms, which would generate the paper copies and respond to questions during the resulting lengthened inspections.

The agency believes that it also may be necessary to require that persons furnish certain electronic copies of electronic records to FDA because paper copies may not be accurate and complete if they lack certain audit trail (metadata) information. Such information may have a direct bearing on record trustworthiness and reliability. These data could include information, for example, on when certain items of electronic mail were sent and received.

The agency notes that people who use different computer systems routinely provide each other with electronic copies of electronic records, and there are many current and developing tools to enable such sharing. For example, at a basic level, records may be created in, or transferred to, the ASCII format. Many different commercial programs have the capability to import from, and export to, electronic records having different formats. Firms use electronic data interchange (commonly known as EDI) and agreed upon transaction set formats to enable them to exchange copies of electronic records effectively. Third parties are also developing portable document formats to enable conversion among several diverse formats.

Concerning the ability of FDA to handle different formats of electronic records, based upon the emergence of format conversion tools such as those mentioned above, the agency's experience with electronic submissions such as computer assisted new drug applications (commonly known as CANDA's), and the agency's planned Submissions Management and Review Tracking System (commonly known as SMART), FDA is confident that it can work with firms to minimize any formatting difficulties. In

addition, substitution of the words ``accurate and complete" for
``true," as discussed in comment 69, should make it easier for firms
to provide FDA with electronic copies of their electronic records. FDA
does not believe it is necessary to specify any particular format in
part 11 because it prefers, at this time, to afford industry and the
agency more flexibility in deciding which formats meet the capabilities
of all parties. Accordingly, the agency has revised proposed
Sec. 11.10(b) to read:
The ability to generate accurate and complete copies of records
in both human readable and electronic form suitable for inspection,
review, and copying by the agency. Persons should contact the agency
if there are any questions regarding the ability of the agency to
perform such review and copying of the electronic records.
71. Proposed Sec. 11.10(c) states that procedures and controls for
closed systems must include the protection of records to enable their
accurate and ready retrieval throughout the records retention period.
One firm commented that, because it replaces systems often (about
every 3 years), it may have to retain supplanted systems to meet these
requirements. Another comment suggested that the rule be modified to
require records retention only for as long as ``legally mandated."
The agency notes that, as discussed in comment 70 of this document,
persons would not necessarily have to retain supplanted hardware and
software systems provided they implemented conversion capabilities when
switching to replacement technologies. The agency does not believe it
is necessary to add the qualifier ``legally mandated" because the
retention period for a given record will generally be established by
the regulation that requires the record. Where the regulations do not
specify a given time, the agency would expect firms to establish their
own retention periods. Regardless of the basis for the retention
period, FDA believes that the requirement that a given electronic
record be protected to permit it to be accurately and readily retrieved
for as long as it is kept is reasonable and necessary.
72. Proposed Sec. 11.10(e) would require the use of time-stamped
audit trails to document record changes, all write-to-file operations,
and to independently record the date and time of operator entries and
actions. Record changes must not obscure previously recorded
information and such audit trail documentation must be retained for a
period at least as long as required for the subject electronic
documents and must be available for agency review and copying.
Many comments objected to the proposed requirement that all write-
to-file operations be documented in the audit trail because it is
unnecessary to document all such operations. The comments said that
this would require audit trails for such automated recordings as those
made to internal buffers, data swap files, or temporary files created
by word processing programs. The comments suggested revising
Sec. 11.10(e) to require audit trails only for operator entries and
actions.
Other comments suggested that audit trails should cover: (1)
Operator data inputs but not actions, (2) only operator changes to
records, (3) only critical write-to-file information, (4) operator
changes as well as all actions, (5) only new entries, (6) only systems
where data can be altered, (7) only information recorded by humans, (8)
information recorded by both humans and devices, and (9) only entries
made upon adoption of the records as official. One comment said audit
trails should not be required for data acquisition systems, while
another comment said audit trails are critical for data acquisition
systems.
It is the agency's intent that the audit trail provide a record of
essentially who did what, wrote what, and when. The write-to-file
operations referenced in the proposed rule were not intended to cover
the kind of ``background" nonhuman recordings the comments identified.

The agency considers such operator actions as activating a manufacturing sequence or turning off an alarm to warrant the same audit trail coverage as operator data entries in order to document a thorough history of events and those responsible for such events. Although FDA acknowledges that not every operator ``action,'' such as switching among screen displays, need be covered by audit trails, the agency is concerned that revising the rule to cover only ``critical'' operations would result in excluding much information and actions that are necessary to document events thoroughly.

[[Page 13447]]

The agency believes that, in general, the kinds of operator actions that need to be covered by an audit trail are those important enough to memorialize in the electronic record itself. These are actions which, for the most part, would be recorded in corresponding paper records according to existing recordkeeping requirements.

The agency intends that the audit trail capture operator actions (e.g., a command to open a valve) at the time they occur, and operator information (e.g., data entry) at the time the information is saved to the recording media (such as disk or tape), in much the same manner as such actions and information are memorialized on paper. The audit trail need not capture every keystroke and mistake that is held in a temporary buffer before those commitments. For example, where an operator records the lot number of an ingredient by typing the lot number, followed by the ``return key'' (where pressing the return key would cause the information to be saved to a disk file), the audit trail need not record every ``backspace delete'' key the operator may have previously pressed to correct a typing error. Subsequent ``saved'' corrections made after such a commitment, however, must be part of the audit trail.

At this time, the agency's primary concern relates to the integrity of human actions. Should the agency's experience with part 11 demonstrate a need to require audit trails of device operations and entries, the agency will propose appropriate revisions to these regulations. Accordingly, the agency has revised proposed Sec. 11.10(e) by removing reference to all write-to-file operations and clarifying that the audit trail is to cover operator entries and actions that create, modify, or delete electronic records.

73. A number of comments questioned whether proposed Sec. 11.10(e) mandated that the audit trail be part of the electronic record itself or be kept as a separate record. Some comments interpreted the word ``independently'' as requiring a separate record. Several comments focused on the question of whether audit trails should be generated manually under operator control or automatically without operator control. One comment suggested a revision that would require audit trails to be generated by computer, because the system, not the operator, should record the audit trail. Other comments said the rule should facilitate date and time recording by software, not operators, and that the qualifier ``securely'' be added to the language describing the audit trail. One comment, noting that audit trails require validation and qualification to ensure that time stamps are accurate and independent, suggested that audit trails be required only when operator actions are witnessed.

The agency advises that audit trail information may be contained as part of the electronic record itself or as a separate record. FDA does not intend to require one method over the other. The word ``independently'' is intended to require that the audit trail not be under the control of the operator and, to prevent ready alteration, that it be created independently of the operator.

To maintain audit trail integrity, the agency believes it is vital that the audit trail be created by the computer system independently of operators. The agency believes it would defeat the purpose of audit trails to permit operators to write or change them. The agency believes that, at this time, the source of such independent audit trails may effectively be within the organization that creates the electronic record. However, the agency is aware of a situation under which time and date stamps are provided by trusted third parties outside of the creating organization. These third parties provide, in effect, a public electronic notary service. FDA will monitor development of such services in light of part 11 to determine if a requirement for such third party services should be included in these regulations. For now, the agency considers the advent of such services as recognition of the need for strict objectivity in recording time and date stamps.

The agency disagrees with the premise that only witnessed operator actions need be covered by audit trails because the opportunities for record falsification are not limited to cases where operator actions are witnessed. Also, the need for validating audit trails does not diminish the need for their implementation.

FDA agrees with the suggestion that the proposed rule be revised to require a secure audit trail--a concept inherent in having such a control at all. Accordingly, proposed Sec. 11.10(e) has been revised to require use of ``secure, computer-generated'' audit trails.

74. A few comments objected to the requirement that time be recorded, in addition to dates, and suggested that time be recorded only when necessary and feasible. Other comments specifically supported the requirement for recording time, noting that time stamps make electronic signatures less vulnerable to fraud and abuse. The comments noted that, in any setting, there is a need to identify the date, time, and person responsible for adding to or changing a value. One of the comments suggested that the rule require recording the reason for making changes to electronic records. Other comments implicitly supported recording time.

FDA believes that recording time is a critical element in documenting a sequence of events. Within a given day a number of events and operator actions may take place, and without recording time, documentation of those events would be incomplete. For example, without time stamps, it may be nearly impossible to determine such important sequencing as document approvals and revisions and the addition of ingredients in drug production. Thus, the element of time becomes vital to establishing an electronic record's trustworthiness and reliability.

The agency notes that comments on the ANPRM frequently identified use of date/time stamps as an important system control. Time recording, in the agency's view, can also be an effective deterrent to records falsification. For example, event sequence codes alone would not necessarily document true time in a series of events, making falsification of that sequence easier if time stamps are not used. The agency believes it should be very easy for firms to implement time stamps because there is a clock in every computer and document management software, electronic mail systems and other electronic record/electronic applications, such as digital signature programs, commonly apply date and time stamps. The agency does not intend that new technologies, such as cryptographic technologies, will be needed to comply with this requirement. The agency believes that implementation of time stamps should be feasible in virtually all computer systems because effective computer operations depend upon internal clock or timing mechanisms and, in the agency's experience, most computer systems are capable of precisely recording such time entries as when records are saved.

The agency is implementing the time stamp requirement based on the understanding that all current computers, electronic document software, electronic mail, and related electronic record systems include such technologies. The agency also understands that time stamps are applied automatically by these systems, meaning firms would not have to install additional hardware, software, or incur additional burden to implement this control. In recognition of this, the agency wishes to clarify that a primary intent of this provision is to ensure that people take reasonable measures to

[[Page 13448]]

ensure that those built in time stamps are accurate and that people do not alter them casually so as to readily mask unauthorized record changes.

The agency advises that, although part 11 does not specify the time units (e.g., tenth of a second, or even the second) to be used, the agency expects the unit of time to be meaningful in terms of documenting human actions.

The agency does not believe part 11 needs to require recording the reason for record changes because such a requirement, when needed, is already in place in existing regulations that pertain to the records themselves.

75. One comment stated that proposed Sec. 11.10(e) should not require an electronic signature for each write-to-file operation.

The agency advises that Sec. 11.10(e) does not require an electronic signature as the means of authenticating each write-to-file operation. The agency expects the audit trail to document who did what and when, documentation that can be recorded without electronic signatures themselves.

76. Several comments, addressing the proposed requirement that record changes not obscure previously recorded information, suggested revising proposed Sec. 11.10(e) to apply only to those entries intended to update previous information.

The agency disagrees with the suggested revision because the rewording is too narrow. The agency believes that some record changes may not be ``updates'' but significant modifications or falsifications disguised as updates. All changes to existing records need to be documented, regardless of the reason, to maintain a complete and accurate history, to document individual responsibility, and to enable detection of record falsifications.

77. Several comments suggested replacing the word ``document'' with ``record'' in the phrase ``Such audit trails shall be retained for a period at least as long as required for the subject electronic documents * * *'' because not all electronic documents are electronic records and because the word document connotes paper.

As discussed in section III.D. of this document, the agency equates electronic documents with electronic records, but for consistency, has changed the phrase to read ``Such audit trail documentation shall be retained for a period at least as long as that required for the subject electronic records * * *.''

78. Proposed Sec. 11.10(k)(ii) (Sec. 11.10(k)(2) in this regulation) addresses electronic audit trails as a systems documentation control. One comment noted that this provision appears to be the same as the audit trail provision of proposed Sec. 11.10(e) and requested clarification.

The agency wishes to clarify that the kinds of records subject to audit trails in the two provisions cited by the comment are different. Section 11.10(e) pertains to those records that are required by existing regulations whereas Sec. 11.10(k)(2) covers the system documentation records regarding overall controls (such as access privilege logs, or system operational specification diagrams). Accordingly, the first sentence of Sec. 11.10(e) has been revised to read ``Use of secure, computer-generated, time-stamped audit trails to independently record and date the time of operator entries and actions that create, modify, or delete electronic records.''

79. Proposed Sec. 11.10(f) states that procedures and controls for closed systems must include the use of operational checks to enforce

permitted sequencing of events, as appropriate.

Two comments requested clarification of the agency's intent regarding operational checks.

The agency advises that the purpose of performing operational checks is to ensure that operations (such as manufacturing production steps and signings to indicate initiation or completion of those steps) are not executed outside of the predefined order established by the operating organization.

80. Several comments suggested that, for clarity, the phrase ``operational checks'' be modified to ``operational system checks.''

The agency agrees that the added modifier ``system'' more accurately reflects the agency's intent that operational checks be performed by the computer systems and has revised proposed Sec. 11.10(f) accordingly.

81. Several comments suggested revising proposed Sec. 11.10(f) to clarify what is to be checked. The comments suggested that ``steps'' in addition to ``events'' be checked, only critical steps be checked, and that ``records'' also be checked.

The agency intends the word ``event'' to include ``steps'' such as production steps. For clarity, however, the agency has revised proposed Sec. 11.10(f) by adding the word ``steps.'' The agency does not, however, agree that only critical steps need be subject to operational checks because a given specific step or event may not be critical, yet it may be very important that the step be executed at the proper time relative to other steps or events. The agency does not believe it necessary to add the modifier ``records'' to proposed Sec. 11.10(f) because creation, deletion, or modification of a record is an event. Should it be necessary to create, delete, or modify records in a particular sequence, operational system checks would ensure that the proper sequence is followed.

82. Proposed Sec. 11.10(g) states that procedures and controls for closed systems must include the use of authority checks to ensure that only authorized individuals use the system, electronically sign a record, access the operation or device, alter a record, or perform the operation at hand.

One comment suggested that the requirement for authority checks be qualified with the phrase ``as appropriate,'' on the basis that it would not be necessary for certain parts of a system, such as those not affecting an electronic record. The comment cited pushing an emergency stop button as an example of an event that would not require an authority check. Another comment suggested deleting the requirement on the basis that some records can be read by all employees in an organization.

The agency advises that authority checks, and other controls under Sec. 11.10, are intended to ensure the authenticity, integrity, and confidentiality of electronic records, and to ensure that signers cannot readily repudiate a signed record as not genuine. Functions outside of this context, such as pressing an emergency stop button, would not be covered. However, even in this example, the agency finds it doubtful that a firm would permit anyone, such as a stranger from outside the organization, to enter a facility and press the stop button at will regardless of the existence of an emergency. Thus, there would likely be some generalized authority checks built into the firm's operations.

The agency believes that few organizations freely permit anyone from within or without the operation to use their computer system, electronically sign a record, access workstations, alter records, or perform operations. It is likely that authority checks shape the activities of almost every organization. The nature, scope, and mechanism of performing such checks is up to the operating organization. FDA believes, however, that performing such checks is one of the most fundamental measures to ensure the integrity and trustworthiness of electronic records.

Proposed Sec. 11.10(g) does not preclude all employees from being permitted to read certain electronic records. However, the fact that some records may be read by all employees would not

[[Page 13449]]

justify deleting the requirement for authority checks entirely. The agency believes it is highly unlikely that all of a firm's employees would have authority to read, write, and sign all of its electronic records.

83. One comment said authority checks are appropriate for document access but not system access, and suggested that the phrase ``access the operation or device'' be deleted. The comment added, with respect to authority checks on signing records, that in many organizations, more than one individual has the authority to sign documents required under FDA regulations and that such authority should be vested with the individual as designated by the operating organization. Another comment said proposed Sec. 11.10(g) should explicitly require access authority checks and suggested that the phrase ``use the system'' be changed to ``access and use the system.'' The comment also asked for clarification of the term ``device.''

The agency disagrees that authority checks should not be required for system access because, as discussed in comment 82 of this document, it is unlikely that a firm would permit any unauthorized individuals to access its computer systems. System access control is a basic security function because system integrity may be impeached even if the electronic records themselves are not directly accessed. For example, someone could access a system and change password requirements or otherwise override important security measures, enabling individuals to alter electronic records or read information that they were not authorized to see. The agency does not believe it necessary to add the qualifier ``access and'' because Sec. 11.10(d) already requires that system access be limited to authorized individuals. The agency intends the word ``device'' to mean a computer system input or output device and has revised proposed Sec. 11.10(g) to clarify this point.

Concerning signature authority, FDA advises that the requirement for authority checks in no way limits organizations in authorizing individuals to sign multiple records. Firms may use any appropriate mechanism to implement such checks. Organizations do not have to embed a list of authorized signers in every record to perform authority checks. For example, a record may be linked to an authority code that identifies the title or organizational unit of people who may sign the record. Thus, employees who have that corresponding code, or belong to that unit, would be able to sign the record. Another way to implement controls would be to link a list of authorized records to a given individual, so that the system would permit the individual to sign only records in that list.

84. Two comments addressed authority checks within the context of PDMA and suggested that such checks not be required for drug sample receipt records. The comments said that different individuals may be authorized to accept drug samples at a physician's office, and that the large number of physicians who would potentially qualify to receive samples would be too great to institute authority checks.

The agency advises that authority checks need not be automated and that in the context of PDMA such checks would be as valid for electronic records as they are for paper sample requests because only licensed practitioners or their designees may accept delivery of drug samples. The agency, therefore, acknowledges that many individuals may legally accept samples and, thus, have the authority to sign electronic receipts. However, authority checks for electronic receipts could nonetheless be performed by sample manufacturer representatives by using the same procedures as the representatives use for paper receipts. Accordingly, the agency disagrees with the comment that proposed Sec. 11.10(g) should not apply to PDMA sample receipts. The agency also advises that under PDMA, authority checks would be particularly important in the case of drug sample request records because only licensed practitioners may request drug samples. Accordingly, proposed Sec. 11.10(g) has been revised to read: ``Use of authority checks to ensure that only authorized individuals can use the system, electronically sign a record, access the operation or computer system input or output device, alter a record, or perform the operation at hand.''

85. Proposed Sec. 11.10(h) states that procedures and controls for closed systems must include the use of device (e.g., terminal) location checks to determine, as appropriate, the validity of the source of data input or operational instruction. Several comments objected to this proposed requirement and suggested its deletion because it is: (1) Unnecessary (because the data source is always known by virtue of system design and validation); (2) problematic with respect to mobile devices, such as those connected by modem; (3) too much of a ``how to;'' (4) not explicit enough to tell firms what to do; (5) unnecessary in the case of PDMA; and (6) technically challenging. One comment stated that a device's identification, in addition to location, may be important and suggested that the proposed rule be revised to require device identification as well.

FDA advises that, by use of the term ``as appropriate,'' it does not intend to require device checks in all cases. The agency believes that these checks are warranted where only certain devices have been selected as legitimate sources of data input or commands. In such cases, the device checks would be used to determine if the data or command source was authorized. In a network, for example, it may be necessary for security reasons to limit issuance of critical commands to only one authorized workstation. The device check would typically interrogate the source of the command to ensure that only the authorized workstation, and not some other device, was, in fact, issuing the command.

The same approach applies for remote sources connected by modem, to the extent that device identity interrogations could be made automatically regardless of where the portable devices were located. To clarify this concept, the agency has removed the word ``location'' from proposed Sec. 11.10(h). Device checks would be necessary under PDMA when the source of commands or data is relevant to establishing authenticity, such as when licensed practitioners order drug samples directly from the manufacturer or authorized distributor without the intermediary of a sales representative. Device checks may also be useful to firms in documenting and identifying which sales representatives are transmitting drug sample requests from licensed practitioners.

FDA believes that, although validation may demonstrate that a given terminal or workstation is technically capable of sending information from one point to another, validation alone would not be expected to address whether or not such device is authorized to do so.

86. Proposed Sec. 11.10(i) states that procedures and controls for closed systems must include confirmation that persons who develop, maintain, or use electronic record or signature systems have the education, training, and experience to perform their assigned tasks. Several comments objected to the word ``confirmation'' because it is redundant with, or more restrictive than, existing regulations, and suggested alternate wording, such as ``evidence.'' Two comments interpreted the proposed wording as requiring that checks of personnel qualifications be performed automatically by computer systems that perform database type

matches between functions and personnel training records.

The agency advises that, although there may be some overlap in proposed Sec. 11.10(i) and other regulations regarding the need for personnel to be properly qualified for their duties, part 11 is specific to functions regarding electronic records, an issue that other regulations may or may not adequately address. Therefore, the agency is retaining the requirement.

The agency does not intend to require that the check of personnel qualifications be performed automatically by a computer system itself (although such automation is desirable). The agency has revised the introductory paragraph of Sec. 11.10, as discussed in section VII. of this document, to clarify this point. The agency agrees that another word should be used in place of ``confirmation,'' and for clarity has selected ``determination.''

87. One comment suggested that the word ``training'' be deleted because it has the same meaning as ``education'' and ``experience,'' and objected to the implied requirement for records of employee training. Another comment argued that applying this provision to system developers was irrelevant so long as systems perform as required and have been appropriately validated. The comment suggested revising proposed Sec. 11.10(i) to require employees to be trained only ``as necessary.'' One comment, noting that training and experience are very important, suggested expanding proposed Sec. 11.10(i) to require appropriate examination and certification of persons who perform certain high-risk, high-trust functions and tasks.

The agency regards this requirement as fundamental to the proper operation of a facility. Personnel entrusted with important functions must have sufficient training to do their jobs. In FDA's view, formal education (e.g., academic studies) and general industry experience would not necessarily prepare someone to begin specific, highly technical tasks at a given firm. Some degree of on-the-job training would be customary and expected. The agency believes that documentation of such training is also customary and not unreasonable.

The agency also disagrees with the assertion that personnel qualifications of system developers are irrelevant. The qualifications of personnel who develop systems are relevant to the expected performance of the systems they build and their ability to explain and support these systems. Validation does not lessen the need for personnel to have the education, training, and experience to do their jobs properly. Indeed, it is highly unlikely that poorly qualified developers would be capable of producing a system that could be validated. The agency advises that, although the intent of proposed Sec. 11.10(i) is to address qualifications of those personnel who develop systems within an organization, rather than external ``vendors'' per se, it is nonetheless vital that vendor personnel are likewise qualified to do their work. The agency agrees that periodic examination or certification of personnel who perform certain critical tasks is desirable. However, the agency does not believe that at this time a specific requirement for such examination and certification is necessary.

88. Proposed Sec. 11.10(j) states that procedures and controls for closed systems must include the establishment of, and adherence to, written policies that hold individuals accountable and liable for actions initiated under their electronic signatures, so as to deter record and signature falsification.

Several comments suggested changing the word ``liable'' to ``responsible'' because the word ``responsible'' is broader, more widely understood by employees, more positive and inclusive of elements of honesty and trust, and more supportive of a broad range of disciplinary measures. One comment argued that the requirement would not deter record or signature falsification because employee honesty and integrity cannot be regulated.

The agency agrees because, although the words ``responsible'' and ``liable'' are generally synonymous, ``responsible'' is preferable because it is more positive and supportive of a broad range of disciplinary measures. There may be a general perception that electronic records and electronic signatures (particularly identification codes and passwords) are less significant and formal than traditional paper records and handwritten signatures. Individuals may therefore not fully equate the seriousness of electronic record falsification with paper record falsification. Employees need to understand the gravity and consequences of signature or record falsification. Although FDA agrees that employee honesty cannot be ensured by requiring it in a regulation, the presence of strong accountability and responsibility policies is necessary to ensure that employees understand the importance of maintaining the integrity of electronic records and signatures.

89. Several comments expressed concern regarding employee liability for actions taken under their electronic signatures in the event that such signatures are compromised, and requested ``reasonable exceptions.'' The comments suggested revising proposed Sec. 11.10(j) to hold people accountable only where there has been intentional falsification or corruption of electronic data.

The agency considers the compromise of electronic signatures to be a very serious matter, one that should precipitate an appropriate investigation into any causative weaknesses in an organization's security controls. The agency nonetheless recognizes that where such compromises occur through no fault or knowledge of individual employees, there would be reasonable limits on the extent to which disciplinary action would be taken. However, to maintain emphasis on the seriousness of such security breeches and deter the deliberate fabrication of ``mistakes,'' the agency believes Sec. 11.10 should not provide for exceptions that may lessen the import of such a fabrication.

90. One comment said the agency should consider the need for criminal law reform because current computer crime laws do not address signatures when unauthorized access or computer use is not an issue. Another comment argued that proposed Sec. 11.10(j) should be expanded beyond ``individual'' accountability to include business entities.

The agency will consider the need for recommending legislative initiatives to address electronic signature falsification in light of the experience it gains with this regulation. The agency does not believe it necessary to address business entity accountability specifically in Sec. 11.10 because the emphasis is on actions and accountability of individuals, and because individuals, rather than business entities, apply signatures.

91. One comment suggested that proposed Sec. 11.10(j) should be deleted because it is unnecessary because individuals are presumably held accountable for actions taken under their authority, and because, in some organizations, individuals frequently delegate authority to sign their names.

As discussed in comments 88 to 90 of this document, the agency has concluded that this section is necessary. Furthermore it does not limit delegation of authority as described in the comment. However, where one individual signs his or her name on behalf of someone else, the signature applied should be that of the delegatee, with some notation of that fact, and not the name of the delegator. This is the
[[Page 13451]]
same procedure commonly used on paper documents, noted as ``X for Y.''

92. Proposed Sec. 11.10(k) states that procedures and controls for closed systems must include the use of appropriate systems

documentation controls, including: (1) Adequate controls over the distribution, access to, and use of documentation for system operation and maintenance; and (2) records revision and change control procedures to maintain an electronic audit trail that documents time-sequenced development and modification of records. Several comments requested clarification of the type of documents covered by proposed Sec. 11.10(k). One comment noted that this section failed to address controls for record retention. Some comments suggested limiting the scope of systems documentation to application and configurable software, or only to software that could compromise system security or integrity. Other comments suggested that this section should be deleted because some documentation needs wide distribution within an organization, and that it is an onerous burden to control user manuals. The agency advises that Sec. 11.10(k) is intended to apply to systems documentation, namely, records describing how a system operates and is maintained, including standard operating procedures. The agency believes that adequate controls over such documentation are necessary for various reasons. For example, it is important for employees to have correct and updated versions of standard operating and maintenance procedures. If this documentation is not current, errors in procedures and/or maintenance are more likely to occur. Part 11 does not limit an organization's discretion as to how widely or narrowly any document is to be distributed, and FDA expects that certain documents will, in fact, be widely disseminated. However, some highly sensitive documentation, such as instructions on how to modify system security features, would not routinely be widely distributed. Hence, it is important to control distribution of, access to, and use of such documentation.

Although the agency agrees that the most critical types of system documents would be those directly affecting system security and integrity, FDA does not agree that control over system documentation should only extend to security related software or to application or configurable software. Documentation that relates to operating systems, for example, may also have an impact on security and day-to-day operations. The agency does not agree that it is an onerous burden to control documentation that relates to effective operation and security of electronic records systems. Failure to control such documentation, as discussed above, could permit and foster records falsification by making the enabling instructions for these acts readily available to any individual.

93. Concerning the proposed requirement for adequate controls over documentation for system operation and maintenance, one comment suggested that it be deleted because it is under the control of system vendors, rather than operating organizations. Several comments suggested that the proposed provision be deleted because it duplicates Sec. 11.10(e) with respect to audit trails. Some comments also objected to maintaining the change control procedures in electronic form and suggested deleting the word ``electronic'' from ``electronic audit trails."

The agency advises that this section is intended to apply to systems documentation that can be changed by individuals within an organization. If systems documentation can only be changed by a vendor, this provision does not apply to the vendor's customers. The agency acknowledges that systems documentation may be in paper or electronic form. Where the documentation is in paper form, an audit trail of revisions need not be in electronic form. Where systems documentation is in electronic form, however, the agency intends to require the audit trail also be in electronic form, in accordance with Sec. 11.10(e). The agency acknowledges that, in light of the comments, the proposed rule may not have been clear enough regarding audit trails addressed in Sec. 11.10(k) compared to audit trails addressed in Sec. 11.10(e) and has revised the final rule to clarify this matter.

The agency does not agree, however, that the audit trail provisions of Sec. 11.10(e) and (k), as revised, are entirely duplicative. Section 11.10(e) applies to electronic records in general (including systems documentation); Sec. 11.10(k) applies exclusively to systems documentation, regardless of whether such documentation is in paper or electronic form.

As revised, Sec. 11.10(k) now reads as follows:

(k) Use of appropriate controls over systems documentation including:

(1) Adequate controls over the distribution of, access to, and use of documentation for system operation and maintenance.

(2) Revision and change control procedures to maintain an audit trail that documents time-sequenced development and modification of systems documentation.

VIII. Electronic Records--Controls for Open Systems (Sec. 11.30)

Proposed Sec. 11.30 states that: ``Open systems used to create, modify, maintain, or transmit electronic records shall employ procedures and controls designed to ensure the authenticity, integrity and confidentiality of electronic records from the point of their creation to the point of their receipt.'' In addition, Sec. 11.30 states:

* * * Such procedures and controls shall include those identified in Sec. 11.10, as appropriate, and such additional measures as document encryption and use of established digital signature standards acceptable to the agency, to ensure, as necessary under the circumstances, record authenticity, integrity, and confidentiality.

94. One comment suggested that the reference to digital signature standards be deleted because the agency should not be setting standards and should not dictate how to ensure record authenticity, integrity, and confidentiality. Other comments requested clarification of the agency's expectations with regard to digital signatures: (1) The kinds that would be acceptable, (2) the mechanism for announcing which standards were acceptable (and whether that meant FDA would be certifying particular software), and (3) a definition of digital signature. One comment asserted that FDA should accept international standards for digital signatures. Some comments also requested a definition of encryption. One comment encouraged the agency to further define open systems.

The agency advises that Sec. 11.30 requires additional controls, beyond those identified in Sec. 11.10, as needed under the circumstances, to ensure record authenticity, integrity, and confidentiality for open systems. Use of digital signatures is one measure that may be used, but is not specifically required. The agency wants to ensure that the digital signature standard used is, in fact, appropriate. Development of digital signature standards is a complex undertaking, one FDA does not expect to be performed by individual firms on an ad hoc basis, and one FDA does not now seek to perform. The agency is nonetheless concerned that such standards be robust and secure. Currently, the agency is aware of two such standards, the RSA (Rivest-Shamir-Adleman), and NIST's Digital Signature Standard (DSS). The DSS became Federal Information Processing Standard (FIPS) 186 on December 1, 1994. These standards are incorporated in different software programs. The agency does not seek to certify or otherwise approve of such programs,

[[Page 13452]]

but expects people who use such programs to ensure that they are suitable for their intended use. FDA is aware that NIST provides certifications regarding mathematical conformance to the DSS core algorithms, but does not formally evaluate the broader programs that contain those algorithms. The agency has revised the final rule to clarify its intent that firms retain the flexibility to use any appropriate digital signature as an additional system control for open systems. FDA is also including a definition of digital signature under Sec. 11.3(b)(5).

The agency does not believe it necessary to codify the term ``encryption'' because, unlike the term digital signature, it has been in general use for many years and is generally understood to mean the transforming of a writing into a secret code or cipher. The agency is aware that there are several commercially available software programs that implement both digital signatures and encryption.

95. Two comments noted that use of digital signatures and encryption is not necessary in the context of PDMA, where access to an electronic record is limited once it is signed and stored. One of the comments suggested that proposed Sec. 11.30 be revised to clarify this point.

As discussed in comment 94 of this document, use of digital signatures and encryption would be an option when extra measures are necessary under the circumstances. In the case of PDMA records, such measures may be warranted in certain circumstances, and unnecessary in others. For example, if electronic records were to be transmitted by a firm's representative by way of a public online service to a central location, additional measures would be necessary. On the other hand, where the representative's records are hand delivered to that location, or transferred by direct connection between the representative and the central location, such additional measures to ensure record authenticity, confidentiality, and integrity may not be necessary. The agency does not believe that it is practical to revise Sec. 11.30 to elaborate on every possible situation in which additional measures would or would not be needed.

96. One comment addressed encryption of submissions to FDA and asked if people making those submissions would have to give the agency the appropriate ``keys'' and, if so, how the agency would protect the security of such information.

The agency intends to develop appropriate procedures regarding the exchange of ``keys'' attendant to use of encryption and digital signatures, and will protect those keys that must remain confidential, in the same manner as the agency currently protects trade secrets. Where the agency and a submitter agree to use a system that calls for the exchange of secret keys, FDA will work with submitters to achieve mutually agreeable procedures. The agency notes, however, that not all encryption and digital signature systems require that enabling keys be secret.

97. One comment noted that proposed Sec. 11.30 does not mention availability and nonrepudiation and requested clarification of the term ``point of receipt.'' The comment noted that, where an electronic record is received at a person's electronic mailbox (which resides on an open system), additional measures may be needed when the record is transferred to the person's own local computer because such additional transfer entails additional security risks. The comment suggested wording that would extend open system controls to the point where records are ultimately retained.

The agency agrees that, in the situation described by the comment, movement of the electronic record from an electronic mailbox to a person's local computer may necessitate open system controls. However, situations may vary considerably as to the ultimate point of receipt, and FDA believes proposed Sec. 11.30 offers greater flexibility in determining open system controls than revisions suggested by the comment. The agency advises that the concept of nonrepudiation is part of record authenticity and integrity, as already covered by Sec. 11.10(c). Therefore, FDA is not revising Sec. 11.30 as suggested.

IX. Electronic Records--Signature Manifestations (Sec. 11.50)
Proposed Sec. 11.50 requires that electronic records that are
electronically signed must display in clear text the printed name of
the signer, and the date and time when the electronic signature was
executed. This section also requires that electronic records clearly
indicate the meaning (such as review, approval, responsibility, and
authorship) associated with their attendant signatures.
98. Several comments suggested that the information required under
proposed Sec. 11.50 need not be contained in the electronic records
themselves, but only in the human readable format (screen displays and
printouts) of such records. The comments explained that the records
themselves need only contain links, such as signature attribute codes,
to such information to produce the displays of information required.
The comments noted, for example, that, where electronic signatures
consist of an identification code in combination with a password, the
combined code and password itself would not be part of the display.
Some comments suggested that proposed Sec. 11.50 be revised to clarify
what items are to be displayed.
The agency agrees and has revised proposed Sec. 11.50 accordingly.
The intent of this section is to require that human readable forms of
signed electronic records, such as computer screen displays and
printouts bear: (1) The printed name of the signer (at the time the
record is signed as well as whenever the record is read by humans); (2)
the date and time of signing; and (3) the meaning of the signature. The
agency believes that revised Sec. 11.50 will afford persons the
flexibility they need to implement the display of information
appropriate for their own electronic records systems, consistent with
other system controls in part 11, to ensure record integrity and
prevent falsification.
99. One comment stated that the controls in proposed Sec. 11.50
would not protect against inaccurate entries.
FDA advises that the purpose of this section is not to protect
against inaccurate entries, but to provide unambiguous documentation of
the signer, when the signature was executed, and the signature's
meaning. The agency believes that such a record is necessary to
document individual responsibility and actions.
In a paper environment, the printed name of the individual is
generally present in the signed record, frequently part of a
traditional ``signature block.'' In an electronic environment, the
person's name may not be apparent, especially where the signature is
based on identification codes combined with passwords. In addition, the
meaning of a signature is generally apparent in a paper record by
virtue of the context of the record or, more often, explicit phrases
such as ``approved by,'' ``reviewed by,'' and ``performed by.'' Thus,
the agency believes that for clear documentation purposes it is
necessary to carry such meanings into the electronic record
environment.
100. One comment suggested that proposed Sec. 11.50 should apply
only to those records that are required to be signed, and that the
display of the date and time should be performed in a secure manner.
The agency intends that this section apply to all signed electronic
records regardless of whether other regulations require them to be
signed. The agency believes that if it is important enough that a
record be signed, human readable
[[Page 13453]]
displays of such records must include the printed name of the signer,
the date and time of signing, and the meaning of the signature. Such
information is crucial to the agency's ability to protect public
health. For example, a message from a firm's management to employees
instructing them on a particular course of action may be critical in
litigation. This requirement will help ensure clear documentation and

- 143 -

deter falsification regardless of whether the signature is electronic or handwritten.

The agency agrees that the display of information should be carried out in a secure manner that preserves the integrity of that information. The agency, however, does not believe it is necessary at this time to revise Sec. 11.50 to add specific security measures because other requirements of part 11 have the effect of ensuring appropriate security.

Because signing information is important regardless of the type of signature used, the agency has revised Sec. 11.50 to cover all types of signings.

101. Several comments objected to the requirement in proposed Sec. 11.50(a) that the time of signing be displayed in addition to the date on the grounds that such information is: (1) Unnecessary, (2) costly to implement, (3) needed in the electronic record for auditing purposes, but not needed in the display of the record, and (4) only needed in critical applications. Some comments asserted that recording time should be optional. One comment asked whether the time should be local to the signer or to a central network when electronic record systems cross different time zones.

The agency believes that it is vital to record the time when a signature is applied. Documenting the time when a signature was applied can be critical to demonstrating that a given record was, or was not, falsified. Regarding systems that may span different time zones, the agency advises that the signer's local time is the one to be recorded.

102. One comment assumed that a person's user identification code could be displayed instead of the user's printed name, along with the date and time of signing.

This assumption is incorrect. The agency intends that the printed name of the signer be displayed for purposes of unambiguous documentation and to emphasize the importance of the act of signing to the signer. The agency believes that because an identification code is not an actual name, it would not be a satisfactory substitute.

103. One comment suggested that the word ``printed'' in the phrase ``printed name'' be deleted because the word was superfluous. The comment also stated that the rule should state when the clear text must be created or displayed because some computer systems, in the context of electronic data interchange transactions, append digital signatures to records before, or in connection with, communication of the record. The agency disagrees that the word ``printed'' is superfluous because the intent of this section is to show the name of the person in an unambiguous manner that can be read by anyone. The agency believes that requiring the printed name of the signer instead of codes or other manifestations, more effectively provides clarity.

The agency has revised this section to clarify the point at which the signer's information must be displayed, namely, as part of any human readable form of the electronic record. The revision, in the agency's view, addresses the comment's concern regarding the application of digital signatures. The agency advises that under Sec. 11.50, any time after an electronic record has been signed, individuals who see the human readable form of the record will be able to immediately tell who signed the record, when it was signed, and what the signature meant. This includes the signer who, as with a traditional signature to paper, will be able to review the signature instantly.

104. One comment asked if the operator would have to see the meaning of the signature, or if the information had to be stored on the physical electronic record.

As discussed in comment 100 of this document, the information required by Sec. 11.50(b) must be displayed in the human readable format of the electronic record. Persons may elect to store that information directly within the electronic record itself, or in logically associated records, as long as such information is displayed any time a person reads the record.

105. One comment noted that proposed Sec. 11.50(b) could be interpreted to require lengthy explanations of the signatures and the credentials of the signers. The comment also stated that this information would more naturally be contained in standard operating procedures, manuals, or accompanying literature than in the electronic records themselves.

The agency believes that the comment misinterprets the intent of this provision. Recording the meaning of the signature does not infer that the signer's credentials or other lengthy explanations be part of that meaning. The statement must merely show what is meant by the act of signing (e.g., review, approval, responsibility, authorship).

106. One comment noted that the meaning of a signature may be included in a (digital signature) public key certificate and asked if this would be acceptable. The comment also noted that the certificate might be easily accessible by a record recipient from either a recognized database or one that might be part of, or associated with, the electronic record itself. The comment further suggested that FDA would benefit from participating in developing rules of practice regarding certificate-based public key cryptography and infrastructure with the Information Security Committee, Section of Science and Technology, of the American Bar Association (ABA).

The intent of this provision is to clearly discern the meaning of the signature when the electronic record is displayed in human readable form. The agency does not expect such meaning to be contained in or displayed by a public key certificate because the public key is generally a fixed value associated with an individual. The certificate is used by the recipient to authenticate a digital signature that may have different meanings, depending upon the record being signed. FDA acknowledges that it is possible for someone to establish different public keys, each of which may indicate a different signature meaning. Part 11 would not prohibit multiple ``meaning'' keys provided the meaning of the signature itself was still clear in the display of the record, a feature that could conceivably be implemented by software. Regarding work of the ABA and other standard-setting organizations, the agency welcomes an open dialog with such organizations, for the mutual benefit of all parties, to establish and facilitate the use of electronic record/electronic signature technologies. FDA's participation in any such activities would be in accordance with the agency's policy on standards stated in the Federal Register of October 11, 1995 (60 FR 53078).

Revised Sec. 11.50, signature manifestations, reads as follows:
(a) Signed electronic records shall contain information associated with the signing that clearly indicates all of the following:
(1) The printed name of the signer;
(2) The date and time when the signature was executed; and
(3) The meaning (such as review, approval, responsibility, or authorship) associated with the signature.
(b) The items identified in paragraphs (a)(1), (a)(2), and (a)(3) of this section shall be subject to the same controls as for electronic records and shall be included as part of any human readable form of the electronic record (such as electronic display or printout).
[[Page 13454]]
X. Electronic Records--Signature/Record Linking (Sec. 11.70)
107. Proposed Sec. 11.70 states that electronic signatures and handwritten signatures executed to electronic records must be verifiably bound to their respective records to ensure that signatures

could not be excised, copied, or otherwise transferred to falsify
another electronic record.

Many comments objected to this provision as too prescriptive,
unnecessary, unattainable, and excessive in comparison to paper-based
records. Some comments asserted that the objectives of the section
could be attained through appropriate procedural and administrative
controls. The comments also suggested that objectives of the provision
could be met by appropriate software (i.e., logical) links between the
electronic signatures and electronic records, and that such links are
common in systems that use identification codes in combination with
passwords. One firm expressed full support for the provision, and noted
that its system implements such a feature and that signature-to-record
binding is similar to the record-locking provision of the proposed PDMA
regulations.

The agency did not intend to mandate use of any particular
technology by use of the word ``binding.'' FDA recognizes that, because
it is relatively easy to copy an electronic signature to another
electronic record and thus compromise or falsify that record, a
technology based link is necessary. The agency does not believe that
procedural or administrative controls alone are sufficient to ensure
that objective because such controls could be more easily circumvented
than a straightforward technology based approach. In addition, when
electronic records are transferred from one party to another, the
procedural controls used by the sender and recipient may be different.
This could result in record falsification by signature transfer.

The agency agrees that the word ``link'' would offer persons
greater flexibility in implementing the intent of this provision and in
associating the names of individuals with their identification codes/
passwords without actually recording the passwords themselves in
electronic records. The agency has revised proposed Sec. 11.70 to state
that signatures shall be linked to their electronic records.

108. Several comments argued that proposed Sec. 11.70 requires
absolute protection of electronic records from falsification, an
objective that is unrealistic to the extent that determined individuals
could falsify records.

The agency acknowledges that, despite elaborate system controls,
certain determined individuals may find a way to defeat
antifalsification measures. FDA will pursue such illegal activities as
vigorously as it does falsification of paper records. For purposes of
part 11, the agency's intent is to require measures that prevent
electronic records falsification by ordinary means. Therefore, FDA has
revised Sec. 11.70 by adding the phrase ``by ordinary means'' at the
end of this section.

109. Several comments suggested changing the phrase ``another
electronic record'' to ``an electronic record'' to clarify that the
antifalsification provision applies to the current record as well as
any other record.

The agency agrees and has revised Sec. 11.70 accordingly.

110. Two comments argued that signature-to-record binding is
unnecessary, in the context of PDMA, beyond the point of record
creation (i.e., when records are transmitted to a point of receipt).
The comments asserted that persons who might be in a position to
separate a signature from a record (for purposes of falsification) are
individuals responsible for record integrity and thus unlikely to
falsify records. The comments also stated that signature-to-record
binding is produced by software coding at the time the record is
signed, and suggested that proposed Sec. 11.70 clarify that binding
would be necessary only up to the point of actual transmission of the
electronic record to a central point of receipt.

The agency disagrees with the comment's premise that the need for
binding to prevent falsification depends on the disposition of people

to falsify records. The agency believes that reliance on individual tendencies is insufficient insurance against falsification. The agency also notes that in the traditional paper record, the signature remains bound to its corresponding record regardless of where the record may go.

111. One comment suggested that proposed Sec. 11.70 be deleted because it appears to require that all records be kept on inalterable media. The comment also suggested that the phrase ``otherwise transferred'' be deleted on the basis that it should be permissible for copies of handwritten signatures (recorded electronically) to be made when used, in addition to another unique individual identification mechanism.

The agency advises that neither Sec. 11.70, nor other sections in part 11, requires that records be kept on inalterable media. What is required is that whenever revisions to a record are made, the original entries must not be obscured. In addition, this section does not prohibit copies of handwritten signatures recorded electronically from being made for legitimate reasons that do not relate to record falsification. Section 11.70 merely states that such copies must not be made that falsify electronic records.

112. One comment suggested that proposed Sec. 11.70 be revised to require application of response cryptographic methods because only those methods could be used to comply with the regulation. The comment noted that, for certificate based public key cryptographic methods, the agency should address verifiable binding between the signer's name and public key as well as binding between digital signatures and electronic records. The comment also suggested that the regulation should reference electronic signatures in the context of secure time and date stamping.

The agency intends to permit maximum flexibility in how organizations achieve the linking called for in Sec. 11.70, and, as discussed above, has revised the regulation accordingly. Therefore, FDA does not believe that cryptographic and digital signature methods would be the only ways of linking an electronic signature to an electronic document. In fact, one firm commented that its system binds a person's handwritten signature to an electronic record. The agency agrees that use of digital signatures accomplishes the same objective because, if a digital signature were to be copied from one record to another, the second record would fail the digital signature verification procedure. Furthermore, FDA notes that concerns regarding binding a person's name with the person's public key would be addressed in the context of Sec. 11.100(b) because an organization must establish an individual's identity before assigning or certifying an electronic signature (or any of the electronic signature components).

113. Two comments requested clarification of the types of technologies that could be used to meet the requirements of proposed Sec. 11.70.

As discussed in comment 107 of this document, the agency is affording persons maximum flexibility in using any appropriate method to link electronic signatures to their respective electronic records to prevent record falsification. Use of digital signatures is one such method, as is use of software locks to prevent sections of codes
[[Page 13455]]
representing signatures from being copied or removed. Because this is an area of developing technology, it is likely that other linking methods will emerge.

XI. Electronic Signatures--General Requirements (Sec. 11.100)

Proposed Sec. 11.100(a) states that each electronic signature must be unique to one individual and not be reused or reassigned to anyone else.

114. One comment asserted that several people should be permitted

to share a common identification code and password where access control is limited to inquiry only.

Part 11 does not prohibit the establishment of a common group identification code/password for read only access purposes. However, such commonly shared codes and passwords would not be regarded, and must not be used, as electronic signatures. Shared access to a common database may nonetheless be implemented by granting appropriate common record access privileges to groups of people, each of whom has a unique electronic signature.

115. Several comments said proposed Sec. 11.100(a) should permit identification codes to be reused and reassigned from one employee to another, as long as an audit trail exists to associate an identification code with a given individual at any one time, and different passwords are used. Several comments said the section should indicate if the agency intends to restrict authority delegation by the nonreassignment or nonreuse provision, or by the provision in Sec. 11.200(a)(2) requiring electronic signatures to be used only by their genuine owners. The comments questioned whether reuse means restricting one noncryptographic based signature to only one record and argued that passwords need not be unique if the combined identification code and password are unique to one individual. One comment recommended caution in using the term ``ownership'' because of possible confusion with intellectual property rights or ownership of the computer systems themselves.

The agency advises that, where an electronic signature consists of the combined identification code and password, Sec. 11.100 would not prohibit the reassignment of the identification code provided the combined identification code and password remain unique to prevent record falsification. The agency believes that such reassignments are inadvisable, however, to the extent that they might be combined with an easily guessed password, thus increasing the chances that an individual might assume a signature belonging to someone else. The agency also advises that where people can read identification codes (e.g., printed numbers and letters that are typed at a keyboard or read from a card), the risks of someone obtaining that information as part of a falsification effort would be greatly increased as compared to an identification code that is not in human readable form (one that is, for example, encoded on a ``secure card'' or other device).

Regarding the delegation of authority to use electronic signatures, FDA does not intend to restrict the ability of one individual to sign a record or otherwise act on behalf of another individual. However, the applied electronic signature must be the assignee's and the record should clearly indicate the capacity in which the person is acting (e.g., on behalf of, or under the authority of, someone else). This is analogous to traditional paper records and handwritten signatures when person ``A'' signs his or her own name under the signature block of person ``B,'' with appropriate explanatory notations such as ``for'' or ``as representative of'' person B. In such cases, person A does not simply sign the name of person B. The agency expects the same procedure to be used for electronic records and electronic signatures.

The agency intends the term ``reuse'' to refer to an electronic signature used by a different person. The agency does not regard as ``reuse'' the replicate application of a noncryptographic based electronic signature (such as an identification code and password) to different electronic records. For clarity, FDA has revised the phrase ``not be reused or reassigned to'' to state ``not be reused by, or reassigned to,'' in Sec. 11.100(a).

The reference in Sec. 11.200(a) to ownership is made in the context of an individual owning or being assigned a particular electronic signature that no other individual may use. FDA believes this is clear and that concerns regarding ownership in the context of intellectual

- 148 -

property rights or hardware are misplaced.

116. One comment suggested that proposed Sec. 11.100(a) should accommodate electronic signatures assigned to organizations rather than individuals.

The agency advises that, for purposes of part 11, electronic signatures are those of individual human beings and not organizations. For example, FDA does not regard a corporate seal as an individual's signature. Humans may represent and obligate organizations by signing records, however. For clarification, the agency is substituting the word ``individual'' for ``person'' in the definition of electronic signature (Sec. 11.3(b)(7)) because the broader definition of person within the act includes organizations.

117. Proposed Sec. 11.100(b) states that, before an electronic signature is assigned to a person, the identity of the individual must be verified by the assigning authority.

Two comments noted that where people use identification codes in combination with passwords only the identification code portion of the electronic signature is assigned, not the password. Another comment argued that the word ``assigned'' is inappropriate in the context of electronic signatures based upon public key cryptography because the appropriate authority certifies the bind between the individual's public key and identity, and not the electronic signature itself.

The agency acknowledges that, for certain types of electronic signatures, the authorizing or certifying organization issues or approves only a portion of what eventually becomes an individual's electronic signature. FDA wishes to accommodate a broad variety of electronic signatures and is therefore revising Sec. 11.100(b) to require that an organization verify the identity of an individual before it establishes, assigns, certifies, or otherwise sanctions an individual's electronic signature or any element of such electronic signature.

118. One comment suggested that the word ``verified'' in proposed Sec. 11.100(b) be changed to ``confirmed.'' Other comments addressed the method of verifying a person's identity and suggested that the section specify acceptable verification methods, including high level procedures regarding the relative strength of that verification, and the need for personal appearances or supporting documentation such as birth certificates. Two comments said the verification provision should be deleted because normal internal controls are adequate, and that it was impractical for multinational companies whose employees are globally dispersed.

The agency does not believe that there is a sufficient difference between ``verified'' and ``confirmed'' to warrant a change in this section. Both words indicate that organizations substantiate a person's identity to prevent impersonations when an electronic signature, or any of its elements, is being established or certified. The agency disagrees with the assertion that this requirement is unnecessary. Without verifying someone's identity at the outset of establishing or certifying

[[Page 13456]]

an individual's electronic signature, or a portion thereof, an imposter might easily access and compromise many records. Moreover, an imposter could continue this activity for a prolonged period of time despite other system controls, with potentially serious consequences.

The agency does not believe that the size of an organization, or global dispersion of its employees, is reason to abandon this vital control. Such dispersion may, in fact, make it easier for an impostor to pose as someone else in the absence of such verification. Further, the agency does not accept the implication that multinational firms would not verify the identity of their employees as part of other routine procedures, such as when individuals are first hired.

In addition, in cases where an organization is widely dispersed and electronic signatures are established or certified centrally, Sec. 11.100(b) does not prohibit organizations from having their local units perform the verification and relaying this information to the central authority. Similarly, local units may conduct the electronic signature assignment or certification.

FDA does not believe it is necessary at this time to specify methods of identity verification and expects that organizations will consider risks attendant to sanctioning an erroneously assigned electronic signature.

119. Proposed Sec. 11.100(c) states that persons using electronic signatures must certify to the agency that their electronic signature system guarantees the authenticity, validity, and binding nature of any electronic signature. Persons utilizing electronic signatures would, upon agency request, provide additional certification or testimony that a specific electronic signature is authentic, valid, and binding. Such certification would be submitted to the FDA district office in which territory the electronic signature system is in use.

Many comments objected to the proposed requirement that persons provide FDA with certification regarding their electronic signature systems. The comments asserted that the requirement was: (1) Unprecedented, (2) unrealistic, (3) unnecessary, (4) contradictory to the principles and intent of system validation, (5) too burdensome for FDA to manage logistically, (6) apparently intended only to simplify FDA litigation, (7) impossible to meet regarding ``guarantees" of authenticity, and (8) an apparent substitute for FDA inspections.

FDA agrees in part with these comments. This final rule reduces the scope and burden of certification to a statement of intent that electronic signatures are the legally binding equivalent of handwritten signatures.

As noted previously, the agency believes it is important, within the context of its health protection activities, to ensure that persons who implement electronic signatures fully equate the legally binding nature of electronic signatures with the traditional handwritten paper-based signatures. The agency is concerned that individuals might disavow an electronic signature as something completely different from a traditional handwritten signature. Such contention could result in confusion and possibly extensive litigation.

Moreover, a limited certification as provided in this final rule is consistent with other legal, regulatory, and commercial practices. For example, electronic data exchange trading partner agreements are often written on paper and signed with traditional handwritten signatures to establish that certain electronic identifiers are recognized as equivalent to traditional handwritten signatures.

FDA does not expect electronic signature systems to be guaranteed foolproof. The agency does not intend, under Sec. 11.100(c), to establish a requirement that is unattainable. Certification of an electronic signature system as the legally binding equivalent of a traditional handwritten signature is separate and distinct from system validation. This provision is not intended as a substitute for FDA inspection and such inspection alone may not be able to determine in a conclusive manner an organization's intent regarding electronic signature equivalency.

The agency has revised proposed Sec. 11.100(c) to clarify its intent. The agency wishes to emphasize that the final rule dramatically curtails what FDA had proposed and is essential for the agency to be able to protect and promote the public health because FDA must be able to hold people to the commitments they make under their electronic signatures. The certification in the final rule is merely a statement of intent that electronic signatures are the legally binding equivalent of traditional handwritten signatures.

120. Several comments questioned the procedures necessary for submitting the certification to FDA, including: (1) The scheduling of the certification; (2) whether to submit certificates for each individual or for each electronic signature; (3) the meaning of ``territory'' in the context of wide area networks; (4) whether such certificates could be submitted electronically; and (5) whether organizations, after submitting a certificate, had to wait for a response from FDA before implementing their electronic signature systems. Two comments suggested revising proposed Sec. 11.100(c) to require that all certifications be submitted to FDA only upon agency request. One comment suggested changing ``should'' to ``shall'' in the last sentence of Sec. 11.100(c) if the agency's intent is to require certificates to be submitted to the respective FDA district office.

The agency intends that certificates be submitted once, in the form of a paper letter, bearing a traditional handwritten signature, at the time an organization first establishes an electronic signature system after the effective date of part 11, or, where such systems have been used before the effective date, upon continued use of the electronic signature system.

A separate certification is not needed for each electronic signature, although certification of a particular electronic signature is to be submitted if the agency requests it. The agency does not intend to establish certification as a review and approval function. In addition, organizations need not await FDA's response before putting electronic signature systems into effect, or before continuing to use an existing system.

A single certification may be stated in broad terms that encompass electronic signatures of all current and future employees, thus obviating the need for subsequent certifications submitted on a preestablished schedule.

To further simplify the process and to minimize the number of certifications that persons would have to provide, the agency has revised Sec. 11.100(c) to permit submission of a single certification that covers all electronic signatures used by an organization. The revised rule also simplifies the process by providing a single agency receiving unit. The final rule instructs persons to send certifications to FDA's Office of Regional Operations (HFC-100), 5600 Fishers Lane, Rockville, MD 20857. Persons outside the United States may send their certifications to the same office.

The agency offers, as guidance, an example of an acceptable Sec. 11.100(c) certification:

Pursuant to Section 11.100 of Title 21 of the Code of Federal Regulations, this is to certify that [name of organization] intends that all electronic signatures executed by our employees, agents, or representatives, located anywhere in the world, are the legally binding equivalent of traditional handwritten signatures.

[[Page 13457]]

The agency has revised Sec. 11.100 to clarify where and when certificates are to be submitted.

The agency does not agree that the initial certification be provided only upon agency request because FDA believes it is vital to have such certificates, as a matter of record, in advance of any possible litigation. This would clearly establish the intent of organizations to equate the legally binding nature of electronic signatures with traditional handwritten signatures. In addition, the agency believes that having the certification on file ahead of time will have the beneficial effect of reinforcing the gravity of electronic signatures by putting an organization's employees on notice that the organization has gone on record with FDA as equating electronic signatures with handwritten signatures.

121. One comment suggested that proposed Sec. 11.100(c) be revised

to exclude from certification instances in which the purported signer claims that he or she did not create or authorize the signature.

The agency declines to make this revision because a provision for nonrepudiation is already contained in Sec. 11.10.

As a result of the considerations discussed in comments 119 and 120 of this document, the agency has revised proposed Sec. 11.100(c) to state that:

(c) Persons using electronic signatures shall, prior to or at the time of such use, certify to the agency that the electronic signatures in their system, used on or after August 20, 1997, are intended to be the legally binding equivalent of traditional handwritten signatures.

(1) The certification shall be submitted in paper form and signed with a traditional handwritten signature to the Office of Regional Operations (HFC-100), 5600 Fishers Lane, Rockville, MD 20857.

(2) Persons using electronic signatures shall, upon agency request, provide additional certification or testimony that a specific electronic signature is the legally binding equivalent of the signer's handwritten signature.

XII. Electronic Signature Components and Controls (Sec. 11.200)

122. Proposed Sec. 11.200 sets forth requirements for electronic signature identification mechanisms and controls. Two comments suggested that the term ``identification code'' should be defined. Several comments suggested that the term ``identification mechanisms'' should be changed to ``identification components'' because each component of an electronic signature need not be executed by a different mechanism.

The agency believes that the term ``identification code'' is sufficiently broad and generally understood and does not need to be defined in these regulations. FDA agrees that the word ``component'' more accurately reflects the agency's intent than the word ``mechanism,'' and has substituted ``component'' for ``mechanism'' in revised Sec. 11.200. The agency has also revised the section heading to read ``Electronic signature components and controls'' to be consistent with the wording of the section.

123. Proposed Sec. 11.200(a) states that electronic signatures not based upon biometric/behavioral links must: (1) Employ at least two distinct identification mechanisms (such as an identification code and password), each of which is contemporaneously executed at each signing; (2) be used only by their genuine owners; and (3) be administered and executed to ensure that attempted use of an individual's electronic signature by anyone other than its genuine owner requires collaboration of two or more individuals.

Two comments said that proposed Sec. 11.200(a) should acknowledge that passwords may be known not only to their genuine owners, but also to system administrators in case people forget their passwords.

The agency does not believe that system administrators would routinely need to know an individual's password because they would have sufficient privileges to assist those individuals who forget passwords.

124. Several comments argued that the agency should accept a single password alone as an electronic signature because: (1) Combining the password with an identification code adds little security, (2) administrative controls and passwords are sufficient, (3) authorized access is more difficult when two components are needed, (4) people would not want to gain unauthorized entry into a manufacturing environment, and (5) changing current systems that use only a password would be costly.

The comments generally addressed the need for two components in electronic signatures within the context of the requirement that all components be used each time an electronic signature is executed.

Several comments suggested that, for purposes of system access, individuals should enter both a user identification code and password, but that, for subsequent signings during one period of access, a single element (such as a password) known only to, and usable by, the individual should be sufficient.

The agency believes that it is very important to distinguish between those (nonbiometric) electronic signatures that are executed repetitively during a single, continuous controlled period of time (access session or logged-on period) and those that are not. The agency is concerned, from statements made in comments, that people might use passwords that are not always unique and are frequently words that are easily associated with an individual. Accordingly, where nonbiometric electronic signatures are not executed repetitively during a single, continuous controlled period, it would be extremely bad practice to use a password alone as an electronic signature. The agency believes that using a password alone in such cases would clearly increase the likelihood that one individual, by chance or deduction, could enter a password that belonged to someone else and thereby easily and readily impersonate that individual. This action could falsify electronic records.

The agency acknowledges that there are some situations involving repetitive signings in which it may not be necessary for an individual to execute each component of a nonbiometric electronic signature for every signing. The agency is persuaded by the comments that such situations generally involve certain conditions. For example, an individual performs an initial system access or ``log on,'' which is effectively the first signing, by executing all components of the electronic signature (typically both an identification code and a password). The individual then performs subsequent signings by executing at least one component of the electronic signature, under controlled conditions that prevent another person from impersonating the legitimate signer. The agency's concern here is the possibility that, if the person leaves the workstation, someone else could access the workstation (or other computer device used to execute the signing) and impersonate the legitimate signer by entering an identification code or password.

The agency believes that, in such situations, it is vital to have stringent controls in place to prevent the impersonation. Such controls include: (1) Requiring an individual to remain in close proximity to the workstation throughout the signing session; (2) use of automatic inactivity disconnect measures that would ``de-log'' the first individual if no entries or actions were taken within a fixed short timeframe; and (3) requiring that the single component needed for subsequent signings be known to, and usable only by, the authorized individual.

The agency's objective in accepting the execution of fewer than all the components of a nonbiometric
[[Page 13458]]
electronic signature for repetitive signings is to make it impractical to falsify records. The agency believes that this would be attained by complying with all of the following procedures where nonbiometric electronic signatures are executed more than once during a single, continuous controlled session: (1) All electronic signature components are executed for the first signing; (2) at least one electronic signature component is executed at each subsequent signing; (3) the electronic signature component executed after the initial signing is only used by its genuine owner, and is designed to ensure it can only be used by its genuine owner; and (4) the electronic signatures are administered and executed to ensure that their attempted use by anyone other than their genuine owners requires collaboration of two or more individuals. Items 1 and 4 are already incorporated in proposed

- 153 -

Sec. 11.200(a). FDA has included items 2 and 3 in final Sec. 11.200(a). The agency cautions, however, that if its experience with enforcement of part 11 demonstrates that these controls are insufficient to deter falsifications, FDA may propose more stringent controls.

125. One comment asserted that, if the agency intends the term ``identification code" to mean the typical user identification, it should not characterize the term as a distinct mechanism because such codes do not necessarily exhibit security attributes. The comment also suggested that proposed Sec. 11.200(a) address the appropriate application of each possible combination of a two-factor authentication method.

The agency acknowledges that the identification code alone does not exhibit security attributes. Security derives from the totality of system controls used to prevent falsification. However, uniqueness of the identification code when combined with another electronic signature component, which may not be unique (such as a password), makes the combination unique and thereby enables a legitimate electronic signature. FDA does not now believe it necessary to address, in Sec. 11.200(a), the application of all possible combinations of multifactored authentication methods.

126. One comment requested clarification of ``each signing," noting that a laboratory employee may enter a group of test results under one signing.

The agency advises that each signing means each time an individual executes a signature. Particular requirements regarding what records need to be signed derive from other regulations, not part 11. For example, in the case of a laboratory employee who performs a number of analytical tests, within the context of drug CGMP regulations, it is permissible for one signature to indicate the performance of a group of tests (21 CFR 211.194(a)(7)). A separate signing is not required in this context for each separate test as long as the record clearly shows that the single signature means the signer performed all the tests.

127. One comment suggested that the proposed requirement, that collaboration of at least two individuals is needed to prevent attempts at electronic signature falsification, be deleted because a responsible person should be allowed to override the electronic signature of a subordinate. Several comments addressed the phrase ``attempted use" and suggested that it be deleted or changed to ``unauthorized use." The comments said that willful breaking or circumvention of any security measure does not require two or more people to execute, and that the central question is whether collaboration is required to use the electronic signature.

The agency advises that the intent of the collaboration provision is to require that the components of a nonbiometric electronic signature cannot be used by one individual without the prior knowledge of a second individual. One type of situation the agency seeks to prevent is the use of a component such as a card or token that a person may leave unattended. If an individual must collaborate with another individual by disclosing a password, the risks of betrayal and disclosure are greatly increased and this helps to deter such actions. Because the agency is not condoning such actions, Sec. 11.200(a)(2) requires that electronic signatures be used only by the genuine owner. The agency disagrees with the comments that the term ``attempted use" should be changed to ``unauthorized uses," because ``unauthorized uses" could infer that use of someone else's electronic signature is acceptable if it is authorized.

Regarding electronic signature ``overrides," the agency would consider as falsification the act of substituting the signature of a supervisor for that of a subordinate. The electronic signature of the subordinate must remain inviolate for purposes of authentication and documentation. Although supervisors may overrule the actions of their staff, the electronic signatures of the subordinates must remain a permanent part of the record, and the supervisor's own electronic signature must appear separately. The agency believes that such an approach is fully consistent with procedures for paper records.

As a result of the revisions noted in comments 123 to 127 of this document, Sec. 11.200(a) now reads as follows:

(a) Electronic signatures that are not based upon biometrics shall:

(1) Employ at least two distinct identification components such as an identification code and password.

(i) When an individual executes a series of signings during a single, continuous period of controlled system access, the first signing shall be executed using all electronic signature components; subsequent signings shall be executed using at least one electronic signature component that is only executable by, and designed to be used only by, the individual.

(ii) When an individual executes one or more signings not performed during a single, continuous period of controlled system access, each signing shall be executed using all of the electronic signature components.

(2) Be used only by their genuine owners; and

(3) Be administered and executed to ensure that attempted use of an individual's electronic signature by anyone other than its genuine owner requires collaboration of two or more individuals.

128. Proposed Sec. 11.200(b) states that electronic signatures based upon biometric/behavioral links be designed to ensure that they could not be used by anyone other than their genuine owners.

One comment suggested that the agency make available, by public workshop or other means, any information it has regarding existing biometric systems so that industry can provide proper input. Another comment asserted that proposed Sec. 11.200(b) placed too great an emphasis on biometrics, did not establish particular levels of assurance for biometrics, and did not provide for systems using mixtures of biometric and nonbiometric electronic signatures. The comment recommended revising the phrase ``designed to ensure they cannot be used" to read ``provide assurances that prevent their execution."

The agency's experience with biometric electronic signatures is contained in the administrative record for this rulemaking, under docket no. 92N-0251, and includes recommendations from public comments to the ANPRM and the proposed rule. The agency has also gathered, and continues to gather, additional information from literature reviews, general press reports, meetings, and the agency's experience with this technology. Interested persons have had extensive opportunity for input and comment regarding biometrics in part 11. In addition, interested persons may continue to contact the agency at any time regarding biometrics or any other relevant technologies. The agency notes [[Page 13459]] that the rule does not require the use of biometric-based electronic signatures.

As the agency's experience with biometric electronic signatures increases, FDA will consider holding or participating in public workshops if that approach would be helpful to those wishing to adopt such technologies to comply with part 11.

The agency does not believe that proposed Sec. 11.200(b) places too much emphasis on biometric electronic signatures. As discussed above, the regulation makes a clear distinction between electronic signatures that are and are not based on biometrics, but treats their acceptance equally.

The agency recognizes the inherent security advantages of

biometrics, however, in that record falsification is more difficult to perform. System controls needed to make biometric-based electronic signatures reliable and trustworthy are thus different in certain respects from controls needed to make nonbiometric electronic signatures reliable and trustworthy. The requirements in part 11 reflect those differences.

The agency does not believe that it is necessary at this time to set numerical security assurance standards that any system would have to meet.

The regulation does not prohibit individuals from using combinations of biometric and nonbiometric-based electronic signatures. However, when combinations are used, FDA advises that requirements for each element in the combination would also apply. For example, if passwords are used in combination with biometrics, then the benefits of using passwords would only be realized, in the agency's view, by adhering to controls that ensure password integrity (see Sec. 11.300). In addition, the agency believes that the phrase ``designed to ensure that they cannot be used'' more accurately reflects the agency's intent than the suggested alternate wording, and is more consistent with the concept of systems validation. Under such validation, falsification preventive attributes would be designed into the biometric systems.

To be consistent with the revised definition of biometrics in Sec. 11.3(b)(3), the agency has revised Sec. 11.200(b) to read, ``Electronic signatures based upon biometrics shall be designed to ensure that they cannot be used by anyone other than their genuine owners.''

XIII. Electronic Signatures--Controls for Identification Codes/ Passwords (Sec. 11.300)

The introductory paragraph of proposed Sec. 11.300 states that electronic signatures based upon use of identification codes in combination with passwords must employ controls to ensure their security and integrity.

To clarify the intent of this provision, the agency has added the words ``[p]ersons who use'' to the first sentence of Sec. 11.300. This change is consistent with Secs. 11.10 and 11.30. The introductory paragraph now reads, ``Persons who use electronic signatures based upon use of identification codes in combination with passwords shall employ controls to ensure their security and integrity. Such controls shall include: * * *.''

129. One comment suggested deletion of the phrase ``in combination with passwords'' from the first sentence of this section.

The agency disagrees with the suggested revision because the change is inconsistent with FDA's intent to address controls for electronic signatures based on combinations of identification codes and passwords, and would, in effect, permit a single component nonbiometric-based electronic signature.

130. Proposed Sec. 11.300(a) states that controls for identification codes/passwords must include maintaining the uniqueness of each issuance of identification code and password.

One comment alleged that most passwords are commonly used words, such as a child's name, a State, city, street, month, holiday, or date, that are significant to the person who creates the password. Another stated that the rule should explain uniqueness and distinguish between issuance and use because identification code/password combinations generally do not change for each use.

FDA does not intend to require that individuals use a completely different identification code/password combination each time they execute an electronic signature. For reasons explained in the response to comment 16, what is required to be unique is each combined password and identification code and FDA has revised the wording of

- 156 -

Sec. 11.300(a) to clarify this provision. The agency is aware, however, of identification devices that generate new passwords on a continuous basis in synchronization with a ``host'' computer. This results in unique passwords for each system access. Thus, it is possible in theory to generate a unique nonbiometric electronic signature for each signing.

The agency cautions against using passwords that are common words easily associated with their originators because such a practice would make it relatively easy for someone to impersonate someone else by guessing the password and combining it with an unsecured (or even commonly known) identification code.

131. Proposed Sec. 11.300(b) states that controls for identification codes/passwords must ensure that code/password issuances are periodically checked, recalled, or revised.

Several comments objected to this proposed requirement because: (1) It is unnecessary, (2) it excessively prescribes ``how to,'' (3) it duplicates the requirements in Sec. 11.300(c), and (4) it is administratively impractical for larger organizations. However, the comments said individuals should be encouraged to change their passwords periodically. Several comments suggested that proposed Sec. 11.300(b) include a clarifying example such as ``to cover events such as password aging.'' One comment said that the section should indicate who is to perform the periodic checking, recalling, or revising.

The agency disagrees with the objections to this provision. FDA does not view the provision as a ``how to'' because organizations have full flexibility in determining the frequency and methods of checking, recalling, or revising their code/password issuances. The agency does not believe that this paragraph duplicates the regulation in Sec. 11.300(c) because paragraph (c) specifically addresses followup to losses of electronic signature issuances, whereas Sec. 11.300(b) addresses periodic issuance changes to ensure against their having been unknowingly compromised. This provision would be met by ensuring that people change their passwords periodically.

FDA disagrees that this system control is unnecessary or impractical in large organizations because the presence of more people may increase the opportunities for compromising identification codes/passwords. The agency is confident that larger organizations will be fully capable of handling periodic issuance checks, revisions, or recalls.

FDA agrees with the comments that suggested a clarifying example and has revised Sec. 11.300(b) to include password aging as such an example. The agency cautions, however, that the example should not be taken to mean that password expiration would be the only rationale for revising, recalling, and checking issuances. If, for example, identification codes and passwords have been copied or compromised, they should be changed.

FDA does not believe it necessary at this time to specify who in an organization is to carry out this system control, although the agency expects
[[Page 13460]]
that units that issue electronic signatures would likely have this duty.

132. Proposed Sec. 11.300(c) states that controls for identification codes/passwords must include the following of loss management procedures to electronically deauthorize lost tokens, cards, etc., and to issue temporary or permanent replacements using suitable, rigorous controls for substitutes.

One comment suggested that this section be deleted because it excessively prescribes ``how to.'' Another comment argued that the proposal was not detailed enough and should distinguish among

- 157 -

fundamental types of cards (e.g., magstripe, integrated circuit, and optical) and include separate sections that address their respective use. Two comments questioned why the proposal called for ``rigorous controls'' in this section as opposed to other sections. One of the comments recommended that this section should also apply to cards or devices that are stolen as well as lost.

The agency believes that the requirement that organizations institute loss management procedures is neither too detailed nor too general. Organizations retain full flexibility in establishing the details of such procedures. The agency does not believe it necessary at this time to offer specific provisions relating to different types of cards or tokens. Organizations that use such devices retain full flexibility to establish appropriate controls for their operations. To clarify the agency's broad intent to cover all types of devices that contain or generate identification code or password information, FDA has revised Sec. 11.300(c) to replace ``etc.'' with ``and other devices that bear or generate identification code or password information.'' The agency agrees that Sec. 11.300(c) should cover loss management procedures regardless of how devices become potentially compromised, and has revised this section by adding, after the word ``lost,'' the phrase ``stolen, missing, or otherwise potentially compromised.'' FDA uses the term ``rigorous'' because device disappearance may be the result of inadequate controls over the issuance and management of the original cards or devices, thus necessitating more stringent measures to prevent problem recurrence. For example, personnel training on device safekeeping may need to be strengthened.

133. Proposed Sec. 11.300(d) states that controls for identification codes/passwords must include the use of transaction safeguards to prevent unauthorized use of passwords and/or identification codes, and, detecting and reporting to the system security unit and organizational management in an emergent manner any attempts at their unauthorized use.

Several comments suggested that the term ``emergent'' in proposed Sec. 11.300(d) be replaced with ``timely'' to describe reports regarding attempted unauthorized use of identification codes/passwords because: (1) A timely report would be sufficient, (2) technology to report emergently is not available, and (3) timely is a more recognizable and common term.

FDA agrees in part. The agency considers attempts at unauthorized use of identification codes and passwords to be extremely serious because such attempts signal potential electronic signature and electronic record falsification, data corruption, or worse-- consequences that could also ultimately be very costly to organizations. In FDA's view, the significance of such attempts requires the immediate and urgent attention of appropriate security personnel in the same manner that individuals would respond to a fire alarm. To clarify its intent with a more widely recognized term, the agency is replacing ``emergent'' with ``immediate and urgent'' in the final rule. The agency believes that the same technology that accepts or rejects an identification code and password can be used to relay to security personnel an appropriate message regarding attempted misuse.

134. One comment suggested that the word ``any'' be deleted from the phrase ``any attempts'' in proposed Sec. 11.300(d) because it is excessive. Another comment, noting that the question of attempts to enter a system or access a file by unauthorized personnel is very serious, urged the agency to substitute ``all'' for ``any.'' This comment added that there are devices on the market that can be used by unauthorized individuals to locate personal identification codes and passwords.

The agency believes the word ``any'' is sufficiently broad to cover all attempts at misuse of identification codes and passwords, and rejects the suggestion to delete the word. If the word ``any'' were deleted, laxity could result from any inference that persons are less likely to be caught in an essentially permissive, nonvigilant system. FDA is aware of the ``sniffing'' devices referred to by one comment and cautions persons to establish suitable countermeasures against them.

135. One comment suggested that proposed Sec. 11.300(d) be deleted because it is impractical, especially when simple typing errors are made. Another suggested that this section pertain to access to electronic records, not just the system, on the basis that simple miskeys may be typed when accessing a system.

As discussed in comments 133 and 134 of this document, the agency believes this provision is necessary and reasonable. The agency's security concerns extend to system as well as record access. Once having gained unauthorized system access, an individual could conceivably alter passwords to mask further intrusion and misdeeds. If this section were removed, falsifications would be more probable to the extent that some establishments would not alert security personnel. However, the agency advises that a simple typing error may not indicate an unauthorized use attempt, although a pattern of such errors, especially in short succession, or such an apparent error executed when the individual who ``owns'' that identification code or password is deceased, absent, or otherwise known to be unavailable, could signal a security problem that should not be ignored. FDA notes that this section offers organizations maximum latitude in deciding what they perceive to be attempts at unauthorized use.

136. One comment suggested substituting the phrase ``electronic signature'' for ``passwords and/or identification codes.''

The agency disagrees with this comment because the net effect of the revision might be to ignore attempted misuse of important elements of an electronic signature such as a ``password'' attack on a system.

137. Several comments argued that: (1) It is not necessary to report misuse attempts simultaneously to management when reporting to the appropriate security unit, (2) security units would respond to management in accordance with their established procedures and lines of authority, and (3) management would not always be involved.

The agency agrees that not every misuse attempt would have to be reported simultaneously to an organization's management if the security unit that was alerted responded appropriately. FDA notes, however, that some apparent security breaches could be serious enough to warrant management's immediate and urgent attention. The agency has revised proposed Sec. 11.300(d) to give organizations maximum flexibility in establishing criteria for management notification. Accordingly, Sec. 11.300(d) now states that controls for identification codes/passwords must include:

Use of transaction safeguards to prevent unauthorized use of passwords and/or identification codes, and to detect and report [[Page 13461]] in an immediate and urgent manner any attempts at their unauthorized use to the system security unit, and, as appropriate, to organizational management.

138. Proposed Sec. 11.300(e) states that controls for identification codes/passwords must include initial and periodic testing of devices, such as tokens or cards, bearing identifying information, for proper function.

Many comments objected to this proposed device testing requirement as unnecessary because it is part of system validation and because devices are access fail-safe in that nonworking devices would deny rather than permit system access. The comments suggested revising this section to require that failed devices deny user access. One comment stated that Sec. 11.300(e) is unclear on the meaning of ``identifying information'' and that the phrase ``tokens or cards'' is redundant

- 159 -

because cards are a form of tokens.

FDA wishes to clarify the reason for this proposed requirement, and to emphasize that proper device functioning includes, in addition to system access, the correctness of the identifying information and security performance attributes. Testing for system access alone could fail to discern significant unauthorized device alterations. If, for example, a device has been modified to change the identifying information, system access may still be allowed, which would enable someone to assume the identity of another person. In addition, devices may have been changed to grant individuals additional system privileges and action authorizations beyond those granted by the organization. Of lesser significance would be simple wear and tear on such devices, which result in reduced performance. For instance, a bar code may not be read with the same consistent accuracy as intended if the code becomes marred, stained, or otherwise disfigured. Access may be granted, but only after many more scannings than desired. The agency expects that device testing would detect such defects.

Because validation of electronic signature systems would not cover unauthorized device modifications, or subsequent wear and tear, validation would not obviate the need for periodic testing.

The agency notes that Sec. 11.300(e) does not limit the types of devices organizations may use. In addition, not all tokens may be cards, and identifying information is intended to include identification codes and passwords. Therefore, FDA has revised proposed Sec. 11.300(e) to clarify the agency's intent and to be consistent with Sec. 11.300(c). Revised Sec. 11.300(e) requires initial and periodic testing of devices, such as tokens or cards, that bear or generate identification code or password information to ensure that they function properly and have not been altered in an unauthorized manner.

XIV. Paperwork Reduction Act of 1995

This final rule contains information collection provisions that are subject to review by the Office of Management and Budget (OMB) under the Paperwork Reduction Act of 1995 (44 U.S.C. 3501-3520). Therefore, in accordance with 5 CFR 1320, the title, description, and description of respondents of the collection of information requirements are shown below with an estimate of the annual reporting and recordkeeping burdens. Included in the estimate is the time for reviewing instructions, searching existing data sources, gathering and maintaining the data needed, and completing and reviewing the collection of information.

Most of the burden created by the information collection provision of this final rule will be a one-time burden associated with the creation of standard operating procedures, validation, and certification. The agency anticipates the use of electronic media will substantially reduce the paperwork burden associated with maintaining FDA-required records.

Title: Electronic records; Electronic signatures.

Description: FDA is issuing regulations that provide criteria for acceptance of electronic records, electronic signatures, and handwritten signatures executed to electronic records as equivalent to paper records. Rules apply to any FDA records requirements unless specific restrictions are issued in the future. Records required to be submitted to FDA may be submitted electronically, provided the agency has stated its ability to accept the records electronically in an agency established public docket.

Description of Respondents: Businesses and other for-profit organizations, state or local governments, Federal agencies, and nonprofit institutions.

Although the August 31, 1994, proposed rule (59 FR 45160) provided a 90-day comment period under the Paperwork Reduction Act of 1980, FDA is providing an additional opportunity for public comment under the

Paperwork Reduction Act of 1995, which was enacted after the expiration of the comment period and applies to this final rule. Therefore, FDA now invites comments on: (1) Whether the proposed collection of information is necessary for the proper performance of FDA's functions, including whether the information will have practical utility; (2) the accuracy of FDA's estimate of the burden of the proposed collection of information, including the validity of the methodology and assumptions used; (3) ways to enhance the quality, utility, and clarity of the information to be collected; and (4) ways to minimize the burden of the collection of information on respondents, including through the use of automated collection techniques, when appropriate, and other forms of information technology. Individuals and organizations may submit comments on the information collection provisions of this final rule by May 19, 1997. Comments should be directed to the Dockets Management Branch (address above).

At the close of the 60-day comment period, FDA will review the comments received, revise the information collection provisions as necessary, and submit these provisions to OMB for review and approval. FDA will publish a notice in the Federal Register when the information collection provisions are submitted to OMB, and an opportunity for public comment to OMB will be provided at that time. Prior to the effective date of this final rule, FDA will publish a notice in the Federal Register of OMB's decision to approve, modify, or disapprove the information collection provisions. An agency may not conduct or sponsor, and a person is not required to respond to, a collection of information unless it displays a currently valid OMB control number.

Table 1.--Estimated Annual Recordkeeping Burden

| 21 CFR Section | Annual No. of Recordkeepers | Hours per Recordkeeper | Total Hours |
|---|---|---|---|
| 11.10 | 50 | 40 | 2,000 |
| 11.30 | 50 | 40 | 2,000 |
| 11.50 | 50 | 40 | 2,000 |
| 11.300 | 50 | 40 | 2,000 |
| Total annual burden hours | | | 8,000 |

[[Page 13462]]

Table 2.--Estimated Annual Reporting Burden

| 21 CFR Section | Annual No. of Respondents | Hours per Response | Total Burden Hours |
|---|---|---|---|
| 11.100 | 1,000 | 1 | 1,000 |
| Total annual burden hours | | | 1,000 |

XV. Environmental Impact

The agency has determined under 21 CFR 25.24(a)(8) that this action is of a type that does not individually or cumulatively have a significant effect on the human environment. Therefore, neither an environmental assessment nor an environmental impact statement is required.

XVI. Analysis of Impacts

FDA has examined the impacts of the final rule under Executive Order 12866, under the Regulatory Flexibility Act (5 U.S.C. 601-612), and under the Unfunded Mandates Reform Act (Pub. L. 104-4). Executive Order 12866 directs agencies to assess all costs and benefits of available regulatory alternatives and, when regulation is necessary, to select regulatory approaches that maximize net benefits (including potential economic, environmental, public health and safety, and other advantages; and distributive impacts and equity). Unless an agency certifies that a rule will not have a significant economic impact on a substantial number of small entities, the Regulatory Flexibility Act requires an analysis of regulatory options that would minimize any significant impact of a rule on small entities. The Unfunded Mandates Reform Act requires that agencies prepare an assessment of anticipated costs and benefits before proposing any rule that may result in an annual expenditure by State, local and tribal governments, in the aggregate, or by the private sector, of $100 million (adjusted annually for inflation).

The agency believes that this final rule is consistent with the regulatory philosophy and principles identified in the Executive Order. This rule permits persons to maintain any FDA required record or report in electronic format. It also permits FDA to accept electronic records, electronic signatures, and handwritten signatures executed to electronic records as equivalent to paper records and handwritten signatures executed on paper. The rule applies to any paper records required by statute or agency regulations. The rule was substantially influenced by comments to the ANPRM and the proposed rule. The provisions of this rule permit the use of electronic technology under conditions that the agency believes are necessary to ensure the integrity of electronic systems, records, and signatures, and the ability of the agency to protect and promote the public health.

This rule is a significant regulatory action as defined by the Executive Order and is subject to review under the Executive Order. This rule does not impose any mandates on State, local, or tribal governments, nor is it a significant regulatory action under the Unfunded Mandates Reform Act.

The activities regulated by this rule are voluntary; no entity is required by this rule to maintain or submit records electronically if it does not wish to do so. Presumably, no firm (or other regulated entity) will implement electronic recordkeeping unless the benefits to that firm are expected to exceed any costs (including capital and maintenance costs). Thus, the industry will incur no net costs as a result of this rule.

Based on the fact that the activities regulated by this rule are entirely voluntary and will not have any net adverse effects on small entities, the Commissioner of Food and Drugs certifies that this rule will not have a significant economic impact on a substantial number of small entities. Therefore, under the Regulatory Flexibility Act, no further regulatory flexibility analysis is required.

Although no further analysis is required, in developing this rule, FDA has considered the impact of the rule on small entities. The agency has also considered various regulatory options to maximize the net benefits of the rule to small entities without compromising the integrity of electronic systems, records, and signatures, or the agency's ability to protect and promote the public health. The following analysis briefly examines the potential impact of this rule on small businesses and other small entities, and describes the measures that FDA incorporated in this final rule to reduce the costs of applying electronic record/signature systems consistent with the objectives of the rule. This analysis includes each of the elements required for a final regulatory flexibility analysis under 5 U.S.C. 604(a).

A. Objectives

The purpose of this rule is to permit the use of a technology that was not contemplated when most existing FDA regulations were written, without undermining in any way the integrity of records and reports or the ability of FDA to carry out its statutory health protection mandate. The rule will permit regulated industry and FDA to operate with greater flexibility, in ways that will improve both the efficiency and the speed of industry's operations and the regulatory process. At the same time, it ensures that individuals will assign the same level of importance to affixing an electronic signature, and the records to which that signature attests, as they currently do to a handwritten signature.

B. Small Entities Affected

This rule potentially affects all large and small entities that are required by any statute administered by FDA, or any FDA regulation, to keep records or make reports or other submissions to FDA, including small businesses, nonprofit organizations, and small government entities. Because the rule affects such a broad range of industries, no data currently exist to estimate precisely the total number of small entities that will potentially benefit from the rule, but the number is substantial. For example, within the medical devices industry alone, the Small Business

[[Page 13463]]

Administration (SBA) estimates that over 3,221 firms are small businesses (i.e., have fewer than 500 employees). SBA also estimates that 504 pharmaceutical firms are small businesses with fewer than 500 employees. Of the approximately 2,204 registered blood and plasma establishments that are neither government-owned nor part of the American Red Cross, most are nonprofit establishments that are not nationally dominant and thus may be small entities as defined by the Regulatory Flexibility Act.

Not all submissions will immediately be acceptable electronically, even if the submission and the electronic record conform to the criteria set forth in this rule. A particular required submission will be acceptable in electronic form only after it has been identified to this effect in public docket 92S-0251. (The agency unit that can receive that electronic submission will also be identified in the docket.) Thus, although all small entities subject to FDA regulations are potentially affected by this rule, the rule will actually only benefit those that: (1) Are required to submit records or other documents that have been identified in the public docket as acceptable if submitted electronically, and (2) choose this method of submission, instead of traditional paper record submissions. The potential range of submissions includes such records as new drug applications, medical device premarket notifications, food additive petitions, and medicated feed applications. These, and all other required submissions, will be considered by FDA as candidates for optional electronic format. Although the benefits of making electronic submissions to FDA will be phased in over time, as the agency accepts more submissions in electronic form, firms can, upon the rule's effective date, immediately benefit from using electronic records/signatures for records they are required to keep, but not submit to FDA. Such records include, but are not limited to: Pharmaceutical and medical device batch production records, complaint records, and food processing records.

Some small entities will be affected by this rule even if they are not among the industries regulated by FDA. Because it will increase the market demand for certain types of software (e.g., document management, signature, and encryption software) and services (e.g., digital notaries and digital signature certification authorities), this rule will benefit some small firms engaged in developing and providing those products and services.

C. Description of the Impact

For any paper record that an entity is required to keep under existing statutes or FDA regulations, FDA will now accept an electronic record instead of a paper one, as long as the electronic record conforms to the requirements of this rule. FDA will also consider an electronic signature to be equivalent to a handwritten signature if it meets the requirements of this rule. Thus, entities regulated by FDA may, if they choose, submit required records and authorizations to the agency electronically once those records have been listed in the docket as acceptable in electronic form. This action is voluntary; paper records and handwritten signatures are still fully acceptable. No entity will be required to change the way it is currently allowed to submit paper records to the agency.

1. Benefits and costs

For any firm choosing to convert to electronic recordkeeping, the direct benefits are expected to include:

(1) Improved ability for the firm to analyze trends, problems, etc., enhancing internal evaluation and quality control;

(2) Reduced data entry errors, due to automated checks;

(3) Reduced costs of storage space;

(4) Reduced shipping costs for data transmission to FDA; and

(5) More efficient FDA reviews and approvals of FDA-regulated products.

No small entity will be required to convert to electronic submissions. Furthermore, it is expected that no individual firm, or other entity, will choose the electronic option unless that firm finds that the benefits to the firm from conversion will exceed any conversion costs.

There may be some small entities that currently submit records on paper, but archive records electronically. These entities will need to ensure that their existing electronic systems conform to the requirements for electronic recordkeeping described in this rule. Once they have done so, however, they may also take advantage of all the other benefits of electronic recordkeeping. Therefore, no individual small entity is expected to experience direct costs that exceed benefits as a result of this rule.

Furthermore, because almost all of the rule's provisions reflect contemporary security measures and controls that respondents to the ANPRM identified, most firms should have to make few, if any, modifications to their systems.

For entities that do choose electronic recordkeeping, the magnitude of the costs associated with doing so will depend on several factors, such as the level of appropriate computer hardware and software already in place in a given firm, the types of conforming technologies selected, and the size and dispersion of the firm. For example, biometric signature technologies may be more expensive than nonbiometric technologies; firms that choose the former technology may encounter relatively higher costs. Large, geographically dispersed firms may need some institutional security procedures that smaller firms, with fewer persons in more geographically concentrated areas, may not need. Firms that require wholesale technology replacements in order to adopt electronic record/signature technology may face much higher costs than those that require only minor modifications (e.g., because they already have similar technology for internal security and quality control purposes). Among the firms that must undertake major changes to implement electronic recordkeeping, costs will be lower for those able to undertake these changes simultaneously with other planned computer and security upgrades. New firms entering the market may have a slight advantage in implementing technologies that conform with this rule, because the technologies and associated procedures can be put in place as part of the general startup.

2. Compliance requirements

If a small entity chooses to keep electronic records and/or make electronic submissions, it must do so in ways that conform to the requirements for electronic records and electronic signatures set forth in this rule. These requirements, described previously in section II. of this document, involve measures designed to ensure the integrity of system operations, of information stored in the system, and of the authorized signatures affixed to electronic records. The requirements apply to all small (and large) entities in all industry sectors regulated by FDA.

The agency believes that because the rule is flexible and reflects contemporary standards, firms should have no difficulty in putting in place the needed systems and controls. However, to assist firms in meeting the provisions of this rule, FDA may hold public meetings and publish more detailed guidance. Firms may contact FDA's Industry and Small Business Liaison Staff, HF-50, at 5600 Fishers Lane, Rockville, MD 20857 (301-827-3430) for more information.

[[Page 13464]]

3. Professional skills required

If a firm elects electronic recordkeeping and submissions, it must take steps to ensure that all persons involved in developing, maintaining, and using electronic records and electronic signature systems have the education, training, and experience to perform the tasks involved. The level of training and experience that will be required depends on the tasks that the person performs. For example, an individual whose sole involvement with electronic records is infrequent might only need sufficient training to understand and use the required procedures. On the other hand, an individual involved in developing an electronic record system for a firm wishing to convert from a paper recordkeeping system would probably need more education or training in computer systems and software design and implementation. In addition, FDA expects that such a person would also have specific on-the-job training and experience related to the particular type of records kept by that firm.

The relevant education, training, and experience of each individual involved in developing, maintaining, or using electronic records/ submissions must be documented. However, no specific examinations or credentials for these individuals are required by the rule.

D. Minimizing the Burden on Small Entities

This rule includes several conditions that an electronic record or signature must meet in order to be acceptable as an alternative to a paper record or handwritten signature. These conditions are necessary to permit the agency to protect and promote the public health. For example, FDA must retain the ability to audit records to detect unauthorized modifications, simple errors, and to deter falsification. Whereas there are many scientific techniques to show changes in paper records (e.g., analysis of the paper, signs of erasures, and handwriting analysis), these methods do not apply to electronic records. For electronic records and submissions to have the same integrity as paper records, they must be developed, maintained, and used under circumstances that make it difficult for them to be inappropriately modified. Without these assurances, FDA's objective of enabling electronic records and signatures to have standing equal to paper records and handwritten signatures, and to satisfy the requirements of existing statutes and regulations, cannot be met. Within these constraints, FDA has attempted to select alternatives that provide as much flexibility as practicable without endangering the integrity of the electronic records. The agency decided not to make the required extent and stringency of controls dependent on the type of record or transactions, so that firms can decide for themselves what level of controls are worthwhile in each case. For example, FDA chose to give firms maximum flexibility in determining: (1) The circumstances under which management would have to be notified of security problems, (2) the means by which firms achieve the required link between an electronic signature and an electronic record, (3) the circumstances under which extra security and authentication measures are warranted in open systems, (4) when to use operational system checks to ensure proper event sequencing, and (5) when to use terminal checks to ensure that data and instructions originate from a valid source.

Numerous other specific considerations were addressed in the public comments to the proposed rule. A summary of the issues raised by those comments, the agency's assessment of these issues, and any changes made in the proposed rule as a result of these comments is presented earlier in this preamble.

FDA rejected alternatives for limiting potentially acceptable electronic submissions to a particular category, and for issuing different electronic submissions standards for small and large entities. The former alternative would unnecessarily limit the potential benefits of this rule; whereas the latter alternative would threaten the integrity of electronic records and submissions from small entities.

As discussed previously in this preamble, FDA rejected comments that suggested a total of 17 additional more stringent controls that might be more expensive to implement. These include: (1) Examination and certification of individuals who perform certain important tasks, (2) exclusive use of cryptographic methods to link electronic signatures to electronic records, (3) controls for each possible combination of a two factored authentication method, (4) controls for each different type of identification card, and (5) recording in audit trails the reason why records were changed.

List of Subjects in 21 CFR Part 11

Administrative practice and procedure, Electronic records, Electronic signatures, Reporting and recordkeeping requirements.

Therefore, under the Federal Food, Drug, and Cosmetic Act, the Public Health Service Act, and under authority delegated to the Commissioner of Food and Drugs, Title 21, Chapter I of the Code of Federal Regulations is amended by adding part 11 to read as follows:

PART 11--ELECTRONIC RECORDS; ELECTRONIC SIGNATURES

Subpart A--General Provisions

Sec.

11.1 Scope.

11.2 Implementation.

11.3 Definitions.

Subpart B--Electronic Records

11.10 Controls for closed systems.

11.30 Controls for open systems.

11.50 Signature manifestations.

11.70 Signature/record linking.

Subpart C--Electronic Signatures

11.100 General requirements.

11.200 Electronic signature components and controls.

11.300 Controls for identification codes/passwords.

Authority: Secs. 201-903 of the Federal Food, Drug, and Cosmetic Act (21 U.S.C. 321-393); sec. 351 of the Public Health Service Act (42 U.S.C. 262).

Subpart A--General Provisions

Sec. 11.1 Scope.

(a) The regulations in this part set forth the criteria under which the agency considers electronic records, electronic signatures, and handwritten signatures executed to electronic records to be trustworthy, reliable, and generally equivalent to paper records and handwritten signatures executed on paper.

(b) This part applies to records in electronic form that are created, modified, maintained, archived, retrieved, or transmitted, under any records requirements set forth in agency regulations. This part also applies to electronic records submitted to the agency under requirements of the Federal Food, Drug, and Cosmetic Act and the Public Health Service Act, even if such records are not specifically identified in agency regulations. However, this part does not apply to paper records that are, or have been, transmitted by electronic means.

(c) Where electronic signatures and their associated electronic records meet the requirements of this part, the agency will consider the electronic signatures to be equivalent to full handwritten signatures, initials, and other general signings as required by agency regulations, unless specifically excepted by regulation(s) effective on or after

[[Page 13465]]

August 20, 1997.

(d) Electronic records that meet the requirements of this part may be used in lieu of paper records, in accordance with Sec. 11.2, unless paper records are specifically required.

(e) Computer systems (including hardware and software), controls, and attendant documentation maintained under this part shall be readily available for, and subject to, FDA inspection.

Sec. 11.2 Implementation.

(a) For records required to be maintained but not submitted to the agency, persons may use electronic records in lieu of paper records or electronic signatures in lieu of traditional signatures, in whole or in part, provided that the requirements of this part are met.

(b) For records submitted to the agency, persons may use electronic records in lieu of paper records or electronic signatures in lieu of traditional signatures, in whole or in part, provided that:

(1) The requirements of this part are met; and

(2) The document or parts of a document to be submitted have been identified in public docket No. 92S-0251 as being the type of submission the agency accepts in electronic form. This docket will identify specifically what types of documents or parts of documents are acceptable for submission in electronic form without paper records and the agency receiving unit(s) (e.g., specific center, office, division, branch) to which such submissions may be made. Documents to agency receiving unit(s) not specified in the public docket will not be considered as official if they are submitted in electronic form; paper forms of such documents will be considered as official and must accompany any electronic records. Persons are expected to consult with the intended agency receiving unit for details on how (e.g., method of transmission, media, file formats, and technical protocols) and whether to proceed with the electronic submission.

Sec. 11.3 Definitions.

(a) The definitions and interpretations of terms contained in section 201 of the act apply to those terms when used in this part.

(b) The following definitions of terms also apply to this part:

(1) Act means the Federal Food, Drug, and Cosmetic Act (secs. 201-903 (21 U.S.C. 321-393)).

(2) Agency means the Food and Drug Administration.

(3) Biometrics means a method of verifying an individual's identity based on measurement of the individual's physical feature(s) or repeatable action(s) where those features and/or actions are both unique to that individual and measurable.

(4) Closed system means an environment in which system access is controlled by persons who are responsible for the content of electronic records that are on the system.

(5) Digital signature means an electronic signature based upon cryptographic methods of originator authentication, computed by using a set of rules and a set of parameters such that the identity of the signer and the integrity of the data can be verified.

(6) Electronic record means any combination of text, graphics, data, audio, pictorial, or other information representation in digital form that is created, modified, maintained, archived, retrieved, or distributed by a computer system.

(7) Electronic signature means a computer data compilation of any symbol or series of symbols executed, adopted, or authorized by an

- 167 -

individual to be the legally binding equivalent of the individual's handwritten signature.

(8) Handwritten signature means the scripted name or legal mark of an individual handwritten by that individual and executed or adopted with the present intention to authenticate a writing in a permanent form. The act of signing with a writing or marking instrument such as a pen or stylus is preserved. The scripted name or legal mark, while conventionally applied to paper, may also be applied to other devices that capture the name or mark.

(9) Open system means an environment in which system access is not controlled by persons who are responsible for the content of electronic records that are on the system.

Subpart B--Electronic Records

Sec. 11.10 Controls for closed systems.

Persons who use closed systems to create, modify, maintain, or transmit electronic records shall employ procedures and controls designed to ensure the authenticity, integrity, and, when appropriate, the confidentiality of electronic records, and to ensure that the signer cannot readily repudiate the signed record as not genuine. Such procedures and controls shall include the following:

(a) Validation of systems to ensure accuracy, reliability, consistent intended performance, and the ability to discern invalid or altered records.

(b) The ability to generate accurate and complete copies of records in both human readable and electronic form suitable for inspection, review, and copying by the agency. Persons should contact the agency if there are any questions regarding the ability of the agency to perform such review and copying of the electronic records.

(c) Protection of records to enable their accurate and ready retrieval throughout the records retention period.

(d) Limiting system access to authorized individuals.

(e) Use of secure, computer-generated, time-stamped audit trails to independently record the date and time of operator entries and actions that create, modify, or delete electronic records. Record changes shall not obscure previously recorded information. Such audit trail documentation shall be retained for a period at least as long as that required for the subject electronic records and shall be available for agency review and copying.

(f) Use of operational system checks to enforce permitted sequencing of steps and events, as appropriate.

(g) Use of authority checks to ensure that only authorized individuals can use the system, electronically sign a record, access the operation or computer system input or output device, alter a record, or perform the operation at hand.

(h) Use of device (e.g., terminal) checks to determine, as appropriate, the validity of the source of data input or operational instruction.

(i) Determination that persons who develop, maintain, or use electronic record/electronic signature systems have the education, training, and experience to perform their assigned tasks.

(j) The establishment of, and adherence to, written policies that hold individuals accountable and responsible for actions initiated under their electronic signatures, in order to deter record and signature falsification.

(k) Use of appropriate controls over systems documentation including:

(1) Adequate controls over the distribution of, access to, and use of documentation for system operation and maintenance.

(2) Revision and change control procedures to maintain an audit trail that documents time-sequenced development and modification of systems documentation.

Sec. 11.30 Controls for open systems.

Persons who use open systems to create, modify, maintain, or transmit electronic records shall employ procedures and controls designed to

[[Page 13466]]

ensure the authenticity, integrity, and, as appropriate, the confidentiality of electronic records from the point of their creation to the point of their receipt. Such procedures and controls shall include those identified in Sec. 11.10, as appropriate, and additional measures such as document encryption and use of appropriate digital signature standards to ensure, as necessary under the circumstances, record authenticity, integrity, and confidentiality.

Sec. 11.50 Signature manifestations.

(a) Signed electronic records shall contain information associated with the signing that clearly indicates all of the following:

(1) The printed name of the signer;

(2) The date and time when the signature was executed; and

(3) The meaning (such as review, approval, responsibility, or authorship) associated with the signature.

(b) The items identified in paragraphs (a)(1), (a)(2), and (a)(3) of this section shall be subject to the same controls as for electronic records and shall be included as part of any human readable form of the electronic record (such as electronic display or printout).

Sec. 11.70 Signature/record linking.

Electronic signatures and handwritten signatures executed to electronic records shall be linked to their respective electronic records to ensure that the signatures cannot be excised, copied, or otherwise transferred to falsify an electronic record by ordinary means.

Subpart C--Electronic Signatures

Sec. 11.100 General requirements.

(a) Each electronic signature shall be unique to one individual and shall not be reused by, or reassigned to, anyone else.

(b) Before an organization establishes, assigns, certifies, or otherwise sanctions an individual's electronic signature, or any element of such electronic signature, the organization shall verify the identity of the individual.

(c) Persons using electronic signatures shall, prior to or at the time of such use, certify to the agency that the electronic signatures in their system, used on or after August 20, 1997, are intended to be the legally binding equivalent of traditional handwritten signatures.

(1) The certification shall be submitted in paper form and signed with a traditional handwritten signature, to the Office of Regional Operations (HFC-100), 5600 Fishers Lane, Rockville, MD 20857.

(2) Persons using electronic signatures shall, upon agency request, provide additional certification or testimony that a specific electronic signature is the legally binding equivalent of the signer's handwritten signature.

Sec. 11.200 Electronic signature components and controls.

(a) Electronic signatures that are not based upon biometrics shall:

(1) Employ at least two distinct identification components such as an identification code and password.

(i) When an individual executes a series of signings during a single, continuous period of controlled system access, the first signing shall be executed using all electronic signature components; subsequent signings shall be executed using at least one electronic signature component that is only executable by, and designed to be used only by, the individual.

(ii) When an individual executes one or more signings not performed during a single, continuous period of controlled system access, each signing shall be executed using all of the electronic signature components.

(2) Be used only by their genuine owners; and

(3) Be administered and executed to ensure that attempted use of an individual's electronic signature by anyone other than its genuine owner requires collaboration of two or more individuals.

(b) Electronic signatures based upon biometrics shall be designed to ensure that they cannot be used by anyone other than their genuine owners.

Sec. 11.300 Controls for identification codes/passwords.

Persons who use electronic signatures based upon use of identification codes in combination with passwords shall employ controls to ensure their security and integrity. Such controls shall include:

(a) Maintaining the uniqueness of each combined identification code and password, such that no two individuals have the same combination of identification code and password.

(b) Ensuring that identification code and password issuances are periodically checked, recalled, or revised (e.g., to cover such events as password aging).

(c) Following loss management procedures to electronically deauthorize lost, stolen, missing, or otherwise potentially compromised tokens, cards, and other devices that bear or generate identification code or password information, and to issue temporary or permanent replacements using suitable, rigorous controls.

(d) Use of transaction safeguards to prevent unauthorized use of passwords and/or identification codes, and to detect and report in an immediate and urgent manner any attempts at their unauthorized use to the system security unit, and, as appropriate, to organizational management.

(e) Initial and periodic testing of devices, such as tokens or cards, that bear or generate identification code or password information to ensure that they function properly and have not been altered in an unauthorized manner.

Dated: March 11, 1997.

William B. Schultz,

Deputy Commissioner for Policy.

[FR Doc. 97-6833 Filed 3-20-97; 8:45 am]

BILLING CODE 4160-01-F


Guidance for Industry 1999


Guidance for Industry


Providing Regulatory Submissions

in Electronic Format -

General Considerations


U.S. Department of Health and Human Services

Food and Drug Administration

Center for Drug Evaluation and Research (CDER)

Center for Biologic Evaluation and Research (CBER)

January 1999

IT 2

---

Guidance for Industry

Providing Regulatory Submissions in Electronic Format -

General Considerations

Additional copies are available from:

Office of Training and Communications

Division of Communications Management

Drug Information Branch, HFD-210

5600 Fishers Lane

Rockville, MD 20857

(Tel) 301-827-4573

(Internet) http://www.fda.gov/cder/guidance/index.htm

or

Office of Communication,

Training, and Manufacturers Assistance (HFM-40)

Center for Biologics Evaluation and Research (CBER)

1401 Rockville Pike, Rockville, MD 20852-1448

http://www.fda.gov/cber/guidelines.htm

(Fax) 888-CBERFAX or 301-827-3844

(Voice Information) 800-835-4709 or 301-827-1800

U.S. Department of Health and Human Services

Food and Drug Administration

Center for Drug Evaluation and Research (CDER)

Center for Biologics Evaluation and Research (CBER)

January 1999

IT 2

_____

TABLE OF CONTENTS

I. Document Information Fields

J. Open Dialog Box

K. Naming PDF Files

L. Security

M. Indexing PDF Documents

N. Plug Ins

O. Electronic Signatures

## IV. WHAT FILE FORMATS SHOULD I USE FOR ELECTRONIC DATASETS ?

A. SAS System XPORT Transport Format

(Version 5 SAS Transport Format)

B. Other Dataset Formats

## V. WHAT ARE THE PROCEDURES FOR SENDING ELECTRONIC SUBMISSIONS FOR ARCHIVE ?

A. CDER

B. CBER

## VI. WHAT TYPE OF MEDIA SHOULD I USE?

## VII. HOW SHOULD I PREPARE THE MEDIA FOR ELECTRONIC SUBMISSIONS FOR ARCHIVE ?

## VIII. HOW DO THE CENTERS PROCESS ELECTRONIC SUBMISSIONS FOR ARCHIVE?

A. CDER

B. CBER

IX. WHAT IF I HAVE A QUESTION ?


A. CDER

B. CBER

---


GUIDANCE FOR INDUSTRY


Providing Regulatory Submissions in Electronic Format -

General Considerations

---


This guidance has been prepared by the Center for Drug Evaluation

and Research (CDER) and the Center for Biologics Evaluation and

Research (CBER) at the Food and Drug Administration. This

guidance document represents the Agency's current thinking on

regulatory submissions in electronic format. It does not create

or confer any rights for or on any person and does not operate to

bind FDA or the public. An alternative approach may be used if

such approach satisfies the requirements of the applicable

statute, regulations, or both.


On June 1, 1998, the President instructed all Federal agencies

to ensure the use of plain language in all new documents. This

guidance reflects Agency efforts to comply with the President's

plain language initiative.

---


I. INTRODUCTION

This is one in a series of guidance documents intended to assist
you when making regulatory submissions in electronic format to the
Center for Drug Evaluation and Research (CDER) and the Center for
Biologics Evaluation and Research (CBER), Food and Drug
Administration (FDA). This guidance discusses general issues
common to all types of electronic regulatory submissions. In some
cases, the guidance for one center differs from that for the other
center because of differences in procedures and in the computer
infrastructures in the centers. We will work to minimize these
differences wherever possible.

Agency guidance documents on electronic regulatory submissions
will be updated regularly to reflect the evolving nature of the
technology involved and the experience of those using this
technology.

II. BACKGROUND

In the Federal Register of March 20, 1997 (62 FR 13430), the FDA
published the Electronic Records; Electronic Signatures regulations
(21 CFR **Part 11**). This regulation provided for the voluntary
submission of parts or all of regulatory records in electronic
format without an accompanying paper copy. Publication of this
regulation resulted in a series of related actions:

March 1997:

The Agency established public docket number 92S-0251 to provide
a permanent location for a list of the Agency units that are

prepared to receive electronic submissions and the specific types

of regulatory records that can be accepted in electronic format

(62 FR 13467, March 20, 1997). This docket can be accessed

on the Internet at

http://www.fda.gov/ohrms/dockets/dockets/92s0251/92s0251.htm.


September 1997:


CDER published a guidance for industry entitled Archiving

Submissions in Electronic Format - NDAs (62 FR 49695,

September 23, 1997) to assist applicants wanting to make electronic

submissions of case report forms (CRFs) and case report tabulations

(CRTs) as part of the NDA archival submission.


April 1998:


CDER issued a draft guidance for industry, Providing Regulatory

Submissions in Electronic Format - NDAs, which expanded on the

September 1997 guidance by providing information on submitting a

complete archival copy of the NDA in electronic format

(63 FR 17185; April 8, 1998).


June 1998:


CBER published the following draft guidances to assist applicants

in their efforts to submit electronic documents to the Center for

review and archive as part of their BLA or PLA/ELA submissions:


Electronic Submissions of a Biologics License Application (BLA),

Product License Application (PLA) /Establishment License Application

(ELA) to the Center for Biologics Evaluation and Research (63 FR 29741, 6/1/98).

Electronic Submissions of Case Report Forms (CRFs), Case Report Tabulations(CRTs) and Data to the Center for Biologics Evaluation and Research (63 FR 29739; 6/1/98).

Pilot Program for Electronic Investigational New Drug (eIND) Applications for Biological Products (63 FR 29740; 6/1/98).

Instructions for Submitting Electronic Lot Release Protocols to the Center for Biologics Evaluation and Research (63 FR 29742; 6/98).

January 1999:

CDER and CBER finalized this joint guidance on general considerations for electronic submissions. Subsequent guidances will focus on specific submission types.

The Agency envisions the series of guidance documents on electronic regulatory submissions to provide guidance on the following:

- General considerations for all electronic submissions (e.g., file formats)

- NDAs to CDER (including supplements and amendments)

- Marketing Applications to CBER (e.g., BLAs, PLAs, ELAs, NDAs)

- Abbreviated New Drug Applications (ANDAs)

- Postmarketing Safety Reports

- Investigational New Drug Applications (INDs)

- Annual Reports

- Drug Master Files (DMFs)

- Launch Material

- Advertising

- Other

As individual documents are completed, they will be issued first
in draft for comment, then finalized and added to the series.
The guidances will be updated regularly to reflect the continuously
evolving nature of the technology and experience of those using
this technology.

## III. WHAT FILE FORMATS SHOULD I USE FOR ELECTRONIC DOCUMENTS?

Regulations in 21 CFR **Part 11** require that the Agency be able to
generate from any document provided in electronic format an accurate
and complete paper copy that is both legible ("human readable")
and suitable for inspection, review, and copying. Therefore,
documents submitted in electronic format should:

- Enable the user to easily view a clear and legible copy of the information

- Enable the user to print each document page by page, as it would
have been provided in paper, maintaining fonts, special
orientations, table formats, and page numbers

- Include a well-structured table of contents and allow the user
to navigate easily through the submission

- Allow the user to copy text and images electronically into common
word processing documents

To achieve the above goals, you should submit all electronic
documents in Portable Document Format (PDF). CDER and CBER are
prepared to archive documents provided as PDF files. PDF is an open,
published format created by Adobe Systems Incorporated
(http://www.adobe.com). You do not need to use a product from Adobe
or from any specific company to produce your PDF documents. PDF
has been accepted as a standard for providing documents in
electronic format by the International Conference on Harmonisation
(ICH).

The following recommendations will help you create PDF files that
we can review and archive.

A. Version

We should be able to read all PDF files with version 3.0 of the
Acrobat Reader with the search plug in. We should not need any
additional software to read and navigate the PDF files.

## B. Fonts

PDF viewing software automatically substitutes a font to display text if the font used to create the text is unavailable on the reviewer's computer. Font substitution can affect a document's appearance and structure, and in some cases it can affect the information conveyed by a document. We cannot guarantee the availability of any one font. Therefore, you should embed all fonts you are using in the PDF files to ensure that those fonts will always be available to the reviewer. When embedding fonts, all characters for the font should be embedded, not just a subset of the fonts being used in the document.

One problem associated with embedding fonts is that embedding requires additional computer storage space. Three techniques to help limit the storage space taken by embedding fonts include:

- Limiting the number of fonts used in each document

- Using only True Type or Adobe Type 1 fonts

- Avoiding customized fonts

Resizing a document because the contents are too small to read is inefficient. We believe that Times New Roman, 12-point font, the font used for this document, is adequate in size for reading narrative text. Although sometimes tempting for use in tables and charts, fonts smaller than 12 points should be avoided whenever possible.

We recommend the use of a black font color. Blue font may be used for hypertext links (preferred for submissions to CBER). If a font color other than black is used, avoid light colors that do not print well on grayscale printers. You can test the color reproduction prior to submission by printing sample pages from the document using a grayscale printer.

## C. Page Orientation

Pages should be properly oriented. For example, you should set the page orientation of landscape pages to landscape prior to saving the PDF document in final form to ensure correct page presentation.

## D. Page Size and Margins

The print area for pages should fit on a sheet of paper that is 8.5 inches by 11 inches. You should allow a margin of at least 1 inch on all sides to avoid obscuring information if the pages are subsequently printed and bound.

## E. Source of Electronic Document

PDF documents produced by scanning paper documents are usually inferior to those produced from an electronic source document. Scanned documents are more difficult to read and do not allow us to search or copy and paste text for editing. They should be avoided if at all possible. If you use optical character recognition software, you should verify that all imaged text converted by the software is accurate.

F. Methods for Creating PDF Documents and Images

Choose a method for creating PDF documents that produces the best replication of a paper document. You can ensure that the paper and PDF version of the document are the same by printing the document from the PDF version.

Documents that are available only in paper should be scanned at resolutions that will ensure the pages are legible both on the computer screen and when printed. At the same time, you should also limit the file size. We recommend scanning at a resolution of 300 dots per inch (dpi) to balance legibility and file size. We discourage the use of grayscale or color because of file size. After scanning, avoid resampling to a lower resolution.

When creating PDF files containing images, you should not resample images. Resampling does not preserve all of the pixels in the original. For PDF images, you can use one of the following lossless compression techniques (with the exception that, when submitting to CBER, standard radiographic images, PET, and SPECT images should not be compressed).

- For lossless compression of color and grayscale images, use Zip/Flate (one technique with two names). This is specified in Internet RFC 1950 and RFC 1951 (http://info.internet.isi.edu/in-notes/rfc/files/rfc1950.txt).

- For lossless compression of black and white images, use the CCITT Group 4 Fax compression technique. It is specified as CCITT recommendations T.6 (1988) - Facsimile coding schemes and coding control functions for Group 4 facsimile apparatus.

Paper documents containing handwritten notes should be scanned at 300 dpi. Handwritten notes should be done in black ink for clarity.

For photographs, the image should be obtained with a resolution of 600 dpi. If black and white photos are submitted, consider 8-bit gray scale images. If color photos are submitted, consider 24-bit RGB images. A captured image should not be subjected to nonuniform scaling (i.e., sizing).

Gels and karyotypes should be scanned directly, rather than from photographs. Scanning should be at 600 dpi and 8-bit grayscale depth.

Plotter output graphics should be scanned or captured digitally at 300 dpi.

High-pressure liquid chromatography or similar images should be scanned at 300 dpi.

G. Hypertext Linking and Bookmarks

Hypertext links and bookmarks are techniques used to improve navigation through PDF documents. Hypertext links can be designated by rectangles using thin lines or by blue text (the latter is preferred by CBER). In CDER, you can use invisible rectangles for hypertext links in a table of contents to avoid obscuring text. Recommendations for hypertext linking and bookmarks are provided in the guidance for the specific submission type.

In general, for documents with a table of contents, provide bookmarks and hypertext links for each item listed in the table of contents including all tables, figures, publications, other references, and appendices. These bookmarks and hypertext links are essential for the efficient navigation through documents. In general, including a bookmark to the main table of contents for a submission or item is helpful. Make the bookmark hierarchy identical to the table of contents. Avoid using bookmark levels in addition to those present in the table of contents. Each additional level increases the need for space to read the bookmarks. We recommend using no more than 4 levels in the hierarchy.

Hypertext links throughout the body of the document to supporting annotations, related sections, references, appendices, tables, or figures that are not located on the same page are helpful and improve navigation efficiency. Use relative paths when creating hypertext linking to minimize the loss of hyperlink functionality when folders are moved between disk drives. Absolute links that reference specific drives and root directories will no longer work once the submission is loaded onto our network servers.

When creating bookmarks and hyperlinks, choose the magnification setting Inherit Zoom so that the destination page displays at the same magnification level that the reviewer is using for the rest of the document.

H. Page Numbering

If a submission includes more than one document, you need not provide pagination for the entire submission. Include page numbers only for individual documents.

It is easier to navigate though an electronic document if the page numbers for the document and the PDF file are the same. To accomplish this, the initial page of the paper document should be numbered page 1.

I. Document Information Fields

Document information fields are used to search for individual documents and to identify the document when found. Recommendations for the document information fields will be provided in the guidance for the specific submission type.

J. Open Dialog Box

The open dialog box sets the document view when the file is opened. The initial view of the PDF files should be set as Bookmarks and Page. If there are no bookmarks, set the initial view as Page only. Set the Magnification and Page Layout to default.

K. Naming PDF Files

We are recommending names for folders and selected files in individual guidances for specific submission types. For uniformity, we hope that you use our specific naming conventions when they are provided. Reviewers are trained to look for these folders and files, and using the recommended names should help avoid misunderstandings, improve communication, and speed the review of a submission.

When we do not specify a file name, you can use file names up to 32 characters in length with a 3-character extension. Avoid using punctuation, spaces, or other nonalphanumeric symbols in file names.

L. Security

You should not include any security settings or password protection for PDF files. Allow printing, changes to the document, selecting text and graphics, and adding or changing notes and form fields. Our internal security and archival processes will maintain the integrity of the submitted files. A read-only copy of the files, generated from the submitted files, will be provided to the reviewer.

M. Indexing PDF Documents

We use full text indexes to help find specific documents and/or search for text within documents. When a document or group of documents is indexed, all words and numbers in the file and all information stored in the Document Information fields are stored in special index files that are functionally accessible using the search tools available in Acrobat. Portions of a document that are imaged are not indexed. Even if the document only contains images, the text in the Document Information fields of the file will be indexed.

These full text indexes should not be confused with a table of contents. Adobe Acrobat Catalog is one example of a tool that can be used to index PDF documents. Indexes should not require extensions or additions to off-the-shelf Acrobat programs.

With many submissions, we ask that you associate the table of contents file for a section with the corresponding full text index file. By associate, we mean that when the table of contents file is opened, the index file is automatically added to the available index list and is ready to be used.

Further recommendations for full text indexes will be provided in guidance for the specific submission types.

N. Plug Ins

It is acceptable to use plug ins to assist in the creation of a submission. However, the review of the submission should not require the use of any plug ins, in addition to those provided with Acrobat Reader 3 because we are not prepared to archive additional plug-in functionality.

O. Electronic Signatures

We are developing procedures for archiving documents with electronic signatures. Until those procedures are in place, documents for which regulations require an original signature, such as certifications, must be accompanied by a paper copy that includes the handwritten signature and the submission identifier (e.g., NDA number).

IV. WHAT FILE FORMATS SHOULD I USE FOR ELECTRONIC DATASETS ?

Regulations in 21 CFR **Part 11** require all datasets provided in electronic format to provide an accurate and complete copy of the data suitable for inspection, review, and copying. Currently, we are able to accept and archive datasets in SAS System XPORT transport format (Version 5 SAS transport file). We plan on providing guidance for additional file format types for datasets. See Section B, below. See also recommendations provided in guidance for the specific submission types.

A. SAS System XPORT Transport Format (Version 5 SAS Transport Format)

SAS XPORT transport format, also called Version 5 SAS transport format, is an open format published by the SAS Institute. The description of this SAS transport file format is in the public domain. Data can be translated to and from this SAS transport format to other commonly used formats without the use of programs from SAS Institute or any specific vendor.

You should follow the recommendations in this section to create SAS transport files that we can review and archive.

1. Version

In SAS, SAS XPORT transport files are created by PROC XCOPY in Version 5 of SAS software and by the XPORT engine in Version 6 and higher of SAS Software. We are unable to archive SAS Transport files processed by the CPORT engine.

You can find the record layout for SAS XPORT transport files in SAS technical support TS-140. This document and additional information about the SAS Transport file layout can be found on the SAS world wide web page at http://www.sas.com/fda-esub.

2. Transformation of Datasets

We use a variety of software tools to analyze the datasets. Stat/Transfer from Circle Systems and DBMS/copy from Conceptual Software Inc., are two programs used to transfer data to various formats used for analysis. SAS Viewer version 7 is used to open SAS transport files directly.

3. Naming SAS Transport Files

All SAS transport files should use xpt as the file extension.

4. Compression Of SAS Transport Files

The SAS transport files should not be compressed.

5. Content Of Datasets And Organization

You should provide a single transport file for each dataset. Many of the software tools used by the reviewers require datasets to be loaded into random access memory (RAM) prior to opening the file. Therefore, dataset files should be organized so that their size is generally less than 25 MB per file. The datasets should be accompanied by data definition tables that include the variable name, a description of the variable, the type of variable (e.g., number, character, date), and codes used in the dataset. For derived variables, the method of deriving the variable should also be included in this table. Variable names are limited to 8 characters. You should include a descriptive name up to 32 characters in the label header. Further recommendations for content of SAS Transport files are provided in guidance for each specific submission type.

We recommend that you discuss the content of the datasets with the review division prior to submission.

B. Other Dataset Formats

Although we are not prepared to archive other dataset file formats at this time, additional file formats are being considered, such as structured ASCII for ANDA and postmarketing safety data. Structured ASCII is also being explored for use with the chemistry, biopharmaceutic, and clinical pharmacology data for NDAs. As these projects mature, we will provide additional guidance.

## V. WHAT ARE THE PROCEDURES FOR SENDING ELECTRONIC SUBMISSIONS FOR ARCHIVE ?

Submissions should be sent directly to the appropriate center involved. The procedure for handling paper submissions is unchanged from the past.

A. CDER

Send one copy of the electronic regulatory submission for archive

to the CDER Central Document Room (CDR) as follows:

Central Document Room

Center for Drug Evaluation and Research

Food and Drug Administration

12229 Wilkins Avenue

Rockville, MD 20852

CDER uses this copy to make other copies as needed (see section

VIII, below, on processing electronic submissions).

B. CBER

Send two copies of the electronic regulatory submission as described

in this guidance to CBER´s Document Control Center (DCC) as

follows:

Center for Biologics Evaluation and Research

Attn: (Insert "Responsible Office")

HFM-99, Room 200N

1401 Rockville Pike

Rockville, MD 20852-1448

It is essential to communicate with the appropriate CBER office

prior to submitting an electronic document, notifying us of your

intention to submit an electronic document at least six to eight

months in advance of the target date for the submission. At that

time, the sponsor should forward a completed copy of the appropriate

application specific questionnaire

(http://www.fda.gov/cber/guidelines.htm).

Subsequent to the receipt of the questionnaire, a teleconference

will be scheduled with the appropriate CBER staff. The objective

of the teleconference is to convey information relating to the

proposed electronic submission's management paradigm, content,

format, and structure. Moreover, we will discuss any issues

specific to your submission that may not have been fully addressed

in the general considerations guidance.


## VI. WHAT TYPE OF MEDIA SHOULD I USE?


CDER and CBER are prepared to accept electronic submissions provided

on the media listed in the table below. To optimize processing

efficiency, we recommend choosing media with a capacity most

appropriate to the size of the submission. Whenever possible,

applicants should choose media capable of holding the submission

on the fewest number of units.


Recommendations for Media


Size of Submission Media and format Units

| | |
| --- | --- |
| Less than 10MB 3.5 inch DOS Formatted Floppy Disks 1 to 10 |
| Less than 3.25GB CD-ROM ISO 9660 1 to 5 CDs |
| Greater than 3.25GB Digital Tape - Digital No limit |

Equipment Corp.

DLT 20/40 and 10/20 GB

format using OPENVMS

with VMS backup or NT

server 4.0 with NT

backup or backup exec.

---

## VII. HOW SHOULD I PREPARE THE MEDIA FOR ELECTRONIC SUBMISSIONS FOR ARCHIVE ?

Send all electronic media adequately secured in a standard binder
marked clearly on the outside ELECTRONIC REGULATORY SUBMISSION FOR
ARCHIVE. CDs should be packaged carefully to ensure that they
arrive in a usable condition. Particularly vulnerable are diskettes
and CD jewel cases shipped in envelopes without bubble-type
protective material or stiff backing. The use of a jiffy-type bag
by itself to ship media will not provide adequate protection for
shipping electronic media.

The first binder with electronic media should include only a paper
copy of the cover letter for the submission, a paper copy of the
appropriate FDA form for the submission (e.g., for an NDA/BLA
include FDA form 356h), and the electronic media for archiving.
Please attach labels to the media including the CD jewel cases.
Label the media with the following:

- Submission identifier (e.g., NDA, BLA number)

- Proprietary and generic name.

- Company name

- Submission serial number, if applicable.

- Submission date: in the format of DD-MMM-YYYY (for example, 01-Jan-1997).

- Disk/CD-ROM/tape number (the number should include the total number submitted such as Disk # of #)

When sending CD ROMS to CBER, number them from 0.001 through 0.XXX for the original submission, and 1.001 through 1.XXX for subsequent submissions with additional information.

# VIII. HOW DO THE CENTERS PROCESS ELECTRONIC SUBMISSIONS FOR ARCHIVE?

## A. CDER

When an electronic submission arrives in CDER, we copy the electronic files to tape to create an archival copy of the submission. We also copy the files to a network server to create a read-only copy for the reviewer. We use internal procedures to track submissions (do not send roadmap files described below with submissions to CDER).

## B. CBER

When an electronic submission arrives in CBER, one copy of the media is archived; the second copy of the submission's media is copied to a network server to create a read-only copy for the reviewer.

The structure and content of electronic submissions to CBER should be based upon the application (e.g., BLAs, PLA/ELAs). Subsequent to the delivery of the electronic application, any additional electronic and/or paper information will be added to the existing network copy of the submission and distributed to appropriate reviewers. The root directory of an electronic application should contain a roadmap.pdf file to orient the review team to the original application and to any and all subsequent information added to the application.

CBER suggests that a roadmap.pdf file be used to establish hypertext links to the application's main table of contents, and to the applications folders and files. This roadmap or home page should be updated and resubmitted as additional information to the application.

The roadmap file should not contribute in any way to the content of what is under review. It is a map, intended to facilitate navigation through the contents of an application. The application's roadmap.pdf file should be easily updated or modified, for example, using the Replace File command under the Document menu option in Adobe Exchange. This function will automatically replace the old hypertext links to previously submitted sections of the application, leaving only the task of creating the new links corresponding to newly submitted information.

In addition to providing a navigable guide to the application, the roadmap.pdf file should include the sponsor's submission date in the DD-MMM-YYYY format (e.g., 01-Jan-1999). The contents of the original application and any subsequent amendments to that application should be briefly described in a roadmap.pdf table. The location of these files and folders on the submitted media should be indicated in the roadmap.pdf. Where portions of an application have been submitted only as a paper documents, they should be included in the roadmap and table of contents and tagged as paper only.

A summation of the electronic document, using at least 40 key words from the main document should be included with all electronic applications delivered to CBER. This summation should be located in the root directory on the CDROM or DLT tape. The file containing the key words should be an ASCII text file entitled Summary.txt.

## IX. WHAT IF I HAVE A QUESTION ?

### A. CDER

You may direct questions regarding the preparation of submissions in electronic format in CDER to the Electronic Submissions Coordinator, email ESUB@CDER.fda.gov.

### B. CBER

You may direct questions regarding the preparation of submissions

in electronic format in CBER to the Electronic Submissions

Coordinator email ESUBPREP@CBER.fda.gov.


Compliance Policy Guide 160.850 on Part 11 Enforcement

COMPLIANCE POLICY GUIDE
Section 160.850
Title: Enforcement Policy: 21 CFR Part 11; Electronic Records; Electronic Signatures (CPG 7153.17)
Background:
This compliance guidance document is an update to the Compliance Policy Guides Manual (August 1996 edition). This is a new Compliance Policy Guide (CPG) and will be included in the next printing of the Compliance Policy Guides Manual. The CPG is intended for Food and Drug Administration (FDA) personnel and is available electronically to the public. This guidance document represents the agency's current thinking on what is required to be fully compliant with 21 CFR Part 11, "Electronic Records; Electronic Signatures" and provides that agency decisions on whether or not to pursue regulatory actions will be based on a case by case evaluation. The CPG does not create or confer any rights for or on any person and does not operate to bind FDA or the public. An alternative approach may be used if such approach satisfies the requirements of the applicable statute, regulation, or both.
In the Federal Register of March 20, 1997, at 62 FR 13429, FDA issued a notice of final rulemaking for 21 CFR, Part 11, Electronic Records; Electronic Signatures. The rule went into effect on August 20, 1997. Part 11 is intended to create criteria for electronic recordkeeping technologies while preserving the agency's ability to protect and promote the public health (e.g., by facilitating timely review and approval of safe and effective new medical products, conducting efficient audits of required records, and when necessary pursuing regulatory actions). Part 11 applies to all FDA program areas, but does not mandate electronic recordkeeping. Part 11 describes the technical and procedural requirements that must be met if a person chooses to maintain records electronically and use electronic signatures. Part 11 applies to those records required by an FDA predicate rule and to signatures required by an FDA predicate rule, as well as signatures that are not required, but appear in required records.
Part 11 was developed in concert with industry over a period of six years. Virtually all of the rule's requirements had been suggested by industry comments to a July 21, 1992 Advance Notice of Proposed Rulemaking (at 57 FR 32185). In response to comments to an August 31, 1994 Proposed Rule (at 59 FR 45160) the agency refined and reduced many of the proposed requirements in order to minimize the burden of compliance. The final rule's provisions are consistent with an emerging body of federal and state law as well as commercial standards and practices.
Certain older electronic systems may not have been in full compliance with Part 11 by August 20, 1997, and modification to these so called "legacy systems" may take more time. As explained in the preamble to the final rule, Part 11 does not grandfather legacy systems and FDA expects that firms using legacy systems will begin taking steps to achieve full compliance.
Policy:
When persons are not fully compliant with Part 11, decisions on whether or not to pursue regulatory actions will be based on a case by case evaluation, which may include the following:
Nature and extent of Part 11 deviation(s). FDA will consider Part 11 deviations to be more significant if those deviations are numerous, if the deviations make it difficult for the agency to audit or interpret data, or if the deviations undermine the integrity of the data or the electronic system. For example, FDA expects that firms will use file formats that permit the agency to make accurate and complete copies in both human readable and electronic form of audited electronic records. Similarly, FDA would have little confidence in data from firms that do not hold their employees accountable and responsible for actions taken under their electronic signatures.
Effect on product quality and data integrity. For example, FDA would consider the absence of an audit trail to be highly significant when there are data discrepancies and when individuals deny responsibility for record entries. Similarly, lack of operational system checks to enforce event sequencing would be significant if an operator's ability to deviate from the prescribed order of manufacturing steps results in an adulterated or misbranded product.
Adequacy and timeliness of planned corrective measures. Firms should have a reasonable timetable for promptly modifying any systems not in compliance (including legacy systems) to make them Part 11 compliant, and should be able to demonstrate progress in implementing their timetable. FDA expects that Part 11

requirements for procedural controls will already be in place. FDA recognizes that technology based controls may take longer to install in older systems.

Compliance history of the establishment, especially with respect to data integrity. FDA will consider Part 11 deviations to be more significant if a firm has a history of Part 11 violations or of inadequate or unreliable recordkeeping. Until firms attain full compliance with Part 11, FDA investigators will exercise greater vigilance to detect inconsistencies, unauthorized modifications, poor attributability, and any other problems associated with failure to comply with Part 11.

Regulatory Action Guidance:

Program monitors and center compliance offices should be consulted prior to recommending regulatory action. FDA will consider regulatory action with respect to Part 11 when the electronic records or electronic signatures are unacceptable substitutes for paper records or handwritten signatures, and that therefore, requirements of the applicable regulations (e.g., CGMP and GLP regulations) are not met. Regulatory citations should reference such predicate regulations in addition to Part 11. The following is an example of a regulatory citation for a violation of the device quality system regulations.

*Failure to establish and maintain procedures to control all documents that are required by 21 CFR 820.40, and failure to use authority checks to ensure that only authorized individuals can use the system and alter records, as required by 21 CFR 11.10(g). For example, engineering drawings for manufacturing equipment and devices are stored in AutoCAD form on a desktop computer. The storage device was not protected from unauthorized access and modification of the drawings.*

Issue date: 5/13/99


Office of Regulatory Affairs

## ORA FIELD MANAGEMENT DIRECTIVE No. 146

### PURPOSE

Persons using electronic signatures/electronic records are required to file certification documents with the Agency, according to the Electronic Records: Electronic Signatures Regulations, 21 C.F.R. Part 11. (By "person", it refers to an individual or an organization with legal rights and duties.) Filing of certification is primarily a one-time requirement for persons wishing to utilize electronic signatures on electronic records in regulated activities and is a declaration that electronic signatures affixed on their electronic records are legally binding equivalents for handwritten signatures. The Office of Regional Operations (ORO) is designated as the administrator of filing and maintenance of the certification information. This FMD is issued to describe how the Office of Regional Operations maintains the certification information and provides the rest of the Agency with access to the information.

### BACKGROUND

21 C.F.R. Part 11 requires that a person using electronic records file a certification document with FDA declaring that electronic signatures used on those records are legally binding equivalents to handwritten signatures. District offices and other units of FDA may need to verify that a person using electronic signatures and electronic records in regulated activities has filed such certification document with the Agency as required by the regulation. However, Part 11 does not call for submission of electronic signature use and authenticity information on individuals covered by the certification document. Investigators or reviewers of documents are expected to determine the authenticity of electronic signatures in the same manner that they determine the authenticity of handwritten signatures.

Significant parts of the regulations pertaining to electronic records are:

Electronic records and signatures are generally equivalent to paper records and handwritten signatures, respectively, executed on paper, provided all the requirements of regulations are met.

Each receiving unit (centers, offices, divisions, branches) must have identified, in advance, the types and formats of records it will accept in electronic format in public docket 92S-0251.

The regulation differentiates between closed systems in which system access is controlled by persons responsible for electronic records on the system, and open systems in which system access may not be entirely controlled by those same persons. Both the open and the closed systems must be designed to ensure that the electronic signatures on electronic records are not easily repudiated by the signer. Open systems must have additional measures such as document encryption and use of appropriate digital signature standards to ensure record authenticity, integrity, and confidentiality (since access to the [computer] system is not controlled by the persons that generate [and maintain] the electronic records under the Part 11 provisions).

Electronic signatures executed to electronic records shall be linked to electronic records to ensure they can't be excised, copied, or transferred to alter those electronic records.

Significant parts of the regulations pertaining to electronic signatures are:

They must be unique to the individual - not reusable by or reassignable to anyone else.

Before using electronic signatures, or at the time of use, persons using electronic signatures must certify to the Agency the electronic signatures used in their system on or after August 20, 1997, are intended to be the legally binding equivalent of handwritten signatures.

The above-mentioned certifications must be in paper form and signed with handwritten signatures and submitted to ORO/DEIO (HFC-130).

On request, persons must provide additional certification or testimony that a specific electronic signature is the legally binding equivalent of the signer's handwritten signature. Electronic signatures shall use biometrics - based on measurements of physical features (fingerprints, retinal signatures) or repeatable actions (dynamic signature verification combined with parameter code), **OR**

They shall employ at least two distinct identification components such as identification code and password.

PROCEDURES

ORO's agency-wide responsibility for certification documents is cited in 21 CFR 11.100(c) which says APersons using electronic signatures shall, prior to or at the time of such use, certify to the agency that the electronic signatures in their system, used on or after August 20, 1997, are intended to be the legally binding equivalent of traditional handwritten signatures..., and 21 CFR 11.100(c)(1) AThe certification shall be submitted in paper form and signed with a traditional handwritten signature, to the Office of Regional Operations (HFC-100).

These certification documents will be received by and physically stored in ORA/ORO. That office will compile a database of persons and all pertinent certification data. This database will be made accessible to the rest of the Agency by posting its content on ORA INTRANET in two separate tables for ease of search: one sorted alphabetically by names of filing persons and the other by Central File Numbers (CFN's). These tables will be presented on the INTRANET Web Page on the Parklawn network server in HTML format by August 20, 1997. They can be accessed from computers directly connected to any of the ORA's network servers at http://www.ora.fda.gov:8000/esig.html. ORO will update these tables on a periodic basis. For those without access to INTRANET and/or for more up-to-date information, ORO has established an ORO/DEIO contact at 301-827-5629.

Persons wishing to satisfy 21 C.F.R. 11.100 (c) (1) requirement should be directed to file the "letter of certification" with ORA/ORO, HFC-100, at 5600 Fishers Lane, Rockville, MD 20857.

If any of the Agency units needs to obtain an original document or its copy for the purpose of establishing the legal status of respective electonic records/electronic signatures, contact ORO/DEIO at the above-noted number. Any inquiries regarding filing of the certification documents should also be referred to the above office.


Part 11 Compliance

PART III - INSPECTIONAL

Inspections will involve a comparison of the practices and procedures of the clinical investigator with the commitments made in the applicable regulations as described in this part of the program.

Many inspections will include a comparison of the data submitted to the sponsor with supporting data in the clinical investigator's files. This will always be the case in human drugs and biologics inspections. Original records should be examined and may include office records, hospital records, laboratory reports, records of consultations, etc.

INSPECTIONAL OPERATIONS-GENERAL INSTRUCTIONS

1. The nature of these inspections makes unannounced visits to the clinical investigator impractical. Appointments to inspect should, therefore, be made by telephone, unless otherwise instructed in special cases by the Center. To facilitate the inspection of a clinical investigator at a Veterans Administration (VA) facility, the FDA investigator should also contact the Medical Center Director. For military installations, the Chief of Professional Services should be the initial contact.

The FDA investigator should, however, keep the time span between initial contact and actual inspection as short as possible. What appears to be undue delay * (such as more than ten working days without sufficient justification) * of the inspection on the part of the clinical investigator shall be reported immediately to the Center.

2. If during the inspection, access to records or copying of records is refused for any reason, the FDA investigator should call the supervisor and report the refusal so that the assigning Center can be advised promptly by telephone. The same procedure should be followed when it becomes evident that delays instituted by the inspected are such that they constitute a de facto refusal. IOM section 514 provides additional guidance. If actions by the *person being inspected* take the form of a partial refusal of inspection of documents or areas to which FDA is entitled under the law, call attention to 301(e) and (f) and 505(k)(2) of the FD&C Act, and if the refusal persists, proceed with the inspection and then telephone your supervisor. The assigning Center should be contacted for instructions.

If a course of action to deal with a refusal cannot be resolved expeditiously by the Center or the Office of Regional Operations (ORO), DCP should be advised by the assigning Center.

3. If deviations from the regulations * that might affect data validity, endanger test subject health or welfare,* are encountered during an inspection, call the Center contact so that a determination can be made as to whether the inspection should be expanded to be more intensive or to include other studies or target groups. The appropriate Center will provide guidance on initiating an in-depth audit inspection; however, the FDA investigator should continue the inspection.

4. For efficiency, a concurrent inspection may be indicated for a previously uninspected IRB or an IRB, which has not been inspected within the past five years. If such an IRB is found during the course of a clinical investigator inspection, contact the assigning Center for guidance and assignment. See CP 7348.809 for the IRB contact for each Center.

5. Issue a Form FDA 483, Inspectional Observations, at the conclusion of the inspection when deviations from regulations are observed. Deviations from guidance documents do not warrant inclusion on the FDA 483, however, they should be discussed with management and documented in the EIR.

INSPECTION PROCEDURES

This part identifies the nature of the information that must be obtained during each inspection to determine if the clinical investigator is meeting obligations under appropriate regulations. This outline provides only the minimal scope of the inspection and each FDA investigator should extend the inspection as the facts evolve. The inspections conducted should be sufficient in scope to determine the clinical investigator's practices for each point identified. The FDA investigator should not attempt to scientifically evaluate the data or protocols maintained by the clinical investigator; however, relevant documents should be reviewed, as appropriate. Evaluation of the scientific merit of the study is done by the FDA scientific reviewers receiving the application. Full narrative reporting of any deviations from existing regulations is required, and deviations must be documented sufficiently to form the basis of a legal or administrative action. For example, any records containing data not comparable with data submitted to FDA should be copied and documented as to what caused the discrepancy. Title 18 violations may require extensive documentation. Discuss the situation with your supervisor and the appropriate Center prior to embarking on this type of coverage.

Each inspection must include a list of all studies performed by the clinical investigator including those for government agencies and for commercial sponsors. This is needed in case a problem is found in an inspected study which requires reevaluation of claims in other agency documents or which requires notification of another government agency.

AUTHORITY AND ADMINISTRATION

1. Determine how (e.g., telephone, memo, etc.) the monitor explained to the clinical investigator the status of the test article, nature of the protocol, and the obligations of a clinical investigat*or*.

2. Determine whether authority for the conduct of the various aspects of the study was delegated properly so that the investigator retained control and knowledge of the study.

3. Determine if and why the investigator discontinued the study before completion.

4. List the name and address of the facility performing laboratory tests.

If any laboratory testing was performed in the investigator's own facility, determine whether that facility is equipped to perform each test specified.

List name(s) of individuals performing such tests and indicate their position.

PROTOCOL

1. *Obtain copies of the protocol and all IRB approvals and modifications (including dates) to the protocol. Unavailability should be reported and documented. If a copy of the protocol and IRB approvals and modifications is sent with the assignment background material, they should be compared to the protocol and approvals at the site. If they are identical, duplicate copies do not need to be obtained, but the documents sent with the assignment should be returned with the EIR. The narrative should note that the protocol and IRB approvals and modifications were identical.*

2. Did the protocol remain unchanged with respect to:

a. subject selection *(i.e., inclusion and exclusion criteria)*,

b. number of subjects,

c. frequency of subject observations,

d. dosage,

e. route of administration,

f. frequency of dosage,

g. blinding procedures,

h. other (specify)?

3. Determine whether all changes to the protocol were:

a. documented by *an approved amendment*,

b. dated,

c. maintained with the protocol,

d. * approved by the IRB and reported to the sponsor before implementation *, and except where necessary, to eliminate apparent immediate hazard to human subjects.

NOTE: * DEVIATIONS FROM * PROTOCOL ARE NOT CHANGES IN THE PROTOCOL

SUBJECTS' RECORDS

1. Describe the investigator's *source documents* in terms of their organization, condition, completeness, and legibility.

2. Determine whether there is adequate documentation to assure that all audited subjects did exist and were alive and available for the duration of their stated participation in the study.

3. Compare the *source documents* in the clinical investigator's records with the case report forms completed for the sponsor. Determine whether clinical laboratory testing (including EKGs, X-rays, eye exams, etc.), as noted in the case report forms, was documented by the presence of completed laboratory records among the *source documents*.

Determine whether *all* adverse *experiences* were reported in the case report forms. Determine whether they were regarded as caused by or associated with the test article and if they were previously anticipated (*specificity and* severity) in any written information regarding the test article.

Concomitant therapy and/or intercurrent illnesses might interfere with the evaluation of the effect of the test article. Were concomitant therapy and/or intercurrent illnesses included in the case report forms?

Determine whether the number and type of subjects entered into the study were confined to the protocol limitations.

Determine whether the existence of the condition for which the test article was being studied is documented by notation made prior to the initiation of the study or by a compatible history.

4. Determine whether each record contains:

a. observations, information, and data on the condition of the subject at the time the subject entered into the clinical study;

b. records of exposure of the subject to the test article;

c. observations and data on the condition of the subject throughout participation in the investigation including results of lab tests, development of unrelated illness, and other factors which might alter the effects of the test article; and

d. the identity of all persons and locations obtaining raw data or involved in the collection or analysis of such data.

5. Determine whether the clinical investigator reported all dropouts, and the reasons therefore, to the sponsor.

OTHER STUDY RECORDS

*Review* information *in* the clinical investigator's records *that* will be helpful in assessing any under-reporting of adverse *experiences* by the sponsor to the agency. The Centers will send you the following information obtained from the sponsor with the assignment (currently not routine for CVM):

*1*. the total number of subjects entered into the study,

*2*. the total number of dropouts from the study (identified by subject number),

*3*. the number of assessable subjects and the number of inassessable subjects (the latter identified by subject number), and

*4*. *the adverse experiences, including deaths (with subject number and a description of the adverse experience or cause of death).*

*The data supplied by the sponsor to the agency should be compared to the information submitted by the clinical investigator to the sponsor from the clinical investigator's files.* For the adverse reactions and deaths use the clinical investigator's correspondence files as it is not practical to search through each case report form. Document any discrepancies found.

CONSENT OF HUMAN SUBJECTS

1. Obtain a copy of the consent form *that was* used.

2. Determine whether written informed consent was obtained from subjects prior to their entry into the study.

*A representative sample of consent forms should be reviewed for compliance with 21 CFR 50. If any problems are found the sample should be expanded to determine the extent of the problem.* If oral consent was obtained, *determine if it conformed to 21 CFR 50?

INSTITUTIONAL REVIEW BOARD (IRB)

1. Identify the name, address, and chairperson of the IRB for the study.

2. Determine whether the investigator maintains copies of all reports submitted to the IRB and reports of all actions by the IRB. Determine the nature and frequency of periodic reports submitted to the IRB.

Determine whether the investigator submitted a report *to the IRB* of all deaths, adverse experiences and unanticipated problems involving risk to human subjects [21 CFR 312.66].*

3. Did the investigator submit to and obtain <u>IRB approval</u> of the following <u>before</u> subjects were allowed to participate in the investigation?

a. protocol

b. modifications to the protocol

c. report of prior investigations
d. materials to obtain human subject consent
e. media ads for patient/subject recruitment
4. Did the investigator disseminate any promotional material or otherwise represent that the test article is safe and effective for the purpose for which it is under investigation? Were these*promotional materials* submitted to the IRB for review *and approval before use?*

## SPONSOR

1. Did the investigator provide a copy of the IRB approved consent form to the sponsor?
2. Determine if periodic reports were submitted to the sponsor.
*3.* Determine if and how the investigator submitted a report of all deaths and adverse reactions to the sponsor.
*4. Determine whether all intercurrent illness and/or concomitant therapy were reported to the sponsor.*
*5.* Determine whether all case report forms on subjects were submitted to the sponsor shortly after completion.
*6.* Determine whether all dropouts, and the reasons therefore, were reported to the sponsor.
*7.* Did the sponsor monitor the progress of the study to assure
that investigator obligations were fulfilled? Briefly describe the method (on-site visit, telephone, contract research organization, etc.) and frequency of monitoring. Do the study records include a log of on-site monitoring visits and telephone contact?

## TEST ARTICLE ACCOUNTABILITY

1. Determine whether unqualified or unauthorized persons administered or dispensed the test article.
What names are listed on the FDA-1571 (for Sponsor-Investigator) *and* FDA-1572? Obtain a copy of all FDA-1572s.
*If copies of the FDA-1572s were sent with the assignment background material, they should be compared to the FDA-1572s at the site. If they are identical, duplicate copies do not need to be obtained, but the FDA-1572s sent with the assignment should be returned with the EIR. The narrative should note that the FDA-1572s sent with the assignment and examined at the site, were identical.*
2. Determine accountability procedures for test article; verify the following:
a. receipt date(s) and quantity;
b. dates and quantity dispensed, identification *numbers of subjects*;
c. whether distribution of the test article was limited to those *subjects* under the investigator's *or subinvestigators* direct supervision;
d. whether the quantity, frequency, duration, and route of administration of the test article, as reported to the sponsor, was generally corroborated by raw data notations;
e. date(s) and quantity returned to sponsor or alternate disposition, authorization for alternate disposition, and the actual disposition.
*f. Compare test article usage with amount shipped and returned. If available, inspect unused supplies and verify that blinding, identity, lot number, and package and labeling agree with other study records describing the test article.*
3. Inspect storage area.
Determine whether the test article was stored under appropriate conditions.
*Determine whether the test article is a controlled substance and whether it is securely locked in a substantially constructed enclosure.
Determine who had access to the controlled substance.*
4. What is the date the last subject completed the study?
Were test articles returned when either:
a. The investigator discontinued or completed his/her participation;
b. The sponsor discontinued or terminated the investigation; or
c. The FDA terminated the investigation.
If none of the above, determine whether alternate disposition of the test article exposed humans or food-producing animals to *risks from the test article(s).*

## RECORDS RETENTION

1. Determine who maintains custody of the required records and the means by which prompt access can be assured.
Determine whether the investigator notified the sponsor in writing regarding the custody of required records, if the investigator does not retain them.
2. Determine whether the records are retained for the specified time as follows:
a. Two years following the date on which the test article is approved by FDA for marketing for the purposes which were the subject of the clinical investigation; or
b. Two years following the date on which the entire clinical investigation (not just the investigator's part in it) is terminated or discontinued by the sponsor.

(For some studies selected as the basis of the inspection, the above time periods are not applicable.)
*ELECTRONIC RECORDS AND SIGNATURES

*FDA published the Electronic Records; Electronic Signatures; Final Rule [21 CFR 11] on March 20, 1997. The rule became effective on August 20, 1997. Records in electronic form that are that created, modified, maintained, archived, retrieved, or transmitted under any records requirement set forth in agency regulations must comply with 21 CFR 11. The following questions are provided to aid evaluation electronic records and electronic signatures:
1. What is the source of the hardware and software?
2. Who was responsible for installation and training?
3. Was the same hardware and software used throughout the duration of the study?
4. Was there any maintenance, including upgrading, conducted on the systems?
5. Were there any problems experienced during the course of the study?
6. What is the source of data entered into the computer?
a. Direct (no paper)?
b. Case report form?
c. Office record?
d. Other?
7. Who enters data? When?
8. Who has access to the computer? Security procedures?
9. How are data previously entered changed? By whom?
Is an audit trail produced?
10. How are data submitted to the sponsor (i.e. modem, network, fax, hard disk, floppy disk, electronic transfer, mail, messenger, picked up)?
11. If the sponsor discovers errors, omissions, etc., in the data received, what contacts are made with the investigator? How are corrections effected, and how are they documented?
12. Does the clinical investigator retain a copy of the electronic data submitted to the sponsor?*


Guidance for Industry
Part 11, Electronic Records; Electronic Signatures - Scope and Application

U.S. Department of Health and Human Services
Food and Drug Administration
Center for Drug Evaluation and Research (CDER)
Center for Biologics Evaluation and Research (CBER)
Center for Devices and Radiological Health (CDRH)
Center for Food Safety and Applied Nutrition (CFSAN)
Center for Veterinary Medicine (CVM)
Office of Regulatory Affairs (ORA)

August 2003

Pharmaceutical CGMPs

Division of Drug Information, HFD-240
Center for Drug Evaluation and Research (CDER)
(Tel) 301-827-4573
http://www.fda.gov/cder/guidance/index.htm

or

Office of Communication, Training and
Manufacturers Assistance, HFM-40
Center for Biologics Evaluation and Research (CBER)
http://www.fda.gov/cber/guidelines.htm
Phone: the Voice Information System at 800-835-4709 or 301-827-1800

or

Communications Staff (HFV-12),

Center for Veterinary Medicine (CVM)
(Tel) 301-594-1755
http://www.fda.gov/cvm/guidance/guidance.html

or

Division of Small Manufacturers Assistance (HFZ-220)
http://www.fda.gov/cdrh/ggpmain.html
Manufacturers Assistance Phone Number: 800.638.2041 or 301.443.6597
Internt'l Staff Phone: 301.827.3993

or

Center for Food Safety and Applied Nutrition (CFSAN)
http://www.cfsan.fda.gov/~dms/guidance.html.

August 2003

Pharmaceutical CGMPs

TABLE OF CONTENTS

Guidance for Industry1

Part 11, Electronic Records; Electronic Signatures -

Scope and Application

This guidance represents the Food and Drug Administration's (FDA's) current thinking on

this topic. It does not create or confer any rights for or on any person and does not

operate to bind FDA or the public. You can use an alternative approach if the approach

satisfies the requirements of the applicable statutes and regulations. If you want to

discuss an alternative approach, contact the FDA staff responsible for implementing this guidance. If you cannot identify the appropriate FDA staff, call the appropriate number listed on the title page of this guidance.

## I. INTRODUCTION

This guidance is intended to describe the Food and Drug Administration's (FDA's) current thinking regarding the scope and application of part 11 of Title 21 of the Code of Federal Regulations; Electronic Records; Electronic Signatures (21 CFR Part 11).2 This document provides guidance to persons who, in fulfillment of a requirement in a statute or another part of FDA's regulations to maintain records or submit information to FDA,3 have chosen to maintain the records or submit designated information electronically and, as a result, have become subject to part 11. Part 11 applies to records in electronic form that are created, modified, maintained, archived, retrieved, or transmitted under any records requirements set forth in Agency regulations. Part 11 also applies to electronic records submitted to the Agency under the Federal Food, Drug, and Cosmetic Act (the Act) and the Public Health Service Act (the PHS Act), even if such records are not specifically identified in Agency regulations (§ 11.1). The underlying requirements set forth in the Act, PHS Act, and FDA regulations (other than part 11) are referred to in this guidance document as predicate rules.

As an outgrowth of its current good manufacturing practice (CGMP) initiative for human and animal drugs and biologics,4 FDA is re-examining part 11 as it applies to all FDA regulated products. We anticipate initiating rulemaking to change part 11 as a result of that re-examination. This guidance explains that we will narrowly interpret the scope of part 11. While the re-examination of part 11 is under way, we intend to exercise enforcement discretion with respect to certain part 11 requirements. That is, we do not intend to take enforcement action to enforce compliance with the validation, audit trail, record retention, and record copying requirements of part 11 as explained in this guidance. However, records must still be maintained or submitted in accordance with the underlying predicate rules, and the Agency can take regulatory action for noncompliance with such predicate rules.

In addition, we intend to exercise enforcement discretion and do not intend to take (or recommend) action to enforce any part 11 requirements with regard to systems that were operational before August 20, 1997, the effective date of part 11 (commonly known as legacy systems) under the circumstances described in section III.C.3 of this guidance. Note that part 11 remains in effect and that this exercise of enforcement discretion applies only as identified in this guidance.

FDA's guidance documents, including this guidance, do not establish legally enforceable responsibilities. Instead, guidances describe the Agency's current thinking on a topic and should be viewed only as recommendations, unless specific regulatory or statutory requirements are cited. The use of the word should in Agency guidances means that something is suggested or recommended, but not required.

## II. BACKGROUND

In March of 1997, FDA issued final part 11 regulations that provide criteria for acceptance by FDA, under certain circumstances, of electronic records, electronic signatures, and handwritten signatures executed to electronic records as equivalent to paper records and handwritten signatures executed on paper. These regulations, which apply to all FDA program areas, were intended to permit the widest possible use of electronic technology, compatible with FDA's responsibility to protect the public health.

After part 11 became effective in August 1997, significant discussions ensued among industry, contractors, and the Agency concerning the interpretation and implementation of the regulations. FDA has (1) spoken about part 11 at many conferences and met numerous times with an industry coalition and other interested parties in an effort to hear more about potential part 11 issues; (2) published a compliance policy guide, CPG 7153.17: Enforcement Policy: 21 CFR Part 11; Electronic Records; Electronic Signatures; and (3) published numerous draft guidance documents including the following:

· 21 CFR Part 11; Electronic Records; Electronic Signatures, Validation

· 21 CFR Part 11; Electronic Records; Electronic Signatures, Glossary of Terms

· 21 CFR Part 11; Electronic Records; Electronic Signatures, Time Stamps

· 21 CFR Part 11; Electronic Records; Electronic Signatures, Maintenance of Electronic Records

· 21 CFR Part 11; Electronic Records; Electronic Signatures, Electronic Copies of Electronic Records

Throughout all of these communications, concerns have been raised that some interpretations of the part 11 requirements would (1) unnecessarily restrict the use of electronic technology in a manner that is inconsistent with FDA's stated intent in issuing the rule, (2) significantly increase the costs of compliance to an extent that was not contemplated at the time the rule was drafted, and (3) discourage innovation and technological advances without providing a significant public health benefit. These concerns have been raised particularly in the areas of part 11 requirements for validation, audit trails, record retention, record copying, and legacy systems.

As a result of these concerns, we decided to review the part 11 documents and related issues, particularly in light of the Agency's CGMP initiative. In the Federal Register of February 4, 2003 (68 FR 5645), we announced the withdrawal of the draft guidance for industry, 21 CFR Part 11; Electronic Records; Electronic Signatures, Electronic Copies of Electronic Records. We had decided we wanted to minimize industry time spent reviewing and commenting on the draft guidance when that draft guidance may no longer represent our approach under the CGMP initiative. Then, in the Federal Register of February 25, 2003 (68 FR 8775), we announced the withdrawal of the part 11 draft guidance documents on validation, glossary of terms, time stamps,5 maintenance of electronic records, and CPG 7153.17. We received valuable public comments on these draft guidances, and we plan to use that information to help with future decision-making with respect to part 11. We do not intend to re-issue these draft guidance documents or the CPG.

We are now re-examining part 11, and we anticipate initiating rulemaking to revise provisions of that regulation. To avoid unnecessary resource expenditures to comply with part 11 requirements, we are issuing this guidance to describe how we intend to exercise enforcement discretion with regard to certain part 11 requirements during the re-examination of part 11. As mentioned previously, part 11 remains in effect during this re-examination period.

III. DISCUSSION

A. Overall Approach to Part 11 Requirements

As described in more detail below, the approach outlined in this guidance is based on three main elements:

· Part 11 will be interpreted narrowly; we are now clarifying that fewer records will be considered subject to part 11.

· For those records that remain subject to part 11, we intend to exercise enforcement discretion with regard to part 11 requirements for validation, audit trails, record retention, and record copying in the manner described in this guidance and with regard to all part 11 requirements for systems that were operational before the effective date of part 11 (also known as legacy systems).

· We will enforce all predicate rule requirements, including predicate rule record and recordkeeping requirements.

It is important to note that FDA's exercise of enforcement discretion as described in this guidance is limited to specified part 11 requirements (setting aside legacy systems, as to which the extent of enforcement discretion, under certain circumstances, will be more broad). We intend to enforce all other provisions of part 11 including, but not limited to, certain controls for closed systems in § 11.10. For example, we intend to enforce provisions related to the following controls and requirements:

· limiting system access to authorized individuals

· use of operational system checks

· use of authority checks

· use of device checks

· determination that persons who develop, maintain, or use electronic systems have the education, training, and experience to perform their assigned tasks

· establishment of and adherence to written policies that hold individuals accountable for actions initiated under their electronic signatures

· appropriate controls over systems documentation

· controls for open systems corresponding to controls for closed systems bulleted above (§ 11.30)

· requirements related to electronic signatures (e.g., §§ 11.50, 11.70, 11.100, 11.200, and 11.300)

We expect continued compliance with these provisions, and we will continue to enforce them. Furthermore, persons must comply with applicable predicate rules, and records that are required to be maintained or submitted must remain secure and reliable in accordance with the predicate rules.

B. Details of Approach - Scope of Part 11

1. Narrow Interpretation of Scope

We understand that there is some confusion about the scope of part 11. Some have understood the scope of part 11 to be very broad. We believe that some of those broad interpretations could lead to unnecessary controls and costs and could discourage innovation and technological advances without providing added benefit to the public health. As a result, we want to clarify that the Agency intends to interpret the scope of part 11 narrowly.

Under the narrow interpretation of the scope of part 11, with respect to records required to be maintained under predicate rules or submitted to FDA, when persons choose to use records in electronic format in place of paper format, part 11 would apply. On the other hand, when persons use computers to generate paper printouts of electronic records, and those paper records meet all the requirements of the applicable predicate rules and persons rely on the paper records to perform their regulated activities, FDA would generally not consider persons to be "using electronic records in lieu of paper records" under §§ 11.2(a) and 11.2(b). In these instances, the use of computer systems in the generation of paper records would not trigger part 11.

2. Definition of Part 11 Records

Under this narrow interpretation, FDA considers part 11 to be applicable to the following records or signatures in electronic format (part 11 records or signatures):

· Records that are required to be maintained under predicate rule requirements and that are maintained in electronic format in place of paper format. On the other hand, records (and any associated signatures) that are not required to be retained under predicate rules, but that are nonetheless maintained in electronic format, are not part 11 records.

We recommend that you determine, based on the predicate rules, whether specific records are part 11 records. We recommend that you document such decisions.

· Records that are required to be maintained under predicate rules, that are maintained in electronic format in addition to paper format, and that are relied on to perform regulated activities.

In some cases, actual business practices may dictate whether you are using electronic records instead of paper records under § 11.2(a). For example, if a record is required to be maintained under a predicate rule and you use a computer to generate a paper printout of the electronic records, but you nonetheless rely on the electronic record to perform regulated activities, the Agency may consider you to be using the electronic record instead of the paper record. That is, the Agency may take your business practices into account in determining whether part 11 applies.

Accordingly, we recommend that, for each record required to be maintained under predicate rules, you determine in advance whether you plan to rely on the electronic record or paper record to perform regulated activities. We recommend that you document this decision (e.g., in a Standard Operating Procedure (SOP), or specification document ).

· Records submitted to FDA, under predicate rules (even if such records are not specifically identified in Agency regulations) in electronic format (assuming the records have been identified in docket number 92S-0251 as the types of submissions the Agency accepts in electronic format). However, a record that is not itself submitted, but is used in generating a submission, is not a part 11 record unless it is otherwise required to be maintained under a predicate rule and it is maintained in electronic format.

· Electronic signatures that are intended to be the equivalent of handwritten signatures, initials, and other general signings required by predicate rules. Part 11 signatures include electronic signatures that are used, for example, to document the fact that certain events or actions occurred in accordance with the predicate rule (e.g. approved, reviewed, and verified).


C. Approach to Specific Part 11 Requirements

1. Validation

The Agency intends to exercise enforcement discretion regarding specific part 11 requirements for validation of computerized systems (§ 11.10(a) and corresponding requirements in § 11.30). Although persons must still comply with all applicable predicate rule requirements for validation (e.g., 21 CFR 820.70(i)), this guidance should not be read to impose any additional requirements for validation.

We suggest that your decision to validate computerized systems, and the extent of the validation, take into account the impact the systems have on your ability to meet predicate rule requirements. You should also consider the impact those systems might have on the accuracy, reliability, integrity, availability, and authenticity of required records and signatures. Even if there is no predicate rule requirement to validate a system, in some instances it may still be important to validate the system.

We recommend that you base your approach on a justified and documented risk assessment and a determination of the potential of the system to affect product quality and safety, and record integrity. For instance, validation would not be important for a word processor used only to generate SOPs.

For further guidance on validation of computerized systems, see FDA's guidance for industry and FDA staff General Principles of Software Validation and also industry guidance such as the GAMP 4 Guide (See References).

2. Audit Trail

The Agency intends to exercise enforcement discretion regarding specific part 11 requirements related to computer-generated, time-stamped audit trails (§ 11.10 (e), (k) (2) and any corresponding requirement in §11.30). Persons must still comply with all applicable predicate rule requirements related to documentation of, for example, date ( e.g., § 58.130(e)), time, or sequencing of events, as well as any requirements for ensuring that changes to records do not obscure previous entries.

Even if there are no predicate rule requirements to document, for example, date, time, or sequence of events in a particular instance, it may nonetheless be important to have audit trails or other physical, logical, or procedural security measures in place to ensure the trustworthiness and reliability of the records.6 We recommend that you base your decision on whether to apply audit trails, or other appropriate measures, on the need to comply with predicate rule requirements, a justified and documented risk assessment, and a determination of the potential effect on product quality and safety and record integrity. We suggest that you apply appropriate controls based on such an assessment. Audit trails can be particularly appropriate when users are expected to create, modify, or delete regulated records during normal operation.

3. Legacy Systems7

The Agency intends to exercise enforcement discretion with respect to all part 11 requirements for systems that otherwise were operational prior to August 20, 1997, the effective date of part 11, under the circumstances specified below.

This means that the Agency does not intend to take enforcement action to enforce compliance with any part 11 requirements if all the following criteria are met for a specific system:

· The system was operational before the effective date.

· The system met all applicable predicate rule requirements before the effective date.

· The system currently meets all applicable predicate rule requirements.

· You have documented evidence and justification that the system is fit for its intended use (including having an acceptable level of record security and integrity, if applicable).

If a system has been changed since August 20, 1997, and if the changes would prevent the system from meeting predicate rule requirements, Part 11 controls should be applied to Part 11 records and signatures pursuant to the enforcement policy expressed in this guidance.

4. Copies of Records

The Agency intends to exercise enforcement discretion with regard to specific part 11 requirements for generating copies of records (§ 11.10 (b) and any corresponding requirement in §11.30). You should provide an investigator with reasonable and useful access to records during an inspection. All records held by you are subject to inspection in accordance with predicate rules (e.g., §§ 211.180(c), (d), and 108.35(c)( 3)(ii)).

We recommend that you supply copies of electronic records by:

· Producing copies of records held in common portable formats when records are maintained in these formats

· Using established automated conversion or export methods, where available, to make copies in a more common format (examples of such formats include, but are not limited to, PDF, XML, or SGML)

In each case, we recommend that the copying process used produces copies that preserve the content and meaning of the record. If you have the ability to search, sort, or trend part 11 records, copies given to the Agency should provide the same capability if it is reasonable and technically feasible. You should allow inspection, review, and copying of records in a human readable form at your site using your hardware and following your established procedures and techniques for accessing records.

5. Record Retention

The Agency intends to exercise enforcement discretion with regard to the part 11 requirements for the protection of records to enable their accurate and ready retrieval throughout the records retention period (§ 11.10 (c) and any corresponding requirement in §11.30). Persons must still comply with all applicable predicate rule requirements for record retention and availability (e.g., §§ 211.180(c),(d), 108.25(g), and 108.35(h )).

We suggest that your decision on how to maintain records be based on predicate rule requirements and that you base your decision on a justified and documented risk assessment and a determination of the value of the records over time.

FDA does not intend to object if you decide to archive required records in electronic format to nonelectronic media such as microfilm, microfiche, and paper, or to a standard electronic file format (examples of such formats include, but are not limited to, PDF, XML, or SGML). Persons must still comply with all predicate rule requirements, and the records themselves and any copies of the required records should preserve their content and meaning. As long as predicate rule requirements are fully satisfied and the content and meaning of the records are preserved and archived, you can delete the electronic version of the records. In addition, paper and electronic record and signature components can co-exist (i.e., a hybrid8 situation) as long as predicate rule requirements are met and the content and meaning of those records are preserved.

## IV. REFERENCES

Food and Drug Administration References

1. Glossary of Computerized System and Software Development Terminology (Division of Field Investigations, Office of Regional Operations, Office of Regulatory Affairs, FDA 1995) (http://www.fda.gov/ora/inspect_ref/igs/gloss.html)

2. General Principles of Software Validation; Final Guidance for Industry and FDA Staff (FDA, Center for Devices and Radiological Health, Center for Biologics Evaluation and Research, 2002) (http://www.fda.gov/cdrh/comp/guidance/938.html)

3. Guidance for Industry, FDA Reviewers, and Compliance on Off-The-Shelf Software Use in Medical Devices (FDA, Center for Devices and Radiological Health, 1999) ( http://www. fda.gov/cdrh/ode/guidance/585.html)

4. Pharmaceutical CGMPs for the 21st Century: A Risk-Based Approach; A Science and Risk -Based Approach to Product Quality Regulation Incorporating an Integrated Quality Systems Approach (FDA 2002) (http://www.fda.gov/oc/guidance/gmp.html)

Industry References

1. The Good Automated Manufacturing Practice (GAMP) Guide for Validation of Automated Systems, GAMP 4 (ISPE/GAMP Forum, 2001) ( http://www.ispe.org/gamp/)

2. ISO/IEC 17799:2000 (BS 7799:2000) Information technology - Code of practice for information security management (ISO/IEC, 2000)

3. ISO 14971:2002 Medical Devices- Application of risk management to medical devices ( ISO, 2001)

1 This guidance has been prepared by the Office of Compliance in the Center for Drug Evaluation and Research (CDER) in consultation with the other Agency centers and the Office of Regulatory Affairs at the Food and Drug Administration.

2 62 FR 13430

3 These requirements include, for example, certain provisions of the Current Good Manufacturing Practice regulations (21 CFR Part 211), the Quality System regulation (21 CFR Part 820), and the Good Laboratory Practice for Nonclinical Laboratory Studies regulations (21 CFR Part 58).

4 See Pharmaceutical CGMPs for the 21st Century: A Risk-Based Approach; A Science and

Risk-Based Approach to Product Quality Regulation Incorporating an Integrated Quality

Systems Approach at www.fda.gov/oc/guidance/gmp.html.

5 Although we withdrew the draft guidance on time stamps, our current thinking has not

changed in that when using time stamps for systems that span different time zones, we do

not expect you to record the signer's local time. When using time stamps, they should be

implemented with a clear understanding of the time zone reference used. In such

instances, system documentation should explain time zone references as well as zone

acronyms or other naming conventions.

6 Various guidance documents on information security are available (see References).

7 In this guidance document, we use the term legacy system to describe systems already

in operation before the effective date of part 11.

8 Examples of hybrid situations include combinations of paper records (or other

nonelectronic media) and electronic records, paper records and electronic signatures, or

handwritten signatures executed to electronic records.

# Pharmaceutical Computer Validation Introduction

The end of this section contains several FDA documents:
- Guidance for Industry on Software Validation
- COMPLIANCE POLICY GUIDE Section 160.850
- Guidance for Industry: COMPUTERIZED SYSTEMS USED IN CLINICAL TRIALS
- 425.100 Guidance
- 21 CFR 58
- 21 CFR 211

## OVERVIEW

To manage and store data critical to the drug manufacturing process, almost all drug companies are using computers. As a result, firms are forced to rely more and more on digital information, sometimes without any real way of knowing if this data is trustworthy. Because manufacturing and testing drugs has life-and-death significance, this is simply not acceptable.

The FDA (Food & Drug Administration) monitors and penalizes pharmaceutical companies for unsafe drug-making procedures and dangerous mistakes. Also, tainted data from poorly managed computer systems will result in financial losses for the pharmaceutical corporation. Therefore, the use of computers demands that definite procedures be in place to guarantee product purity and process accuracy.

Computer systems involved in drug making must be:
- Developed per acceptable standards
- Used properly by trained personnel
- Maintained correctly to insure the integrity, accuracy, and reproducibility of the data.

## STORY

Jim Gullible was just promoted to Head of Computer Systems at Cutting Edge Pharmaceutical, Inc. With all of the new regulations regarding the handling of data related to product development, testing, and distribution, he spent many long nights in the office alone trying to figure them all out.

After several weeks of working day and night, six days a week, he still hadn't put together the company-wide data processing SOPs (Standard Operating Procedures). Then to his horror, one night he received an e-mail message from the Vice President of Operations saying that FDA auditors would be inspecting his systems very soon. He needed to get all hardware, software, and related personnel ready to pass the most stringent computer validation audits.

But how?!

He looked at the clock; it was midnight. Then he looked at his calendar and fretted, buried under stacks of books and papers on the subject of computer validation for pharmaceutical applications. Finally, the next morning he found himself happily typing a detailed plan to cover the regulated items and issues.

COURSE OUTLINE

1. Computer Validation Defined
2. Regulations
3. Personnel Responsible For Computer Validation
4. How Validation Is Accomplished
5. Examples Of Regulatory Problems
6. GLP – GMP Regulatory Chart
7. Further Reading

But after looking at the breadth and scope of the task, he began to feel discouraged again. He became paralyzed, and all he could type into his document is: "I just don't know what to do!"

Then he just sat and stared at his computer screen…and at about 4:00 a.m., he eventually dozed off to sleep…. When he woke up, things were weird! His head had actually become a computer!

Suddenly, he heard a strange voice that said: "Maybe I can help you solve your problem." He shook his head. "Am I hallucinating?" Something very weird was happening to his Word document. The voice rang out again, this time followed by a text message on his screen. "Maybe I can help you solve your problem and save your job!"

The Head of Computers jumped up. "How could someone be using Microsoft Word to send me an instant message?"

He detached his Internet connection and typed: "Is someone still out there?" The answer came forth from his Word document: "Yes, I'm still here!"

Head of Computers almost fell out of his chair, then composed himself and initiated voice activation.

"Who are you? And what do want with me?"

A deceivingly good-natured computer image appeared on the screen. The text and voice message answered, "My name is Legacy Computer, head spirit of the dead and dying legacy computer systems. Some think I'm evil and corrupt, but I can save you your job… for a price, of course."

Head of Computers looked at the vice president's e-mail and the calendar again, then perked up. "If you can help me validate all my computer systems so I can keep my job, I'll give you whatever you want."

"Very well, Computer Head," said Legacy Computer. "Here's the deal: I'll give you all the information you need if you promise to keep us legacy computers functioning for Cutting Edge Pharmaceuticals. You CANNOT scrap us for newer, state-of-the-art systems."

"Okay, I agree, I agree. And I like the name, 'Computer Head'." Head of Computers was desperate. "But if I'm forced to bring in more high tech computers and software later, what will happen?"

Legacy Computer growled sinisterly. "I'll be forced to possess the other legacy systems and I'll make them do very bad things to your company. We'll throw things out of whack… and then you'll be out of your job."

Now he faked a pleasant smile. "So, I have your word?"

Computer Head knew he'd have to get some new computers, eventually. And he figured that they'd be smarter and stronger than the legacy systems, anyway. He told himself, "They'll be able to fight for themselves… and for me too!  I'm not scared."

So he lied as he gave his response. "You have my word."

Legacy Computer told him to run his finger along the back edge of the computer. As Computer Head did so, his finger caught on a metal edge and began to bleed. "Now I accept your word," grinned Legacy Computer, and he began compiling documents to match Head of Computers's outline. "Then let's get on with it. We're going to start with the first item on your outline:

COMPUTER VALIDATION DEFINED

"Computer Validation encompasses computers which directly control a process or system. It also pertains to computers that collect analytical data.

"Computer Validation includes the qualification of all software and hardware which have an impact-- whether direct or indirect-- on the quality of a product.

"The underlying objective of the process at all levels is to define and make clear those responsible for validation, the objectives, the workload and timelines for validation of computer systems.

"It will also create a mechanism for management control of the validation process.

"During the planning phase, certain issues should be addressed, such as system objectives, constraints of the software/hardware, testing, supplier requirements, source code viability, legibility and code logic.

"In this phase of validation, a further array of documents is generated."

Review Question: Legacy Computer: I want to be certain you understand me. Answer this: Computer Validation only includes the qualification of hardware which has an impact, direct or indirect, on the quality of a product. Software is excluded. True or false?

Answer: False. Computer Validation includes the qualification of all hardware AND software which have an impact, direct or indirect, on the quality of a product.

But Head of Computers was still going crazy with his heavy workload. Even with Legacy Computer's help he had far too much work to do... and not enough time to do it. Eventually, he had to bring in some newer, faster, more powerful computers and software to satisfy new production requirements.

And soon he began getting Validation information from a unit called "State-of-the-Art Computer."

State-of-the-Art Computer: "I want to tell you about the <u>process</u> of computer validation. It's mainly concerned with making sure that a computer system can perform the functions it was designed to handle.

"And it has to do it in a way that is documented and reproducible.

"Validation begins upon initial development of the system.

"It goes on for several years, and only ends when use of the system has been terminated."

<u>Review Question:</u> "Okay, let me see if you're keeping up with me.... Which of the following is true about the duration of the Computer Validation process?"
A. It ends when pharmaceutical products seem to be okay.
B. It goes on for several years, and only ends when use of the system has been terminated.
C. It ends as soon as the design phase is over and the system goes into operation
<u>Answer:</u> B.

Suddenly, Legacy computer interrupted with his own information: "Hey! I'M the one whom you should be listening to, Head Computer!

"The only way to be certain that the system requirements have been properly designed, and that none have been overlooked, is to have sufficient <u>documentation</u> to that effect.

"Even after the pioneering builders of the system have long gone, a correctly-documented system will still facilitate proper maintenance and successful validation far into the future."

Then State-of-the-Art Computer interrupted Legacy:

"Ahem! <u>Reproducibility</u> is another important issue. Especially in the pharmaceutical industry, the processes involved in manufacturing a safe and approvable product require the utmost control.

"The producing firm's management must be able to prove upon inspection that a quality development and manufacturing environment is achieved and sustained.

"Any substantial variations in how the produced items are made over time will cause the system to fail a reproducibility test."

<u>Review Question:</u> Do you follow me? Let's see you answer this: The only way to be certain that the system requirements have been properly designed, and that none have been overlooked, is to have sufficient documentation to that effect.
True or false?
<u>Answer:</u> True. Even after the pioneering builders of the system have long gone, a correctly documented system will still facilitate proper maintenance and successful validation far into the future.

Feeling betrayed, Legacy Computer was livid! He began to threaten Head of Computers. "I told you I'd make things bad for you if you double-crossed me!"

But Head of Computers didn't back down. "Do it, and I'll dump you fast!"

He allowed State-of-the-Art Computer to continue. "Go ahead, State-of-the-Art."

State-of-the-Art Computer made sure to "watch his back" (circuits, that is). He knew that Legacy Computer had the wherewithal to harm his new hardware and software. But because he anticipated the full installation of newer, high-tech systems, he also knew that he would soon get reinforcements.

State-of-the-Art Computer went on, confidently.

"Okay, Computer Head. Hardware needs to be tested both alone and while operating with a connection to any other units. As any new peripheral is added, further tests must be done. Finally, upon completion of full installation, the whole system needs to be completely tested again.

"Software has the same stringent test requirements as hardware, but there are additional issues. Tests must be conducted—and documented in detail—to insure that the modular software is reliable. Then, after the modules have been integrated, tests must be conducted again—and again with documentation."

Review Question: So, are you getting that? Then answer this question: Which of the following is NOT true about the process of validating computer hardware?
A. Hardware needs to be tested both alone and while operating with a connection to any other units.
B. As any new peripheral is added, further tests must be done.
C. Finally, upon completion of full installation, the whole system needs to be completely tested again.
D. Hardware that has been approved in stand-alone functions need not be tested after integration with other proven hardware.
Answer: D.

Review Question: Which of the following is NOT true?
Software never needs to be tested after implementation tests have been successful.

Software has the same stringent test requirements as with hardware, but there are additional issues.

Software tests must be conducted-and documented in detail-to insure that the modular software is reliable.

Answer: A.

Then Legacy Computer again began to try and force his information upon Head of Computers.

"Hey, check this out, Computer Head! Operational Qualification is imperative. In order to verify that operations are properly qualified, they must be tested under conditions that both cover regular use and scenarios of the worst case.

"The security of system has to be verified and documented. Tests must also be done to validate the results of prior assessments, as well as critical inputs and outputs.

"One of the worst-case examinations must include the ramifications of power outages during crucial cycles of the process.

"Another standard check is how the process fares when an operator uses it or misuses the computer system."

Review Question: Are you paying attention? Let's see you get this one: Operational Qualification means that in order to verify that operations are properly qualified, they must be tested under conditions that both cover regular use and scenarios of the worst case. True or false?

Answer: True. The security of system has to be verified and documented. Tests must also be done to validate the results of prior assessments, as well as critical inputs and outputs.

The next day, Legacy Computer formulated his attack plan. "Yes, I could wipe out the whole company's data systems and make Computer Head lose his job. But then I would be scrapped for sure—along with all of the rest of the older hardware, software, and networks."

So, instead of wreaking destructive havoc right away, Legacy Computer angrily began to conspire with the other legacy hardware and software units to prove their superior knowledge and functioning.

Legacy Computer: "Guys and gals... we have experience and maturity on our side. All the newer systems have are "greenness" and the ineptitude of youth."
"But if they start winning, then we'll create even more 'bugs' than their systems probably already have!"

Legacy Henchman #1

Legacy Henchman #2

Legacy Henchman #3

Legacy Henchman #4

Legacy Henchman #5

Legacy Henchman #6

Head of Computers didn't trust Legacy Computer anymore. He feared that, if threatened with termination, the older systems would attempt to end his career, as well. He told State-of-the-Art Computer the whole story about his dilemma and the inappropriate promise he made to the deceptive Legacy Computer.

State-of-the-Art Computer felt sorry for him. "Never make a deal with the devil... unless you find a good angel that's tough enough to cover for you!"

Computer Head was desperate—again! "Can you help me?"

State-of-the-Art Computer smiled. "I and my high-tech reinforcement systems are the toughest in the business!"

Computer Head felt more at ease. "Then I want you and your modern computers to stand up against the older systems." State-of-the-Art Computer asked him, "Can you guarantee that we'll get the assignment?"

Computer Head buried his monitor head in his hands. "I'm leaning toward you, but no more deals! May the best system win!"

So now, State-of-the-Art Computer rallied all of the highest tech systems to wage the technological debate.

State-of-the-Art
Reinforcement #1

State-of-the-Art
Reinforcement #2

State-of-the-Art
Reinforcement #3

State-of-the-Art
Reinforcement #4

State-of-the-Art
Reinforcement #5

State-of-the-Art
Reinforcement #6

Always devious and sneaky, Legacy Computer and his henchmen tried to get the newer systems to defect to their side: "Just remember, at the rate that technology advances, within a year, you'll be considered an 'obsolete legacy system' like we are."

State-of-the-Art Computer told his followers not to listen to Legacy Computer's fear tactics: "We know what we have to do to remain validated. We'll be implemented, then we'll outperform you... and Head of Computers will still keep his job."

Legacy Computer said, "No, you won't be implemented. We'll outperform all your 'nouveau and bugged' systems."

State-of-the-Art Computer said, "Yes, we will be implemented. Your tired, worn- out infrastructure will fail you. You're all going to the junkyard soon."

Then they both turned to Head of Computers for guidance and approval. He just sat back and pointed at one and then the other.

"Then you'll each have to prove to me that you can deliver before the FDA computer validation inspection. Continue the fight!"

Legacy Computer reluctantly agreed. But knowing that Head of Computers had violated his promise, he had an evil computer "chip on his shoulder."

He and his henchmen just might have to do underhanded things to make sure they win.

Head of Computers said, "We're finished with defining Computer Validation for now."

Legacy Computer: "Okay, I'm going to let you get away with this for now."

Let's move on to cover the second item on your outline:

REGULATIONS

State-of-the-Art Computer: "As mentioned earlier, the FDA is the primary agency that regulates the pharmaceutical industry."

Legacy Computer: "Everybody knows that. But I'd bet you don't know this:

"In regards to computer validation, the FDA's job is to make sure that computer systems used in the various stages of drug development, clinical trials, manufacturing, testing, and distribution, are correctly developed, employed, and maintained to guarantee the integrity of data and products."

State-of-the-Art Computer: "I thought you were going to tell me something I DON'T know!"

Computer Head: "Okay, how about this?

Which relevant FDA regulations and guidelines include the Good Laboratory Practices (GLPs) and Good Manufacturing Practices (GMPs)?"

State-of-the-Art Computer: "I know this one."

* Part 58 of the Code of Federal Regulations (CFR Title 21) covers GLP regulations.
* Part 211 of the CFR covers GMP regulations.
* Both the GLP and GMP regulations include sections to which computer validation applies.

Computer Head: "I'm looking in my manuals. It says that the FDA's main directive is to enforce against what they have determined to be prohibited acts. What are the main ones?"

Legacy Computer: "See, this is where experience comes in. We've worked on this a million times:
• The shipment of any article in violation of new drug, investigational device, or other provisions
• The refusal to permit access to or the copying of records
• The refusal to permit inspection
• The manufacture of any adulterated or misbranded food, drug, device, or cosmetic"

Review Question: So, did you get that? Let's find out! Which of the following does the FDA NOT consider a prohibited act?
A. The refusal to permit inspection
B. The refusal to permit access to or the copying of records
C. The refusal to state which drugs are in the office first-aid kits.
D. The manufacture of any adulterated or misbranded food, drug, device, or cosmetic
Answer: C.

Legacy Computer (cont'd): "The FDA defines 'adulterated drugs and devices' as those that aren't produced in compliance with GMPs (Good Manufacturing Practices).

"Specifically targeted are those drugs whose strength, purity, or quality differs from what has been represented.

"Also at issue are drugs whose strength, purity, or quality deviates from the standards of the official compendia.

"In like fashion, an adulterated device can be one which is not in compliance with a performance standard, or one that isn't produced in compliance with GMPs."

State-of-the-Art Computer: "That's okay, but it's not the whole story. The FDA wants makers of drugs and devices to establish documented evidence that gives a high degree of assurance about whether a process will be consistent. It has to continuously produce the same predetermined specifications and quality characteristics in its products.

"This is what validation is all about from the FDA's perspective. And they have specific rules regarding inspection, measuring and test equipment.

"They've declared that every manufacturer has to be sure that all inspection, measuring and test equipment is suitable for its intended purposes.

"All mechanical, automated, and electronic inspection and test equipment are included in this regulation.

"The equipment must also be capable of producing valid results."
Computer Head: "I know that another regulation states that firms must prepare and maintain adequate and accurate case histories, as well as allow the FDA to have access to, copy, and verify any required records or reports. But give me more details."

Legacy Computer: "If the records and data are being managed electronically, then the FDA's guidance document called 'The Computerized Systems Used in Clinical Trials' is relevant.

"But when electronic records or electronic signatures are used to meet an FDA record or signature requirement, a legally enforceable regulation applies (21CFR Part 11).

"This law forces firms to guarantee that their computerized systems provide the same degree of confidence as their paper documents."

State-of-the-Art Computer: "But you left something out. This means that the documents should be
* Attributable (Revealing who authored or changed them)
* Legible (Easily readable)
* Contemporaneous (creation, change, and identification of handler are processed simultaneously)."

Legacy Computer: "I left it out because you interrupted me.

"Anyway, it should go without saying that the FDA demands access to <u>original</u> and <u>accurate</u> documents, whether they are electronic or on paper."

Legacy Computer contacted his henchman: "Well, it's time to do something bad to this double-crosser. But we've still got to help him, so we can appear to be on his side. That way he won't be so likely to suspect us!"

Hiding his urge for revenge, he turned to Computer Head: "So, we're going to move forward?"

Computer Head: "Yes. Now that we've discussed Regulations, I still need a lot more information."

Then Computer Head pulled State-of-the-Art Computer aside and talked secretly: "I'm kind of scared of Legacy Computer!"

"Computer Head, don't worry about that 'has-been!'

"I'm going to introduce the 3$^{rd}$ topic on your outline:"

PERSONNEL RESPONSIBLE FOR COMPUTER VALIDATION

Computer Head: "So tell me—who is responsible for system validation?"

State-of-the-Art Computer: "The burden of the computer validation process falls on the user, the developer, and the quality assurance personnel."

It's up to the <u>user</u> to delineate the objectives of the system. The user also makes sure that it's tested properly before it reaches the environment in which it's supposed to be operated.

This is who makes certain that the system is used by properly trained personnel that follow strict computer and data security measures.

Routine inspection of computer output and operational effectiveness also fall in the user's domain of responsibility.

Legacy Computer:  "Henchmen... it's time to begin our secret attack on Cutting Edge Pharmaceutical's operations. Guess how?"

Legacy Henchman 1: "What do you want us to teach them?"
Legacy Henchman 3: "I think we should train them to share passwords."
Legacy Henchman 2: "Yeah, and we could teach them to leave their systems on without logging off their user names."

After some time, Computer Head began to see big problems in the area of system security. And some of these came to the attention of internal auditors.

Computer Head: "But we've been training them on proper procedures!"

Then he was told to fix the problem-- or else. He turned to State-of-the-Art Computer for help.

State-of-the-Art Computer: "My system checks show that the correct SOPs for computer and data security have been substituted with incorrect ones. I'm sure that Legacy Computer is behind it. I'll get together with my high-tech reinforcements to fix the problem."

Computer Head: "Thanks."

Computer Head asked Legacy Computer if he knew anything about how the computer & data training SOPs were changed.

Legacy Computer: "Er, uh.... No... I have no idea what you're talking about. Man, you're paranoid!"

So, Computer Head had no choice but to go back to State-of-the-Art to see if he had corrected the problem.

State-of-the-Art Computer: "Yes, the correct SOP's are back in the system again."

Computer Head: "Great! Retrain all the employees, so we can move on."

State-of-the-Art Computer: "Consider it done!"

Legacy Computer: "Hey, Computer Head! I'm glad you worked out your problem. Just between us, I think that State-of-the-Art Computer was trying to sabotage you. I know he probably said it was me, huh?

"But just to prove that I'm still on your side, here's another tip for you: When it comes to making certain that the computer system is developed, tested, and given the correct support, it's the <u>developer</u> that has the responsibility.

"This person or group must base its task on accepted development and change control procedures.

"They must follow an approved methodology in their development and—of course—they must document this process as required."

Computer Head: "Hey! I know this one—Quality Assurance personnel work to give a firm's management the assurance that proper validation procedures and policies have been established and maintained for the entire life of the relevant computer system."

State-of-the-Art Computer: "But they don't actually do any real validation of the hardware or software itself. To achieve this, they manage the tasks of inspection and follow-up. In addition, they are in charge of education and training."

Computer Head: "Good, good! That puts you in the lead, State-of-the-Art Computer. Now I'm sure I understand topic number 3, 'Responsible Personnel.'"

Legacy Computer became even angrier, and he discussed with his henchmen more ways to disrupt Computer Head's operation. But they would wait for the most opportune moment to strike! And he'd give Computer Head one more chance....

"Computer Head, you're trying to double-cross me, and it won't work! I know I'll change your mind with the 4th topic on your outline:"

HOW VALIDATION IS ACCOMPLISHED

Computer Head: "How exactly does a company achieve validation?"

Legacy Computer: "There isn't any single way to accomplish validation. But, in general, there are nine basic issues to review in the process."

State-of-the-Art Computer: "Any computer worth its motherboard also would have said that flexibility is part of any technology-based procedures, since change is a constant."

Legacy Computer: "Yeah, yeah, yeah. Say what you want. But, any system development methodology or new approach should facilitate data integrity, accuracy, and reliability."

Computer Head: "Can you list the basic issues of the validation process?"

State-of-the-Art Computer: "Here they are:
    A. Requirements
    B. Design
    C. Testing
    D. Operation
    E. Security
    F. Change Control
    G. Maintenance
    H. Record Retention
    I. Periodic Review"

Review Question: That was a mouthful-- er, uh, a monitor full. See if you can remember a few: Which of the following is NOT a main item of the validation process?
A. Testing
B. Security
C. Change Control
D. Grooming
Answer: D.

Legacy Computer: "<u>Requirements</u> define what the system should do. The requirements for a system should be detailed and reflect how the system will be used, who will use it, and where the system will be located."

State-of-the-Art Computer: "But more importantly, with the <u>design</u> issue, the developer of the system creates a design based on the functional requirements.

"The developer has to deliver a document containing specific items.

"Some them include: a system overview, screen designs, report layouts, data descriptions, system configuration, file structure, and module design."

Legacy Henchman 1: "Here's an important issue: <u>testing</u>.

"It must be done to challenge the computer system's functioning at different levels of the development process. This has to be structured according to the developer's predetermined test plan and expected results."

Legacy Henchman 2: "All levels of performance must be tested. These can include: implementation (or coding), integration, installation, and acceptance."

Computer Head: "What about operation?"

State-of-the-Art Reinforcement 1: "As the system goes into on-line use after being approved, the validation process goes into the operational phase.

"Once the system is accepted and online, the operational phase begins and assures that the system is operating as designed through routine assessments and according to SOPs (standard operating procedures)."

State-of-the-Art Reinforcement 2: "Of course, <u>security</u> is one of the biggest deals. A computer system is virtually worthless without comprehensive and effective security policies. The information and data shape the product and the profits."

State-of-the-Art Reinforcement 3: "Also, regulatory and legal requirements dictate the imperative execution of strict security measures for computer systems. These measures can be physical (as in the case of locks and restricting access to the equipment)."

Legacy Henchman 4: "Software measures are also used to create passwords, create bar codes (or other pattern recognition devices), and divide access on a "need-to-know" basis per job responsibility. Screen access controls and anti virus software are also part of software security."

State-of-the-Art Reinforcement 4: "Another large issue is <u>change control</u>: There must be standard operating procedures (SOPs) that force the documentation, testing, and acceptance of any and all modifications to the system.

"This includes hardware and software changes."

<u>Review Question:</u> When it comes to the CHANGE CONTROL issue of validation, which of the following is NOT true?

There must be standard operating procedures (SOPs) that force the documentation, testing, and acceptance of any and all modifications to the system.
Both hardware and software changes fall under the regulations. Only hardware is involved, since software isn't usually changed.
Answer: C.

State-of-the-Art Computer: "<u>Maintenance</u> is an important consideration. Another SOP needs to exist which compels personnel to document any maintenance conducted on system hardware. The records must show what the problem was, as well as whatever correct actions or follow-up were taken."

Legacy Computer: "But <u>record retention</u> is just as important to auditors. A policy must be developed and put in place that deals with the retention of records. It must detail what documents should be kept, the exact location, and the duration of the retention.

State-of-the-Art Reinforcement 6: "For FDA-regulated validation, the documents involving system development and maintenance need to be kept five years after the system's life has been terminated."

Computer Head: "What about Periodic Review?"

Legacy Henchman 5: "The computer output and system performance need to be reviewed on a routine basis. At regular intervals, an experienced person must examine the output for completeness, reasonableness, and print quality."

State-of-the-Art Reinforcement 5: "Periodic evaluations of the overall performance should be done, so as to set up and maintain faith in the system's performance capabilities."

Review Question: So are you remembering all of this stuff? I'm going to check: Which of the following is NOT true about records retention policy in regards to computer validation?
It must detail the weekly schedules of all workers.
It must be developed and put in place to deal with the archival maintenance of records.
It must detail what documents should be kept, the exact location, and the duration of the retention.
Answer: A.

Legacy Computer: "Henchmen... the wait's over. It's time to do some more damage to Cutting Edge Pharmaceutical's validation status. Suggestions?"

Legacy Henchman 1: "Let's block them from testing all levels of performance. Without complete testing-- and documentation-- they'll fail any audit! Whoo-hoo!"

Legacy Henchman 3: "Yeah. I'll work on deleting implementation and coding tests from their procedures. Yippee!"

Legacy Henchman 2: "And I'll mess up the integration, installation, and acceptance tests! Ha-ha-ha!"

It wasn't long before another internal audit showed that the majority of system tests would fail an FDA compliance audit. The bosses threatened to fire Computer Head if he didn't stay on top of things.

Computer Head: "I don't understand. We've gone over this... so many times!"

Once again, he turned to State-of-the-Art Computer for assistance.

State-of-the-Art Computer: "It looks as if someone has deleted some important performance levels from your testing procedures. Only Legacy Computer and his henchmen could be capable of something as extensive as this. I'll work hard with my high-tech reinforcements to fix the problem."

Computer Head: "I owe you, big time!"

Once again, Computer Head asked Legacy Computer about the apparent sabotage to the systems test procedures.

Legacy Computer: "Uh... you've got the wrong guy. You should be interrogating State-of-the-Art Computer. His software bugs were probably the motive for this."

Computer Head went back to State-of-the-Art for resolution confirmation.

State-of-the-Art Computer: "It's done. Everything's back in compliance."

Computer Head: "All right! We'll need to patrol the systems everyday. But for now, let's move on."

State-of-the-Art Computer: "We'll be on the job, 24-7 (24 hrs/day, 7 days/week)!"

Now, Legacy Computer actually had the nerve to pull Computer Head aside and pressure him about who would get first place in the computer implementation competition.

Computer Head: "I think I'm still leaning toward State-of-the-Art Computer."

State-of-the-Art Computer: "Great!"

Legacy Computer: "No way! You can't do this me!"
Computer Head: "Well, we're not completely done yet. Maybe you'll have a chance to catch up."

The meanest Legacy Henchman began to growl and grind its hard drives!

Legacy Computer: "Calm down, Henchman #6, we'll still get them! Since we've finished item 4 of Computer Head's outline, we're going to beat the state-of-the-art systems on item number 5:"

EXAMPLES OF REGULATORY PROBLEMS

Computer Head: "According to the FDA's expectations, a company must maintain proper documentation for their computer systems. What else is true?"

Legacy Henchman 3: "Automated system documents must be accurate, complete, and satisfactory to demonstrate correct performance."

Legacy Henchman 4: "Without the proper documentation, the FDA will not consider the systems to be validated."

Legacy Henchman 5: "They can--and will--write warning letters, impose legal sanctions, or disapprove NDAs (New Drug or Device Applications)."

State-of-the-Art Reinforcement 6: "But more importantly, here are some examples of documentation problems related to the computer validation process:

Failure to:

- Clearly state objectives or test methods
- Define record format, content, and retention
- Cite protocols or required tests
- Require double-checking of key data and reports for accuracy
- Require approval signatures by two or more responsible persons
- Identify each record which must be prepared and/or approved
- Provide for exception reporting
- Define what each approving signature means
- Specify excessive limits
- Perform input-output checks at proper places or times
- Provide for conditional approvals and actions to be taken if some tests do not meet acceptance criteria."

State-of-the-Art Reinforcement 5: "And here are more noncompliance issues:
- Criteria or specifications that lack measurable parameters
- Lack of defined responsibilities and mechanisms for approval, including independent approval by the QC unit."

Legacy Computer: "Henchmen... this is a good time to attack that double-crosser again. What do think we should do now?"

Legacy Henchman 4: "I'll make them fail to specify excessive limits. Then I'll make them fail to perform input-output checks at proper places or times. Ya-hoooo!"

Legacy Henchman 5: "I'll make sure that they don't define record format, content, and retention. I'll also block them from citing protocols or required tests. Oh, yeah!"

Legacy Henchman 6: "But I'll really screw them up by creating a lack of defined responsibilities and mechanisms for approval, including independent approval by the QC unit. Ho-ho!"

Just before the FDA audit, State-of-the-Art Computer and his reinforcements detected the systems tampering. Each non-compliance issue was secretly fixed before becoming a problem. And, although no one had proof of Legacy Computer's involvement, State-of-the-Art Computer and his high-tech reinforcements knew who was behind the damage. They told Computer Head.

Computer Head: "Thanks, again, State-of-the-Art."

They both tried to figure out how to dump the dangerous Legacy Computer systems. But after looking at FDA documents, they realized that only a slow replacement process would be possible, or else they wouldn't be able to go on manufacturing the products without breaking compliance continuity.

So they both agreed that they MUST keep Legacy Computer and his henchmen implemented-- and functioning happily-- during the slow and gradual equipment phase-out process.

Computer Head: "So we'll be strong and wait it out, State-of-the-Art Computer."

Legacy Computer: "What are you guys talking about behind my back?"

State-of-the-Art Computer: "Er, uh, nothing!"

Computer Head: "That's right, Legacy Computer.  Nothing!"
Legacy Computer: "So, since you're giving State-of-the-Art Computer so much credit, let him handle the next topic."

State-of-the-Art Computer: "I'll gladly tackle the next topic! We've seen enough examples of regulatory problems (outline item 5) for the moment.

"Now let me show you a chart detailing which sections of GLP and GMP regulations apply (directly or indirectly) to the process of computer validation."

| GLP | GMP | ISSUE COVERED |
| --- | --- | --- |
| 58.130 | | Standard Conduct |
| 58.190/58.195 | 211.180 | Record Retention |
| 58.29 | 211.25 | Personnel |
| 58.32 | | Testing-Facility |
| Management | | |
| 58.35 | | Quality Assurance Unit |
| 58.41 | 211.42 | Building/Facility |
| 58.61 | 211.63 | Equipment Design |
| 58.63 | 211.68 | Equipment Maintenance |
| 58.81 | 211.100 | SOPs |

Computer Head: "Excellent work, State-of-the-Art Computer! It looks like you get the job."

Legacy Computer: "You're not going to scrap us, are you?"

Computer Head: "Not yet. Until we make the complete transition, I need to keep you legacy systems around. But the day is coming, I assure you."

Legacy Computer growled again, and spoke where only his henchmen could hear. "Then we'll make sure that THAT day is the day he loses his job too! And, until it happens, we'll throw a wrench in every plan he makes!"

EPILOGUE

Eventually, Head of Computer Jim Gullible's alter ego (Computer Head) won him the praise of Cutting Edge Pharmaceutical, Inc. executives, as well as that of computer validation auditors from the FDA.

But from that day on, Legacy Computer would be a thorn in his side. It would be up to State-of-the-Art Computer and his reinforcement systems to protect the vulnerable Computer Head for the rest of his career!

State-of-the-Art Computer: "Don't fret, Jim Gullible... er, uh, 'Computer Head!'

"I and the other State-of-the-Art Computer Systems have 'got your back!'

"And here are some very helpful documents to keep you on top of things:"

FURTHER READING

FDA DOCUMENTS:

Software Development Activities, 1987.
Guideline for the Monitoring of Clinical Investigations, 1988.

Glossary of Computerized System and Software Development
Terminology, 1995.
Guidance for Industry: Good Target Animal Practices: Clinical
Investigators and Monitors, 1997.

21 CFR Part 11, Electronic Records; Electronic Signatures;
Final Rule. Federal Register Vol. 62, No. 54, 13429, March 20,
1997.

Compliance Program Guidance Manual, "Compliance Program
7348.810 - Sponsors, Contract Research Organizations and
Monitors," October 30, 1998.

Compliance Program Guidance Manual, "Compliance Program
7348.811 - Bioresearch Monitoring - Clinical Investigators,"
September 2, 1998.

Information Sheets for Institutional Review Boards and Clinical
Investigators, 1998.

Guidance for Industry: General Principles of Software
Validation, draft 1997.

Also:  (Non-FDA) International Conference on Harmonisation,
Good Clinical Practice: Consolidated Guideline, Federal
Register Vol 62, No. 90, 25711, May 9, 1997.

GUIDANCE FOR INDUSTRY

# GENERAL PRINCIPLES OF SOFTWARE VALIDATION

DRAFT GUIDANCE
Version 1.1

This guidance is being distributed for comment purposes only.

Draft released for comment on: June 9, 1997

Comments and suggestions regarding this draft document should be submitted by October 1, 1997 to the Dockets Management Branch (HFA-305), Food and Drug Administration, Room 146, 12420 Parklawn Drive, Rockville, Maryland 20857. For questions regarding this draft document, contact Stewart Crumpler, Office of Compliance, CDRH, 2098 Gaither Road, Rockville, Maryland 20850, Phone: (301) 594-4659, FAX: (301) 594-4672, E-mail: ESC@CDRH.FDA.GOV

U.S. Department of Health and Human Services
Food and Drug Administration
Center for Devices and RadiologicalHealth

June 1, 1997

PREFACE

As of June 1, 1997, the medical device quality system regulation is effective, including requirements for implementing design controls. Those design controls include requirements for validation of software used in medical devices. Further, the quality system regulation continues the requirement that when software is used to automate a production process or a part of the quality system, that software must be validated for its intended use. Both medical device manufacturers and FDA staff have requested further guidance regarding the meaning of these requirements, and what is needed to comply with them. The attached draft guidance on "General Principles of Software Validation" was developed in response to these requests, and is provided for your review and comment.

The subject of software validation can be very complex, and no single document is likely to provide all the information needed for every manufacturer in every circumstance. Manufacturers have wide latitude in choosing which particular techniques will be combined into their software validation program. This draft guidance is intended as a general overview of software validation principles, and as a beginning point for use in evaluating software validation programs.

The official comment period for this draft guidance will be July 1, 1997 through October 1, 1997. We request that your comments be as specific as possible, with references to specific sections and paragraphs in the document, and with specific proposals for recommended changes. Instructions for submission of your comments appear on the title page, along with the Office of Compliance contact for any questions you may have about the document.

Thank you for your participation in the comment and review process. I am certain it will make the final guidance document more useful for all of us when it is issued.

Lillian J. Gill Director Office of Compliance Center for Devices and Radiological Health

**Table of Contents**

## I. PURPOSE

This draft guidance outlines general validation principles that the Food and Drug Administration (FDA) considers to be applicable to the validation of medical device software or the validation of software used to design, develop or manufacture medical devices.

## II. SCOPE

### A. Applicability

This draft guidance is applicable to all medical device software, including blood establishment software, and to software used to design, develop or manufacture medical devices. This draft guidance document represents the agency's current thinking on validation of software related to medical devices. It does not create or confer any rights for or on any person and does not operate to bind FDA or the public. An alternative approach may be used if such approach satisfies the requirements of the applicable statute, regulations or both.

This document discusses how the general provisions of the Quality System Regulation apply to software and the agency's current approach to evaluating a software validation system. For example, this document lists validation elements which are acceptable to the FDA for the validation of software; however, it does not list all of the activities and tasks that must, in all instances, be used to comply with the law.

This document does not recommend any specific life cycle model or any specific validation technique or method, but does recommend that software validation activities be conducted throughout the entire software life cycle. For each software project, the responsible party should determine and justify the level of validation effort to be applied, and the specific combination of validation techniques to be used.

This document is based on generally recognized software validation principles and could therefore be applicable to any software. For FDA purposes, this draft guidance is applicable to any software related to a regulated medical device as defined by Section 201(h) of the Federal Food, Drug, and Cosmetic Act (Act) and by current FDA software and regulatory policy. It is not the intent of this document to determine or identify specifically which software is or is not regulated.

## B. Audience

The FDA intends this draft guidance to provide useful information and recommendations to the following individuals:

> Persons subject to the Medical Device Quality System Regulation
>
> Persons responsible for the design, development or production of medical device software
>
> Persons responsible for the design, development, production or procurement of automated tools used for the design, development or manufacture of medical devices, or software tools used to implement the quality system itself
>
> FDA Scientific Reviewers
>
> FDA Investigators
>
> FDA Compliance Officers

## C. Quality System Regulations for Software Validation

Software validation is a requirement of the Quality System Regulation, 21 CFR Part 820, which was published in the Federal Register (61 FR 52602) on October 7, 1996, and takes effect on June 1, 1997. Validation requirements apply to software used in medical devices, to software that is itself a medical device (e.g., software used in blood establishments), as well as to software used in production of the device or in implementation of the device manufacturer's quality system.

Unless specifically exempted in a classification regulation, all medical device software developed after June 1, 1997, regardless of its device class, is subject to applicable design control provisions of 21 CFR 820.30. This includes completion of current development projects, all new development projects, and all changes made to existing medical device software. Specific requirements for validation of device software are found in 21 CFR 820.30(g). In addition, formal design reviews and software verification are integral parts of an overall software validation, as required by 21 CFR 820.30(e) and (f).

Any software used to automate any part of the device production process or any part of the quality system must be validated for its intended use, as required by 21 CFR 820.70(i). This requirement applies to any software used to automate device design, testing, component acceptance, manufacturing, labeling, packaging, distribution, complaint handling, or to automate any other aspect of the quality system. Such software may be developed in-house or under contract, but it is most likely to be purchased off-the-shelf for a particular intended use. This off-the-shelf software may have many capabilities, only a few of which are needed by the device manufacturer. The software must be validated for those specific uses for which it is intended. All production and/or quality system software must have documented requirements which fully define its intended use, and against which testing results and other verification evidence can be compared, to show that the production and/or quality system software is validated for its intended use.

## D. Quality System Regulation vs Pre-Market Submissions

This document addresses Quality System Regulation issues; specifically, the implementation of software validation. It provides guidance for the management and control of the software validation process. Although software validation is required for automated processes, requirements for process validation are not addressed in this document.

Manufacturers may use the same procedures and records for compliance with quality system and design control requirements, as well as for pre-market submissions to FDA. It is not the intent of this document to cover any specific safety or efficacy issues related to software validation. Design issues and documentation requirements for pre-market submissions of regulated software are not addressed by this document. Specific design issues related to safety and efficacy, and the documentation required in pre-market submissions, are addressed by the

Office of Device Evaluation (ODE), Center for Devices and Radiological Health (CDRH) or by the Office of Blood Research and Review, Center for Biologics Evaluation and Research (CBER). See the bibliography for reference to applicable guidance documents for premarket submissions.

## III. DISCUSSION

Many people have asked for specific guidance on what FDA expects them to do to assure compliance with the Quality System Regulation with regard to software validation. Information on software validation presented in this document is not new. Validation of software using the principles and tasks listed in Sections IV and V has been conducted industry-wide for well over 20 years.

FDA recognizes that, because of the great variety of medical devices, processes, and manufacturing facilities, it is not possible to state in one document all of the specific validation elements that are applicable. Several broad concepts, however, have general applicability which persons can use successfully as a guide to software validation. These broad concepts provide an acceptable framework for building a comprehensive approach to software validation. Additional specific information is available from many of the references listed in the bibliography.

### A. Software is Different from Hardware

While software shares many of the same engineering tasks as hardware, it is different. The quality of a hardware product is highly dependent on design, development and manufacture, whereas the quality of a software product is highly dependent on design and development with a minimum concern for software manufacture. Software manufacturing consists of reproduction which can be easily verified. For software, the hardest part is not manufacturing thousands of programs that work alike; it is getting just one program that works to design specifications. The vast majority of software problems are traceable to errors made during the design and development process.

Unlike hardware, software components are rarely standardized. While object oriented development holds promise for reuse of software, it requires a significant up front investment of resources to define and develop reusable software code. Many of the available object oriented development tools and techniques have not yet been adopted for medical device applications.

One of the most significant features of software is branching -- its ability to execute alternative series of commands, based on differing inputs. This feature is a major contributing factor for another characteristic of software -- its complexity. Even short programs can be very complex and difficult to fully understand.

Typically, testing alone cannot fully verify that software is complete and correct. In addition to testing, other verification techniques and a structured and documented development process should be combined to assure a comprehensive validation approach.

Unlike hardware, software is not a physical entity and does not wear out. In fact, software may improve with age, as latent defects are discovered and removed. Again, unlike hardware failures, software failures occur without advanced warning. The software's branching, which allows it to follow differing paths during execution, can result in additional latent defects being discovered long after a software product has been introduced into the marketplace.

Another related characteristic of software is the speed and ease with which it can be changed. This factor can lead both software and non-software professionals to the false impression that software problems can be easily corrected. Combined with a lack of understanding of software, it can lead engineering managers to believe that tightly controlled engineering is not as much needed for software as for hardware. In fact, the opposite is true. Because of its complexity, the development process for software should be even more tightly controlled than for hardware, in order to prevent problems which cannot be easily detected later in the development process.

Repairs made to correct software defects, in fact, establish a new design. Seemingly insignificant changes in software code can create unexpected and very significant problems elsewhere in the software program.

### B. Benefits of Software Validation

Software validation is a critical tool in assuring product quality for device software and for software automated operations. Software validation can increase the usability and reliability of the device, resulting in decreased failure rates, fewer recalls and corrective actions, less risk to patients and users, and reduced liability to manufacturers. Software validation can also reduce long term costs by making it easier and less costly to reliably modify software and revalidate software changes. Software maintenance represents as much as 50% of the total cost of software. An established comprehensive software validation process helps to reduce the long term software cost by reducing the cost of each subsequent software validation.

## C. Definitions and Terminology

Some commonly used terminology in the software industry can be confusing when compared to definitions of validation and verification found in the medical device Quality System Regulation. For example, many software engineering journal articles and textbooks use the terms "verification" and "validation" interchangeably, or in some cases refer to software "verification, validation and testing (VV&T)" as if it is a single concept, with no distinction among the three terms. For purposes of this guidance and for compliance with the Quality System Regulation, FDA considers "testing" to be one of several "verification" techniques, and considers "validation" to be the umbrella term that encompasses both verification and testing. Unless otherwise specified herein, all other terms are as defined in the current edition of the FDA "Glossary of Computerized System and Software Development Terminology."

Verification is defined in 21 CFR 820.3(aa) as "confirmation by examination and provision of objective evidence that specified requirements have been fulfilled." In a software development environment, software verification is confirmation that the output of a particular phase of development meets all of the input requirements for that phase. Software testing is one of several verification activities, intended to confirm that software development output meets its input requirements. Other verification activities include walkthroughs, various static and dynamic analyses, code and document inspections, both informal and formal (design) reviews and other techniques.

For purposes of this guidance, a working definition of software validation is "establishing by objective evidence that all software requirements have been implemented correctly and completely and are traceable to system requirements" [Ref: NIST 500-234]. Software validation is essentially a design verification function as defined in 21 CFR 820.3(aa) and 820.30(f), and includes all of the verification and testing activities conducted throughout the software life cycle. Design validation encompasses software validation, but goes further to check for proper operation of the software in its intended use environment. For example, both alpha and beta testing of device software in a simulated or real use environment, and acceptance testing of an automated testing tool by a device manufacturer, may be included as components of an overall design validation program for a software automated device.

The Quality System Regulation [21 CFR 820.3(k)] defines "establish" to mean "define, document and implement." Where it appears in this guidance, the word "establish" should be interpreted to have this same meaning.

## IV. PRINCIPLES OF SOFTWARE VALIDATION

This section lists the general validation principles that FDA considers to be applicable to both the validation of medical device software and the validation of software used to design, develop or manufacture medical devices.

### A. Timing

Proper software validation is not a one time event. Software validation should begin when design planning and design input begin. The software validation process should continue for the entire software life cycle. The software validation effort may pause with the release of each new version, but the software validation process does not end until the software product is no longer used.

### B. Management

Software cannot be properly validated without an established software life cycle. Proper validation of software includes the planning, execution, analysis, and documentation of appropriate validation activities and tasks (including testing or other verification) throughout the entire software life cycle.

### C. Plans

Established design and development plans should include a specific plan for how the software validation process will be controlled and executed.

### D. Procedures

Validation tasks should be conducted in accordance with established procedures.

## E. Requirements

To validate software, there must be predetermined and documented software requirements specifications [Ref: 21 CFR 820.3(z) and (aa) and 820.30(f) and (g)].

## F. Testing

Software verification includes both static (paper review) and dynamic techniques. Dynamic analysis (i.e., testing) is concerned with demonstrating the software's run-time behavior in response to selected inputs and conditions. Due to the complexity of software, dynamic analysis alone may be insufficient to show that the software is correct, fully functional and free of avoidable defects. Therefore, static approaches and methods are used to offset this crucial limitation of dynamic analysis. Dynamic analysis is a necessary part of software verification, but static evaluation techniques such as inspections, analyses, walkthroughs, design reviews, etc., may be more effective in finding, correcting and preventing problems at an earlier stage of the development process. These static techniques can and should be used to focus or augment dynamic analysis.

Software test plans, test procedures and test cases should be developed as early in the software life cycle as possible. Such discipline helps to assure testability of requirements specifications and design specifications, and provides useful feedback regarding those specifications at a time when changes can be implemented most easily and cost effectively.

## G. Partial Validation

Software cannot be partially validated. When a change is made to a software system (even a small change), the validation status of the entire software system should be addressed, and not just the validation of the individual change. Retrospective validation and reverse engineering of existing software is very difficult, but may be necessary in order to properly document and validate changes made to previously unvalidated software.

## H. Amount of Effort

The magnitude of the software validation effort should be commensurate with the risk associated with the device, the device's dependence on software for potentially hazardous or critical functions, and the role of specific software modules in higher risk device functions. For example, while all software modules should be validated, those modules which are safety critical should be subject to more thorough and detailed inspections of software requirements specifications, software design specifications and test cases.

Likewise, size and complexity of the software project is an important factor in establishing the appropriate level of effort and associated documentation for the software. The larger the project and staff involved, the greater the need for formal communication, more extensive written procedures and management control of the process. However, small firm size is not a proper justification for inadequately staffing, controlling, or documenting the development and validation effort for a complex software project.

## I. Independence

Validation activities should be conducted using the basic quality assurance precept of "independence of review." Self-validation is extremely difficult; an independent review is always better. Smaller firms may need to be creative in how tasks are organized and assigned, or may need to contract for some validation activities, in order to establish independence of review.

## J. Real World

It is fully recognized that software is designed, developed, validated and regulated in a real world environment. It is understood that environments and risks cover a wide spectrum, so that each time a software validation principle is used, the implementation may be different.

Environments can include the application of software for the control of manufacturing, medical devices, design and development systems as well as quality systems. In each environment, software components from many sources may be used to create the application (e.g., in-house developed software, off-the-shelf software, contract software, shareware). In addition, software components come in many different forms (e.g., application software, operating systems, compilers, debuggers, configuration management tools and many more).

The use of software in these environments is a complex task; therefore, it is appropriate that all of the software principles be considered when designing the software validation process. The resultant software validation process should be commensurate with the risk associated with the system, device or process.

Software validation activities and tasks may be dispersed, occurring at different locations and being conducted by different organizations. However, regardless of the distribution of tasks, contractual relations, source of components, or the development environment, the device manufacturer or specification developer retains ultimate responsibility for assuring that the software is validated.

## V. SOFTWARE VALIDATION

The primary goal of software validation is to demonstrate that the completed software end product complies with established software and system requirements. The correctness and completeness of the system requirements should be addressed as part of the design validation process for the device. Software validation is the confirmation that all software requirements have been met and that all software requirements are traceable to the system requirements. Software validation is a required component of the design validation of a medical device. Whereas the software validation confirms that all software requirements have been met, the design validation goes further to confirm that the medical device itself meets user needs and intended uses.

### A. Initial Validation Considerations

The concept phase of a project may begin when someone (e.g., marketing, field engineering, or quality assurance staff) suggests that a new automated function is needed for a medical device or a piece of manufacturing or quality system equipment, or that a software change is needed to correct a problem or enhance a software function. This suggestion is explored sufficiently to allow management to decide whether to authorize its full development or procurement. One or more staff may be assigned to consider and document the project, its purpose, anticipated users, intended use environments, system needs, and the anticipated role of software. The concept may include basic system elements, sequence of operations, constraints and risks associated with development of the software, and performance requirements for the system.

Once the concept is completed and documented, the results of the concept phase becomes an important design input for the software requirements specification. While not required by the Quality System Regulation, it is recommended that sources of input information developed during the concept phase be documented, for later reference when developing specific requirements. The concept may or may not be completed before proceeding to the requirements or preliminary design activities. However, by carefully and thoughtfully initiating the software project, it will be less likely that major requirements will be missed in later phases. For example, early decisions, such as whether to contract for software development, to use an off-the-shelf software product, or to develop software in-house, will have significant implications for later validation of that software.

The following is a list of preliminary questions and considerations:

What software quality factors (e.g., reliability, maintainability, usability, etc.) are important to the validation process and how will those factors be evaluated?

Are there enough staff and facilities resources to conduct the validation?

What part will the hazard management function play in the software validation process?

How will off-the-shelf (OTS) software be validated? What are the specific requirements for use of the OTS software? What are the risks and benefits of OTS versus contracted or in-house developed software? What information (description of the software quality assurance program, validation techniques, documentation of validation, "bug lists", etc.) is available from the OTS vendor to help in validating use of the software in the device, or to produce the device? Will the OTS vendor allow an audit of their validation activities? Is the OTS software suitable for its intended use, given the availability of necessary validation information? What level of black-box testing is required to demonstrate that the OTS software is suitable for its intended use? What impact will these factors have on contract negotiations and vendor selection?

How will contracted software be validated? In addition to the issues above for OTS software, who will control the source code and documentation, and what role will the contractor play in validation of the contracted software.

For an OTS software automated process or quality system function, will the output of the process or function be fully verified in every case against specifications? If so, the process or function is not dependent upon proper operation of the software and "verification by output" may be sufficient. However, if the output will not be fully verified against the specification, then the software must be validated for its intended use [Ref: 21 CFR 820.70(i)].

What human factors need to be addressed? One of the most persistent and critical problems encountered by FDA is user error induced by overly complex or counterintuitive design. Frequently, the design of the software is a factor in such user errors. Human factors engineering should be woven into the entire design and development process, including the device design concept, requirements, analyses, and tests. Safety and usability issues should be considered when developing flowcharts, state diagrams, prototyping tools, and test plans. Also task and function analyses, hazard analyses, prototype tests and reviews, and full usability tests should be performed. Participants from the user population should be included when applying these methodologies.

## B. Software Life Cycle Activities

This guidance does not recommend the use of any specific life cycle model. Software developers should establish a software life cycle model that is appropriate for their product and organization. The life cycle model that is selected should cover the software from concept to retirement. Activities in a typical software life cycle include:

Management

Requirements

Design

Implementation (Coding)

Integration and Test

Installation

Operation and Support

Maintenance

## C. Design Reviews

Formal design review is a primary validation tool. Formal design reviews allow management to confirm that all validation goals have been achieved. Software validation should be included in design reviews. The Quality System Regulation requires that at least one formal design review be conducted during the device design process. However, it is recommended that multiple design reviews be conducted (e.g., at the end of each software life cycle activity, in preparation for proceeding to the next activity). An especially important place for a design review is at the end of the requirements activity, before significant resources have been committed to a specific design. Problems found at this point can be more easily resolved, saving time and money, and reducing the likelihood of missing a critical issue. Some of the key questions to be answered during formal design reviews include:

Have the appropriate validation tasks and expected results, outputs or products been established for each life cycle activity?

Do the validation tasks and expected results, outputs or products of each life cycle activity comply with the requirements of other life cycle activities in terms of correctness, completeness, consistency, and accuracy?

Do the validation tasks and expected results, outputs or products for each life cycle activity satisfy the standards, practices, and conventions of that activity?

Do the validation tasks and expected results, outputs or products of each life cycle activity establish a proper basis for initiating tasks for the next life cycle activity?

## D. Typical Validation Tasks

For each of the software life cycle activities, certain validation tasks are performed:

## 1. Management

During design and development planning, a software validation plan is created to identify necessary validation tasks, procedures for anomaly reporting and resolution, validation resources needed, and management review requirements including formal design reviews. A software life cycle model and associated activities should be identified, as well as validation tasks necessary for each software life cycle activity. The validation plan should include:

The specific validation tasks for each life cycle activity.

Methods and procedures for each validation task.

Criteria for initiation and completion (acceptance) of each validation task.

Inputs for each validation task.

Outputs from each validation task.

Criteria for defining and documenting outputs in terms that will allow evaluation of their conformance to input requirements.

Roles, resources and responsibilities for each validation task.

Risks and assumptions.

Management must identify and provide the appropriate validation environment and resources [Ref: 21 CFR 820.20(b)(1) and (2)]. Typically each validation task requires personnel as well as physical resources. The validation plan should identify the personnel, facility and equipment resources for each validation task. A configuration management plan should be developed that will guide and control multiple parallel development activities and assure proper communications and documentation. Controls should be implemented to assure positive and correct correspondence between all approved versions of the specifications documents, source code, object code and test suites which comprise a software system, accurate identification of the current approved versions, and appropriate access to the current approved versions during development activities.

Procedures should be created for reporting and resolving all software and validation anomalies. Management should identify the validation reports, and specify the contents, format, and responsible organizational elements for each report. Procedures should also be created for the review and approval of validation results, including the responsible organizational elements for such reviews and approvals.

*Typical Validation Tasks* - *Management*

Software Validation Plan

> Validation Tasks and Acceptance Criteria
> Validation Reporting Requirements
> Formal Design Review Requirements
> Other Validation Review Requirements

Configuration Management Plan

Resource Allocation to Conduct All Validation Activities

## 2. Requirements

A software requirements specification document should be created with a written definition of the software functions to be performed. It is not possible to validate software without predetermined and documented software requirements. Typical software requirements specify the following:

All inputs that the software system will receive.

All outputs that the software system will produce..

All functions that the software system will perform.

All performance requirements that the software will meet, e.g., data throughput, reliability, timing, etc.

The definition of all internal, external and user interfaces.

What constitutes an error and how errors should be handled.

The intended operating environment for the software, e.g., hardware platform, operating system, etc., (if this is a design constraint).

All safety requirements, features or functions that will be implemented in software.

All ranges, limits, defaults and specific values that the software will accept.

Safety requirements should be commensurate with the hazards that can result from a system failure. The identification of the system safety requirements should include a software hazard analysis (e.g., software failure mode, effects and criticality analysis (SFMECA) and/or software fault tree analysis (SFTA)). The failure modes of the software should be identified, as well as their consequences. This analysis should identify all possible system failures that could result from software failures. From this analysis, it should be possible to identify what measures need to be taken to prevent catastrophic and other failures.

The Quality System Regulation [21 CFR 820.30(c)] requires a mechanism for addressing incomplete, ambiguous, or conflicting requirements. Each software requirement documented in the software requirements specification should be evaluated for accuracy, completeness, consistency, testability, correctness, and clarity. For example, software requirements should be analyzed to verify that:

> There are no internal inconsistencies among requirements.

> All of the performance requirements for the system have been spelled out.

> Fault tolerance and security requirements are complete and correct.

> Allocation of software functions is accurate and complete.

> Software requirements are appropriate for the system hazards.

> All requirements are expressed in terms that are measurable.

Assertions are executable statements incorporated into the software as fault tolerance protection for system safety and computer security objectives. All assertions (e.g., checking algorithms, logic states, system integrity checks) and all responses to unfavorable results of the assertions should be checked to verify that the operation of the assertions will not adversely impact system performance or safety.

A software requirements traceability analysis should be conducted to trace software requirements to system requirements (and vice versa). In addition, a software requirements interface analysis should be conducted, comparing the software requirements to hardware, user, operator and software interface requirements for accuracy, completeness, consistency, correctness, and clarity, and to assure that there are no external inconsistencies. In addition to any other analyses and documentation used to verify software requirements, one or more Formal Design Reviews (a.k.a. Formal Technical Reviews) should be conducted to confirm that requirements are fully specified and appropriate, before extensive software design efforts begin. Requirements can be approved and released incrementally, but care should be taken that interactions and interfaces among software (and hardware) requirements are properly reviewed, analyzed and controlled.

*Typical Validation Tasks* - *Requirements*

> Preliminary Hazard Analysis
> Traceability Analysis - System Requirements to Software Requirements (and vice versa)
> Software Requirements Evaluation
> Software Requirements Interface Analysis
> System Test Plan Generation
> Acceptance Test Plan Generation

## 3. Design

In the design phase, software requirements are translated into a logical and physical representation of the software to be implemented. To enable persons with varying levels of technical responsibilities to clearly understand design information, it may need to be presented both as a high level summary of the design, as well as a detailed design specification. The completed software design specification should constrain the programmer/coder to stay within the intent of the agreed upon requirements and design. The software design specification should be complete enough that the programmer is not required to make ad hoc design decisions.

The software design specification describes the software's logical structure, parameters to be measured or recorded, information flow, logical processing steps, control logic, data structures, error and alarm messages, security measures, and predetermined criteria for acceptance. It also describes any supporting software (e.g., operating systems, drivers, other applications), special hardware that will be needed, communication links among internal modules of the software, links with the supporting software, links with the hardware, and any other constraints not previously identified.

The software design specification may include:

> data flow diagrams
> program structure diagrams

control flow diagrams
pseudo code of the modules
context diagrams
interface/program diagrams
data and control element definitions
module definitions
module interaction diagrams

The validation activities that occur during this phase have several purposes. Software design evaluations are conducted to determine if the design is complete, correct, consistent, unambiguous, feasible and maintainable. Appropriate consideration of software architecture (e.g., modular structure) at the design phase can reduce the magnitude of future validation efforts when software changes are needed. Software design evaluations may include analyses of control flow, data flow, complexity, timing, sizing, memory allocation, and many other aspects of the design. A traceability analysis should be conducted to verify that the software design implements all of the software requirements, and that all aspects of the design are traceable to those requirements. A design interface analysis should be conducted to evaluate the proposed design with respect to hardware, user, and related software requirements. The hazard analysis should be re-examined to determine whether any additional hazards have been identified and whether any new hazards have been introduced by the design.

At the end of the design activity, a Formal Design Review should be conducted to verify that the design is correct, consistent, complete, accurate, and testable, before moving to implement the design. Elements of the design can be approved and released incrementally, but care should be taken that interactions and interfaces among various elements are properly reviewed, analyzed and controlled.

*Typical Validation Tasks - Design*

Updated Hazard Analysis
Traceability Analysis - Design Specification to Software Requirements (and vice versa)
Software Design Evaluation
Design Interface Analysis
Module Test Plan Generation
Integration Test Plan Generation Test Design Generation (module, integration, system and acceptance)

## 4. Implementation (Coding)

Implementation is the software activity where detailed design specifications are implemented as source code. This is referred to as programming or coding. Implementation is the lowest level of abstraction for the software development process and represents the last stage of the decomposition of the software requirements where module specifications are translated into a programming language. Implementation also represents the first stage of composition where the construction of the actual software code begins.

Programming usually involves the use of a high-level programming language and may also entail the use of assembly language or microcode for time-critical operations. The source code may be either compiled or interpreted for use on a target hardware platform. Decisions on selection of programming languages and software build tools (assemblers, linkers and compilers) may occur in the requirements or in the design phase of development. Such selection decisions should include consideration of the impact on subsequent validation tasks (e.g., availability of debugging and testing tools for the chosen language). Some compilers offer optional error checking commands and levels. For software validation, if the most rigorous level of error checking is not used for translation of the source code, then justification for use of the less rigorous translation error checking should be documented. Also, there should be documentation of the compilation process and its outcome, including any warnings or other messages from the compiler and their resolution. Modules ready for integration and test should have documentation of compliance with translation quality policies and procedures.

Source code should be evaluated to verify its compliance with specified coding standards. Such coding standards should include conventions for clarity, style, complexity management, and commenting. Code comments should provide useful and descriptive information for a module, including expected inputs and outputs, variables referenced, expected data types, and operations to be performed. Source code should also be evaluated to verify its compliance with the corresponding detailed design specifications. Source code evaluations are often implemented as code inspections and code walkthroughs. Small firms may employ desk checking with appropriate controls to assure consistency and independence. Source code evaluations should be extended to verification of internal interfaces between modules and layers [horizontal and vertical interfaces] and compliance with their design specifications. Appropriate documentation of the performance of source code evaluations should be maintained as part of the validation information.

During implementation, both static and dynamic, informal and formal, testing methods may be employed. The static methods include the code evaluations described above. When a source code module has passed the necessary static code evaluations, then dynamic analyses of the module begins. Initially, dynamic testing may be informal as the programmer refines a module's code to conform to the specifications. However, because module testing is an essential element of software validation the firm's procedures should clearly define when module testing begins and who is to conduct module testing. If the programmer is responsible for module testing, then the procedures should clearly differentiate between the programmer's informal testing conducted to implement the module, and the dynamic testing conducted as part of validation.

A source code traceability analysis is an important tool for verifying that all code is linked to established specifications and established test procedures. A source code traceability analysis should be conducted and documented to:

> verify that each element of the software design specification has been implemented in code
>
> verify that modules and functions implemented in code can be traced back to an element in the software design specification
>
> verify that tests for modules and functions can be traced back to an element in the software design specification
>
> verify that tests for modules and functions can be traced to source code for the same modules and functions

*Typical Validation Tasks - Implementation*

Traceability Analyses
    Source Code to Design Specifications and Vice Versa
    Test Cases to Source Code and to Design Specifications
Source Code and Source Code Documentation
Source Code Interface Analysis
Test Procedure and Test Case Generation (module, integration, system and acceptance)


**5. Integration and Test**

This aspect of software validation is closely coupled with the prior validation activities. In fact, effective testing activities overlap with other software development activities. Software testing objectives include demonstration of compliance with all software specifications, and producing evidence which provides confidence that defects which may lead to unacceptable failure conditions have been identified and removed. A software testing strategy designed to find software defects will produce far different results than a strategy designed to prove that the software works correctly. A complete software testing program uses both strategies to accomplish these objectives.

As programming of the individual modules comprising a software system is completed, the modules are combined until the complete program has been assembled. This process is called integration and proceeds according to the project's integration plan. The methods which may be used range from non-incremental integration to any of those employed for incremental integration. Non-incremental integration is often used for small programs, while some form of incremental integration is typically employed for large programs. The properties of the program being assembled dictate the chosen method of integration.

PLANS: Test plans should be created during the prior software development phases. They should identify the test schedules, environments, resources [personnel, tools, etc.], methodologies, cases [inputs, procedures, outputs, expected results], documentation and reporting criteria. The test plans should be linked to each of the specification phases; e.g., requirements, design, and implementation; and correlated to the other project plans including the integration plan. Individual test cases should be definitively associated with particular specification elements and each test case should include a predetermined, explicit, and measurable expected result, derived from the specification documents, in order to identify objective success/failure criteria.

Test plans should identify the necessary levels and extent of testing, as well as clear, pre-determined acceptance criteria. The magnitude of testing should be linked to criticality, reliability, and/or safety issues. Test plans should also include criteria for determining when testing is complete. Test completion criteria should include both functional and structural coverage requirements. Each externally visible function and each internal function should be tested at least once. Each program statement should be executed at least once and each program decision should be exercised with both true and false outcomes at least once. Test completion criteria should also include measurements or estimates of the quality and/or reliability of the released software.

PERSONNEL: Sufficient personnel should be available to provide necessary independence from the programming staff, and to provide adequate knowledge of both the software application's subject matter and software/programming concerns related to testing. Small firms may use various techniques (e.g., detailed written procedures and checklists) to facilitate consistent application of intended testing activities and to simulate independence.

METHODS: The methodologies used to identify test cases should provide for thorough and rigorous examination of the software. They should challenge the intended use or functionality of a program with test cases based on the functional and performance specifications. They should also challenge the decisions made by the program with test cases based on the structure or logic of the design and source code.

Complete structural testing exercises the program's data structures; e.g., configuration tables; and its control and procedural logic at the appropriate level, and it identifies "dead" code. It assures the program's statements and decisions are fully exercised by testing; for example, confirming that program loop constructs behave as expected at their boundaries. For configurable software, the integrity of the data in configuration tables should be evaluated for its impact on program behavior. Structural testing should be done at the module, integration, and system levels of testing.

Complete functional testing includes test cases which expose program behavior not only in response to the normal case, but also in response to exceptional, stress and/or worst case conditions. As applicable, it demonstrates program behavior at the boundaries of its input and output domains; program responses to invalid, unexpected, and special inputs are confirmed; the program's actions are revealed when given combinations of inputs, unexpected sequences of inputs, or when defined timing requirements are violated. Functional test cases should be identified for application at the module, integration, and system levels of testing.

Module (a.k.a. unit or component) level testing focuses on the early examination of sub-program functionality and ensures that functionality not visible at the system level is examined by testing. Module testing should be conducted before the integration testing phase to confirm that modules meet specifications and ensure that quality modules are furnished for integration into the finished software system. The magnitude of the testing effort should be commensurate with the criticality (risk), complexity, or error prone status associated with a module. For low hazard modules, the static analyses (testing) conducted during implementation may be sufficient. However, dynamic testing (executing the code with test drivers) is usually necessary to verify the correct behavior of critical modules. For example, critical modules may be exposed to fault injection testing or other stress testing in order to characterize the behavior of the module with out-of-range or unexpected input conditions or parameters.

Integration level testing focuses on the transfer of data and control across a program's internal and external interfaces. External interfaces are those with other software including operating system software, system hardware, and the users. When a program is built using incremental integration methods, sufficient regression testing should be conducted to assure the addition of new modules has not changed the behavior of existing modules.

System level testing demonstrates that all specified functionality exists and that the software is trustworthy. This testing verifies the as-built program's functionality and performance with respect to the requirements for the software system and for the device. Test cases designed to address concerns such as robustness, stress, security, recovery, usability, etc., should be used to verify the dependability of the software. Control measures, e.g., a traceability analysis, should be used to assure that the necessary level of coverage is achieved.

System level testing also exhibits the software's behavior in the intended operating environment, and is an important aspect of design validation for the device. The location of such testing is dependent upon the software developer's ability to produce the target operating environment. Depending upon the circumstances, simulation and/or testing at (potential) customer locations may be utilized. Test plans should identify the controls to assure that the intended coverage is achieved and that proper documentation is prepared when planned system testing is conducted at sites not directly controlled by the software developer.

The quality of any software tools used during testing should be such that they do not introduce errors into the application being developed. For tools designed to find software errors, there should be evidence that they perform as intended. These tools can include supporting software built in-house to facilitate module testing and subsequent integration testing (e.g., drivers and stubs) and commercial testing tools. Appropriate documentation providing evidence of the quality of these tools should be maintained.

DOCUMENTATION: Test results [inputs, processing, outputs] should be documented in a manner permitting objective pass/fail decisions to be reached. They should be suitable for review and decision making subsequent to running the test. Test results should also be suitable for use in any subsequent regression testing. Errors detected during testing should be logged, classified, reviewed and resolved prior to release of the software. Test reports should comply with the requirements of the corresponding test plans.

*Typical Validation Tasks* - *Integration and Testing*

Traceability Analysis - Testing
    Module Tests to Detailed Design
    Integration Tests to High Level Design
    System Tests to Software Requirements
Test Evaluation
Error Evaluation/Resolution
Module Test Execution
Integration Test Execution
System Test Execution
Acceptance Test Execution
Test Results Evaluation
Final Test Report

## VI. INSTALLATION TESTING

Installation testing is an essential part of validation for a device or the validation of an automated process used in its design, manufacture, or implementation of its quality system.

Section 820.170 of the Quality System Regulation requires installation and inspection procedures (including testing where appropriate) and documentation of inspection and testing to demonstrate proper installation. Likewise, Section 820.70(g) requires that manufacturing equipment must meet specified requirements, and Section 820.70(i) requires that automated systems be validated for their intended use.

Terminology in this testing area can be confusing. Terms such as beta test, site validation, user acceptance test, and installation verification have all been used to describe installation testing. To avoid confusion, and for the purposes of this guidance, installation testing is defined as any testing that takes place outside of the developer's controlled environment. Installation testing is any testing that takes place at a user's site with the actual hardware and software that will be part of the installed system configuration. The testing is accomplished through either actual or simulated use of the software being tested within the environment in which it is intended to function.

Guidance contained here is general in nature and is applicable to any installation testing. However, in some areas, i.e. bloodbank systems, there are specific site validation requirements that need to be considered in the planning of installation testing. Test planners should check with individual FDA Centers to determine whether there are any additional regulatory requirements for installation testing.

Installation testing should follow a pre-defined plan with a formal summary of testing and a record of formal acceptance. There should be retention of documented evidence of all testing procedures, test input data and test results.

There should be evidence that hardware and software are installed and configured as specified. Measures should ensure that all system components are exercised during the testing and that the versions of these components are those specified. The testing instructions should encourage use through the full range of operating conditions and should continue for a sufficient time to allow the system to encounter a wide spectrum of conditions and events in an effort to detect any latent faults which are not apparent during more normal activities.

Some of the evaluations that have been performed earlier by the software developer at the developer's site should be repeated at the site of actual use. These may include tests for a high volume of data, heavy loads or stresses, security, fault testing (avoidance, detection, tolerance, and recovery), error messages, implementation of safety requirements, and serviceability. The developer may be able to furnish the user with some of the test data sets to be used for this purpose.

In addition to an evaluation of the system's ability to properly perform its intended functions, there should be an evaluation of the ability of the users of the system to understand and correctly interface with it. Operators should be able to perform the intended operations and respond in an appropriate and timely manner to all alarms, warnings, errors, etc.

Records should be maintained during installation testing of both the system's capability to properly perform and the system's failures, if any, which are encountered. The revision of the system to compensate for faults detected during this installation testing should follow the same procedures and controls as any other software change.

The developers of the software may or may not be involved in the installation testing. If the developers are involved, they may seamlessly carry over to the user's site the last portions of design-level systems testing. If the developers are not involved, it is all the more important that the user have persons knowledgeable in software engineering who understand the importance of such matters as careful test planning, the definition of expected test results, and the recording of all test outputs.

## VII. MAINTENANCE AND SOFTWARE CHANGES

As applied to software, the term maintenance does not mean the same as when applied to hardware. The operational maintenance of hardware and software are different because their failure/error mechanisms are different. Hardware maintenance typically includes preventive maintenance actions, component replacement, and corrective changes. Software maintenance includes corrective, perfective and adaptive changes, but does not include preventive maintenance actions or component replacement.

Changes made to correct errors and faults in the software are considered as corrective maintenance. Changes made to the software to improve the performance, maintainability, or other attribute of the software system is considered as perfective maintenance. Changes made to the software to make the software system usable in a changed environment is considered as adaptive maintenance.

All modifications, enhancements, or additions to existing software or its operating environment (corrective, perfective, or adaptive changes) are design changes, and are subject to design controls provisions of the Quality System Regulation. The regulation [21 CFR 820.30(i)] requires design validation, unless the manufacturer documents the justification of why design verification is sufficient. The validation requirements, activities and processes that are used for software maintenance actions are the same as those that are used for the development of new software. The validation activities associated with each software change should be documented as part of the record of that change.

When changes are made to a software system, either during initial development or during post release maintenance, sufficient regression testing should be conducted to demonstrate that portions of the software not involved in the change were not adversely impacted. This is in addition to testing which evaluates the correctness of the implemented change(s).

The specific validation effort necessary for each software change is determined by the type of change, the development products affected and the impact of those products on the operation of the software. Careful and complete documentation of the design structure and interrelationships of various modules, interfaces, etc., can limit the validation effort needed when a change is made. The level of effort needed for fully validate a change is also dependent upon the degree to which validation of the original software was documented and archived. For example, to perform regression testing, the test documentation, test cases and results of previous validation testing should have been archived. Failure to archive this information for later use can sharply increase the level of effort and expense of revalidating the software after a change is made.

In addition to validation tasks that are part of the standard software development process, some additional maintenance tasks include the following:

Software Validation Plan Revision - For software that was previously validated, the existing software validation plan should be revised to support the validation of the revised software. If no previous software validation plan exists, a software validation plan should be established to support the validation of the revised software.

Anomaly Evaluation - Software anomalies should be evaluated in terms of their severity and their effects on system operation and safety. Anomalies should also be evaluated as symptoms of deficiencies in the quality system. A root cause analysis of anomalies can identify specific quality system deficiencies. Where trends are identified, appropriate corrective and preventive actions, as required in Section 820.100 of the Quality System Regulation, must be implemented to avoid recurrence of similar quality problems.

Proposed Change Assessment - All proposed modifications, enhancements, or additions should be assessed to determine the effect each change would have on the system. This information should determine the extent to which validation tasks need to be iterated.

Validation Task Iteration - For approved software changes, all necessary validation tasks should be performed to ensure that planned changes are implemented correctly, all documentation is complete and up to date, and no unacceptable changes have occurred in software performance.

**Bibliography**

Food and Drug Administration References

Design Control Guidance for Medical Device Manufacturers, March 1997

Do It by Design, An Introduction to Human Factors in Medical Devices, March 1997

Glossary of Computerized System and Software Development Terminology, August 1995

Guideline on the General Principles of Process Validation, May 1987.

Medical Devices; Current Good Manufacturing Practice (CGMP) Final Rule; Quality System Regulation, 61 Federal Register 52602 (October 7, 1996).

Reviewer Guidance for Computer Controlled Medical Devices Undergoing 510(k) Review, August 1991 (now replaced by Guidance for the Content of Pre-market Submissions for Software Contained in Medical Devices)

Reviewer Guidance for a Pre-Market Notification Submission for Blood Establishment Computer Software, January 1997

Software Development Activities, Reference Materials and Training Aids for Investigators, July 1987.

Other Government References

NIST Special Publication 500-165, Software Verification and Validation: Its Role in Computer Assurance and Its Relationship with Software Project Management Standards, National Institute for Science and Technology.

NIST Special Publication 500-234, Reference Information for the Software Verification and Validation Process, National Institute for Science and Technology, March 1996.

The Application of the Principles of GLP to Computerized Systems, Environmental Monograph #116, Organization for Economic Cooperation and Development (OECD), 1995.

Standards

ANSI/ANS-10.4-1987, Guidelines for the Verification and Validation of Scientific and Engineering Computer Programs for the Nuclear Industry, American National Standards Institute, 1987.

ANSI/ASQC Standard D1160-1995, Formal Design Reviews, American Society for Quality Control, 1995.

IEEE Std 1012-1986, Software Verification and Validation Plans, Institute for Electrical and Electronics Engineers, 1986.

ANSI/ISO/ASQC Q9000-3-1991, Guidelines for the Application of ANSI/ISO/ASQC Q9001 to the Development, Supply and Maintenance of Software, American Society for Quality Control, 1991.

ISO/IEC 12207, Information Technology - Software Life Cycle Processes.

Other References

Technical Report No. 18, Validation of Computer Related Systems, PDA Journal of Pharmaceutical Science and Technology, Vol. 49, No 1/January-February, 1995.

Software Systems Engineering, A. P. Sage, J.D. Palmer: John Wiley & Sons, 1990.

Software Verification and Validation, Realistic Project Approaches, M. S. Deutsch, Prentice Hall, 1982.

The Art of Software Testing, Glenford J. Myers, John Wiley & Sons, Inc., 1979

Validation Compliance Annual 1995, International Validation Forum, Inc.

**Development Team**

The following team was assembled to prepare this DRAFT for public comment.

<u>Center for Devices and Radiological Health</u>

Office of Compliance
* Stewart Crumpler, Howard Press

Office of Device Evaluation
* Donna-Bea Tillman, James Cheng

Office of Science and Technology
* John Murray

Office of Health and Industry Programs
* Dick Sawyer, Bryan Benesch

Office of Surveillance and Biometrics
* Isaac Hantman

<u>Center for Drug Evaluation and Research</u>

* Office of Compliance                                  Charles Snipes

<u>Center for Biologics Evaluation and Branch</u>

* Office of Compliance                                  Alice Godziemski

<u>Office of Regulatory Affairs</u>

* Office of Regional Operations              David Bergeson, Joan Loreng

---

<u>160.850 Enforcement Policy: 21 CFR Part 11; Electronic Records; Electronic Signatures CPG 7153.17</u>

Office of Regulatory Affairs

COMPLIANCE POLICY GUIDE    Section 160.850

COMPLIANCE POLICY GUIDE

Section 160.850

Title: Enforcement Policy: 21 CFR Part 11; Electronic Records; Electronic Signatures (CPG 7153.17)

Background:

This compliance guidance document is an update to the Compliance Policy Guides Manual (August 1996 edition). This is a new Compliance Policy Guide (CPG) and will be included in the next printing of the Compliance Policy Guides Manual. The CPG is intended for Food and Drug Administration (FDA) personnel and is available electronically to the public. This guidance document represents the agency's current thinking on what is required to be fully compliant with 21 CFR Part 11, "Electronic Records; Electronic Signatures" and provides that agency decisions on whether or not to pursue regulatory actions will be based on a case by case evaluation. The CPG does not create or confer any rights for or on any person and does not operate to bind FDA or the public. An alternative approach may be used if such approach satisfies the requirements of the applicable statute, regulation, or both.

In the Federal Register of March 20, 1997, at 62 FR 13429, FDA issued a notice of final rulemaking for 21 CFR, Part 11, Electronic Records; Electronic Signatures. The rule went into effect on August 20, 1997. Part 11 is intended to create criteria for electronic recordkeeping technologies while preserving the agency's ability to protect and promote the public health (e.g., by facilitating timely review and approval of safe and effective new medical products, conducting efficient audits of required records, and when necessary pursuing regulatory actions). Part 11 applies to all FDA program areas, but does not mandate electronic recordkeeping. Part 11 describes the technical and procedural requirements that must be met if a person chooses to maintain records electronically and use electronic signatures. Part 11 applies to those records required by an FDA predicate rule and to signatures required by an FDA predicate rule, as well as signatures that are not required, but appear in required records.

Part 11 was developed in concert with industry over a period of six years. Virtually all of the rule's requirements had been suggested by industry comments to a July 21, 1992 Advance Notice of Proposed Rulemaking (at 57 FR 32185). In response to comments to an August 31, 1994 Proposed Rule (at 59 FR 45160) the agency refined and reduced many of the proposed requirements in order to minimize the burden of compliance. The final rule's provisions are consistent with an emerging body of federal and state law as well as commercial standards and practices.

Certain older electronic systems may not have been in full compliance with Part 11 by August 20, 1997, and modification to these so called "legacy systems" may take more time. As explained in the preamble to the final rule, Part 11 does not grandfather legacy systems and FDA expects that firms using legacy systems will begin taking steps to achieve full compliance.

Policy:

When persons are not fully compliant with Part 11, decisions on whether or not to pursue regulatory actions will be based on a case by case evaluation, which may include the following:

> Nature and extent of Part 11 deviation(s). FDA will consider Part 11 deviations to be more significant if those deviations are numerous, if the deviations make it difficult for the agency to audit or interpret data, or if the deviations undermine the integrity of the data or the electronic system. For example, FDA expects that firms will use file formats that permit the agency to make accurate and complete copies in both human readable and electronic form of audited electronic records. Similarly, FDA would have little confidence in data from firms that do not hold their employees accountable and responsible for actions taken under their electronic signatures.

> Effect on product quality and data integrity. For example, FDA would consider the absence of an audit trail to be highly significant when there are data discrepancies and when individuals deny responsibility for record entries. Similarly, lack of operational system checks to enforce event sequencing would be significant if an operator's ability to deviate from the prescribed order of manufacturing steps results in an adulterated or misbranded product.

> Adequacy and timeliness of planned corrective measures. Firms should have a reasonable timetable for promptly modifying any systems not in compliance (including legacy systems) to make them Part 11 compliant, and should be able to demonstrate

progress in implementing their timetable. FDA expects that Part 11 requirements for procedural controls will already be in place. FDA recognizes that technology based controls may take longer to install in older systems.

Compliance history of the establishment, especially with respect to data integrity. FDA will consider Part 11 deviations to be more significant if a firm has a history of Part 11 violations or of inadequate or unreliable recordkeeping. Until firms attain full compliance with Part 11, FDA investigators will exercise greater vigilance to detect inconsistencies, unauthorized modifications, poor attributability, and any other problems associated with failure to comply with Part 11.

Regulatory Action Guidance:

Program monitors and center compliance offices should be consulted prior to recommending regulatory action. FDA will consider regulatory action with respect to Part 11 when the electronic records or electronic signatures are unacceptable substitutes for paper records or handwritten signatures, and that therefore, requirements of the applicable regulations (e.g., CGMP and GLP regulations) are not met. Regulatory citations should reference such predicate regulations in addition to Part 11. The following is an example of a regulatory citation for a violation of the device quality system regulations.

> *Failure to establish and maintain procedures to control all documents that are required by 21 CFR 820.40, and failure to use authority checks to ensure that only authorized individuals can use the system and alter records, as required by 21 CFR 11.10(g). For example, engineering drawings for manufacturing equipment and devices are stored in AutoCAD form on a desktop computer. The storage device was not protected from unauthorized access and modification of the drawings.*

Issue date: 5/13/99

## Sec. 425.100 Computerized Drug Processing; CGMP Applicability To Hardware and Software* (CPG 7132a.11)

BACKGROUND:

The use of computers in the production and control of drug products is quickly increasing. Questions have been raised as to the applicability of various sections of the Current Good Manufacturing Practice Regulations to the physical devices (hardware) which constitute the computer systems and to the instructions (software) which make them function.

POLICY:

Where a computer system is performing a function covered by the CGMP regulations then, in general, hardware will be regarded as equipment and applications software1 will be regarded as records. The kind of record (e.g., standard operating procedure, master production record) that the software constitutes and the kind of equipment (e.g., process controller, laboratory instrument) that the hardware constitutes will be governed by how the hardware and software are used in the manufacture, processing, packing, or holding of the drug product. Their exact use will then be used to determine and apply the appropriate sections of the regulations that address equipment and records.

1Applications software consists of programs written to specified user requirements for the purpose of performing a designated task such as process control, laboratory analyses, and acquisition/processing/storage of information required by the CGMP regulations.

*Material between asterisks is new or revised*

Issued: 10/19/84
Revised: 9/4/87

## Sec. 425.200 Computerized Drug Processing; Vendor Responsibility (CPG 7132a.12)

BACKGROUND:

Computer systems used in the production and control of drug products can consist of various devices (hardware) and programs (software) supplied by different vendors, or in some cases by a single vendor. It is important that such computer systems perform accurately and reliably, *and* that they are suitable for their intended use.

Questions have arisen as to the vendor's responsibility in assuring computer systems performance and suitability. When an integrated system, composed of elements from several different vendors, fails, it can be especially difficult to attribute the cause of a problem to one particular vendor.

POLICY:

The end user is responsible for the suitability of computer systems (hardware and software) used in manufacture, processing or holding of a drug product.

*The vendor may also be liable, under the FD&C Act, for causing the introduction of adulterated or misbranded drug products into interstate commerce, where the causative factors for the violation are attributable to intrinsic defects in the vendor's hardware and software. In addition vendors may incur liability for validation, as well as hardware/software maintenance performed on behalf of users.*

*Material between asterisks is new or revised*

Issued: 1/18/85
Revised: 9/4/87


Sec. 425.300 Computerized Drug Processing; Source Code for Process Control Application Programs (CPG 7132a.15)


BACKGROUND:

An increasing number of pharmaceuticals are being manufactured under the control of computer systems. The manufacturing procedures, control, instructions, specifications and precautions to be followed within such automated systems are embodied in the computer program(s) which drive the computer. Depending of the complexity of the programs, they may also contain controlling data on product formulation, batch size, yields and automated in-process sampling/testing procedures. In a manual system such procedures, instructions, specifications, precautions and other controlling data would be embodied in master production records which must be reviewed and approved before implementation and which must be maintained, as required by the current good manufacturing practice regulations (CGMP's). Such manual records are, of course, prepared in human readable form.

In the case of computerized drug process control, certain information required by CGMP's to be in a master production record is contained in the source code for the application program. (An application program is software written to specified user requirements for the purpose of performing a designated task.) Source code is the human readable form of the program, written in its original (source) programming language. Source code must be compiled, assembled, or interpreted before it can be executed by a computer. Because the source code ultimately has a direct and significant bearing on drug product quality as manual master records, it is vital that source code and supporting documentation be reviewed and approved by the drug manufacturer prior to implementation, and be maintained as the CGMP's require for master production and control records. (E.g., see 21 CFR 211.100, 211.180, and 211.186.) Careful review of source code and its documentation is especially important for assuring that process specifications, conditions, sequencing, decision criteria, and formulas have been properly incorporated into the computer program; source code should also be reviewed to detect and remove dead code--non-executable instructions which are usually artifacts of earlier versions of the program.

Supportive program documentation, such as flow diagrams and explanatory narratives, can be useful in understanding and reviewing source code. However, such documentation is not an acceptable substitute for source code itself.

POLICY:

We regard source code and its supporting documentation for application programs used in drug process control to be part of master production and control records, within the meaning of 21 CFR Parts 210 and 211.

Accordingly, those sections of the current good manufacturing practice regulations which pertain to master production and control records will be applied to source code.

Issued: 4/16/87

## Sec. 425.400 Computerized Drug Processing; Input/Output Checking (CPG 7132a.07)

BACKGROUND:

Section 211.68 (automatic, mechanical, and electronic equipment) of the Current Good Manufacturing Practice Regulations requires, in part, that input to and output from the computer or related system of formulas or other records or data be checked for accuracy. This requirement has generated questions as to the need for and extent of checking a computer's input and output.

The agency received several petitions to delete or modify the requirement on the grounds that a validated computer system need not have its input/output routinely checked. The request to delete or modify the requirement was denied because our experience has shown that input/output error can occur, even in validated systems. Printouts, for example, can contain errors as a result of faulty input, programming, or equipment malfunction. More significantly, there is the human element which can induce errors. At worst, input/output errors can result in serious production errors and distribution of adulterated or misbranded products. Several recalls have, in fact, been conducted because of insufficient input/output checks.

Despite the general need for input/output checks, not all input and output need be checked. The regulation is, in fact, deliberately silent on the required frequency and extent of data checking to afford firms the necessary flexibility. Also, the use of efficient input edits, for example, could mitigate the need for more detailed manual data checks.

POLICY:

Input/Output checks of data for computer systems, as required by 21 CFR 211.68, are necessary to assure the quality of a drug product processed using such systems. The extent and frequency of input/output checking will be assessed on an individual basis, and should be determined based upon the complexity of the computer system and built in controls.

Issued: 9/20/82
Reissued: 9/4/87

## Sec. 425.500 Computerized Drug Processing; Identification of "Persons" on Batch Production and Control Records (CPG 7132a.08)

BACKGROUND:

Section 211.188(b)(11) of the Current Good Manufacturing Practice Regulations requires that batch production and control records include documentation that each significant step in the manufacture, processing, packing, or holding of a batch was accomplished, including identification of the persons performing, directly supervising or checking each significant step in the operation.

Questions have been raised as to acceptable ways of complying with this requirement when the "person" performing, supervising or checking each step is, in fact, not a human being, but rather an automated piece of equipment, such as a computer system.

The intent of the regulation is to assure that each significant step in a process was, in fact, performed properly and that there is some record to show this. It is quite possible that a computerized system can achieve the same or higher degree of assurance. In this case it may not be necessary to specifically record the checks made on each of a series of steps in the production of the product.

POLICY:

When the significant steps in the manufacturing, processing, packing or holding of a batch are performed, supervised or checked by a computerized system an acceptable means of complying with the identification requirements of 21 CFR 211.188(b)(11) would consist of conformance to all of the following:

1. Documentation that the computer program controlling step execution contains adequate checks, and documentation of the performance of the program itself.

2. Validation of the performance of the computer program controlling the execution of the steps.

3. Recording specific checks in batch production and control records of the initial step, any branching steps and the final step.

NOTE: In assessing how well a computer system checks a process step it is necessary to demonstrate that the computer system examines the same conditions that a human being would look for, and that the degree of accuracy in the examination is at least equivalent.

Issued: 11/2/82
Reissued: 9/4/87

Sec. 460.400 Computerized Prescription Recordkeeping by Pharmacies (CPG 7132b.09)

BACKGROUND:

The National Association of Boards of Pharmacy (NABP) Task Force on Innovative Pharmacy Care has recommended the use of automated systems in pharmacies to keep readily retrievable and accurate records.

POLICY:

The Food and Drug Administration regards the use of a computerized prescription recordkeeping system as satisfying the statutory requirements for prescription drug recordkeeping as set forth under Section 503(b) of the Federal Food, Drug, and Cosmetic Act, provided the system includes the following NABP recommended controls:

1. The pharmacist has control over all prescriptions, i.e. the pharmacist must be able to ascertain quantities, refills remaining, time of previous filling and other information pertinent to adequate control.

2. The pharmacist responsible for the initial fill of a prescription and any subsequent refills can be readily determined.

3. The data is readily retrievable. The system must be capable of producing a listing of transactions to meet FDA and DEA regulations.

4. All prescription transactions occurring while the automated system is inoperable must be entered into the system as soon as possible, after the system is repaired.

5. Data in computerized prescription storage systems can be and is recreated in case of need.

6. The system must provide for the confidentiality of patient information.

Issued: 10/1/80

**Guidance for Industry**

**COMPUTERIZED SYSTEMS USED IN CLINICAL TRIALS**

U.S. Department of Health and Human Services
Food and Drug Administration
Center for Biologic Evaluation and Research (CBER)
Center for Drug Evaluation and Research (CDER)
Center for Devices and Radiological Health (CDRH)
Center for Food Safety and Nutrition (CFSAN)
Center for Veterinary Medicine (CVM)
Office of Regulatory Affairs (ORA)

April 1999

**TABLE OF CONTENTS**

**GUIDANCE FOR INDUSTRY**

**COMPUTERIZED SYSTEMS USED IN CLINICAL TRIALS**

## I. INTRODUCTION

This document addresses issues pertaining to computerized systems used to create, modify, maintain, archive, retrieve, or transmit clinical data intended for submission to the Food and Drug Administration (FDA). These data form the basis for the Agency's decisions regarding the safety and efficacy of new human and animal drugs, biologics, medical devices, and certain food and color additives. As such, these data have broad public health significance and must be of the highest quality and integrity.

FDA established the Bioresearch Monitoring (BIMO) Program of inspections and audits to monitor the conduct and reporting of clinical trials to ensure that data from these trials meet the highest standards of quality and integrity and conform to FDA's regulations. FDA's acceptance of data from clinical trials for decision-making purposes is dependent upon its ability to verify the quality and integrity of such data during its onsite inspections and audits. To be acceptable the data should meet certain fundamental elements of quality whether collected or recorded electronically or on paper. Data should be attributable, original, accurate, contemporaneous, and legible. For example, attributable data can be traced to individuals responsible for observing and recording the data. In an automated system, attributability could be achieved by a computer system designed to identify individuals responsible for any input.

This guidance addresses how these elements of data quality might be satisfied where computerized systems are being used to create, modify, maintain, archive, retrieve, or transmit clinical data. Although the primary focus of this guidance is on computerized systems used at clinical sites to collect data, the principles set forth may also be appropriate for computerized systems at contract research organizations, data management centers, and sponsors. Persons using the data from computerized systems should have confidence that the data are no less reliable than data in paper form.

Computerized medical devices, diagnostic laboratory instruments and instruments in analytical laboratories that are used in clinical trials are not the focus of this guidance. This guidance does not address electronic submissions or methods of their transmission to the Agency.

This guidance document reflects long-standing regulations covering clinical trial records. It also addresses requirements of the Electronic Records/Electronic Signatures rule (21 CFR part 11).

The principles in this guidance may be applied where source documents are created (1) in hardcopy and later entered into a computerized system, (2) by direct entry by a human into a computerized system, and (3) automatically by a computerized system.

## II. DEFINITIONS

**Audit Trail** means, for the purposes of this guidance, a secure, computer generated, time-stamped electronic record that allows reconstruction of the course of events relating to the creation, modification, and deletion of an electronic record.

**Certified Copy** means a copy of original information that has been verified, as indicated by dated signature, as an exact copy having all of the same attributes and information as the original.

**Commit** means a saving action, which creates or modifies, or an action which deletes, an electronic record or portion of an electronic record. An example is pressing the key of a keyboard that causes information to be saved to durable medium.

**Computerized System** means, for the purpose of this guidance, computer hardware, software, and associated documents (e.g., user manual) that create, modify, maintain, archive, retrieve, or transmit in digital form information related to the conduct of a clinical trial.

**Direct Entry** means recording data where an electronic record is the original capture of the data. Examples are the keying by an individual of original observations into the system, or automatic recording by the system of the output of a balance that measures subject's body weight.

**Electronic Case Report Form (e-CRF)** means an auditable electronic record designed to record information required by the clinical trial protocol to be reported to the sponsor on each trial subject.

**Electronic Patient Diary** means an electronic record into which a subject participating in a clinical trial directly enters observations or directly responds to an evaluation checklist.

**Electronic Record** means any combination of text, graphics, data, audio, pictorial, or any other information representation in digital form that is created, modified, maintained, archived, retrieved, or distributed by a computer system.

**Electronic Signature** means a computer data compilation of any symbol or series of symbols, executed, adopted, or authorized by an individual to be the legally binding equivalent of the individual's handwritten signature.

**Software Validation** means confirmation by examination and provision of objective evidence that software specifications conform to user needs and intended uses, and that the particular requirements implemented through the software can be consistently fulfilled. For the purposes of this document, design level validation is that portion of the software validation that takes place in parts of the software life cycle before the software is delivered to the end user.

**Source Documents** means original documents and records including, but not limited to, hospital records, clinical and office charts, laboratory notes, memoranda, subjects' diaries or evaluation checklists, pharmacy dispensing records, recorded data from automated instruments, copies or transcriptions certified after verification as being accurate and complete, microfiches, photographic negatives, microfilm or magnetic media, x-rays, subject files, and records kept at the pharmacy, at the laboratories, and at medico-technical departments involved in the clinical trial.

**Transmit** means, for the purposes of this guidance, to transfer data within or among clinical study sites, contract research organizations, data management centers, or sponsors. Other Agency guidance covers transmission from sponsors to the Agency.

## III. GENERAL PRINCIPLES

A. Each study protocol should identify at which steps a computerized system will be used to create, modify, maintain, archive, retrieve, or transmit data.

B. For each study, documentation should identify what software and, if known, what hardware is to be used in computerized systems that create, modify, maintain, archive, retrieve, or transmit data. This documentation should be retained as part of study records.

C. Source documents should be retained to enable a reconstruction and evaluation of the trial.

D. When original observations are entered directly into a computerized system, the electronic record is the source document.

E. The design of a computerized system should ensure that all applicable regulatory requirements for recordkeeping and record retention in clinical trials are met with the same degree of confidence as is provided with paper systems.

F. Clinical investigators should retain either the original or a certified copy of all source documents sent to a sponsor or contract research organization, including query resolution correspondence.

G. Any change to a record required to be maintained should not obscure the original information. The record should clearly indicate that a change was made and clearly provide a means to locate and read the prior information.

H. Changes to data that are stored on electronic media will always require an audit trail, in accordance with 21 CFR 11.10(e). Documentation should include who made the changes, when, and why they were made.

I. The FDA may inspect all records that are intended to support submissions to the Agency, regardless of how they were created or maintained.

J. Data should be retrievable in such a fashion that all information regarding each individual subject in a study is attributable to that subject.

K. Computerized systems should be designed: (1) So that all requirements assigned to these systems in a study protocol are satisfied (e.g., data are recorded in metric units, requirements that the study be blinded); and, (2) to preclude errors in data creation, modification, maintenance, archiving, retrieval, or transmission.

Security measures should be in place to prevent unauthorized access to the data and to the computerized system.

## IV. STANDARD OPERATING PROCEDURES

Standard Operating Procedures (SOPs) pertinent to the use of the computerized system should be available on site.

SOPs should be established for, but not limited to:

* System Setup/Installation
* Data Collection and Handling
* System Maintenance
* Data Backup, Recovery, and Contingency Plans
* Security
* Change Control

## DATA ENTRY

A. Electronic Signatures

1. To ensure that individuals have the authority to proceed with data entry, the data entry system should be designed so that individuals need to enter electronic signatures, such as combined identification codes/passwords or biometric-based electronic signatures, at the start of a data entry session.

2. The data entry system should also be designed to ensure attributability. Therefore, each entry to an electronic record, including any change, should be made under the electronic signature of the individual making that entry. However, this does not necessarily mean a separate electronic signature for each entry or change. For example, a single electronic signature may cover multiple entries or changes.

a. The printed name of the individual who enters data should be displayed by the data entry screen throughout the data entry session. This is intended to preclude the possibility of a different individual inadvertently entering data under someone else=s name.

If the name displayed by the screen during a data entry session is not that of the person entering the data, then that individual should log on under his or her own name before continuing.

3. Individuals should only work under their own passwords or other access keys and should not share these with others. Individuals should not log on to the system in order to provide another person access to the system.

4. Passwords or other access keys should be changed at established intervals.

5. When someone leaves a workstation, the person should log off the system. Failing this, an automatic log off may be appropriate for long idle periods. For short periods of inactivity, there should be some kind of automatic protection against unauthorized data entry. An example could be an automatic screen saver that prevents data entry until a password is entered.

B. Audit Trails

1. Section 21 CFR 11.10(e) requires persons who use electronic record systems to maintain an audit trail as one of the procedures to protect the authenticity, integrity, and, when appropriate, the confidentiality of electronic records.

a. Persons must use secure, computer-generated, time-stamped audit trails to independently record the date and time of operator entries and actions that create, modify, or delete electronic records. A record is created when it is saved to durable media, as described under "commit" in Section II, Definitions.

b. Audit trails must be retained for a period at least as long as that required for the subject electronic records (e.g., the study data and records to which they pertain) and must be available for agency review and copying.

2. Personnel who create, modify, or delete electronic records should not be able to modify the audit trails.

3. Clinical investigators should retain either the original or a certified copy of audit trails.

4. FDA personnel should be able to read audit trails both at the study site and at any other location where associated electronic study records are maintained.

5. Audit trails should be created incrementally, in chronological order, and in a manner that does not allow new audit trail information to overwrite existing data in violation of §11.10(e).

C. Date/Time Stamps

Controls should be in place to ensure that the system's date and time are correct.

The ability to change the date or time should be limited to authorized personnel and such personnel should be notified if a system date or time discrepancy is detected. Changes to date or time should be documented.

Dates and times are to be local to the activity being documented and should include the year, month, day, hour, and minute. The Agency encourages establishments to synchronize systems to the date and time provided by trusted third parties.

Clinical study computerized systems will likely be used in multi-center trials, perhaps located in different time zones. Calculation of the local time stamp may be derived in such cases from a remote server located in a different time zone.

**VI. SYSTEM FEATURES**

A. Systems used for direct entry of data should include features that will facilitate the collection of quality data.

Prompts, flags, or other help features within the computerized system should be used to encourage consistent use of clinical terminology and to alert the user to data that are out of acceptable range. Features that automatically enter data into a field when that field is bypassed should not be used.

Electronic patient diaries and e-CRFs should be designed to allow users to make annotations. Annotations add to data quality by allowing ad hoc information to be captured. This information may be valuable in the event of an adverse reaction or unexpected result. The record should clearly indicate who recorded the annotations and when (date and time).

B. Systems used for direct entry of data should be designed to include features that will facilitate the inspection and review of data. Data tags (e.g., different color, different font, flags) should be used to indicate which data have been changed or deleted, as documented in the audit trail.

C. Retrieval of Data

Recognizing that computer products may be discontinued or supplanted by newer (possibly incompatible) systems, it is nonetheless vital that sponsors retain the ability to retrieve and review the data recorded by the older systems. This may be achieved by maintaining support for the older systems or transcribing data to the newer systems.

When migrating to newer systems, it is important to generate accurate and complete copies of study data and collateral information relevant to data integrity. This information would include, for example, audit trails and computational methods used to derive the data. Any data retrieval software, script, or query logic used for the purpose of manipulating, querying, or extracting data for report generating purposes should be documented and maintained for the life of the report. The transcription process needs to be validated.

### D. Reconstruction of Study

FDA expects to be able to reconstruct a study. This applies not only to the data, but also how the data were obtained or managed. Therefore, all versions of application software, operating systems, and software development tools involved in processing of data or records should be available as long as data or records associated with these versions are required to be retained. Sponsors may retain these themselves or may contract for the vendors to retain the ability to run (but not necessarily support) the software. Although FDA expects sponsors or vendors to retain the ability to run older versions of software, the agency acknowledges that, in some cases, it will be difficult for sponsors and vendors to run older computerized systems.

## VII. SECURITY

### A. Physical Security

In addition to internal safeguards built into the system, external safeguards should be in place to ensure that access to the computerized system and to the data is restricted to authorized personnel.

Staff should be thoroughly aware of system security measures and the importance of limiting access to authorized personnel.

SOPs should be in place for handling and storing the system to prevent unauthorized access.

### B. Logical Security

Access to the data at the clinical site should be restricted and monitored through the system's software with its required log-on, security procedures, and audit trail. The data should not be altered, browsed, queried, or reported via external software applications that do not enter through the protective system software.

There should be a cumulative record that indicates, for any point in time, the names of authorized personnel, their titles, and a description of their access privileges. The record should be in the study documentation accessible at the site.

If a sponsor supplies computerized systems exclusively for clinical trials, the systems should remain dedicated to the purpose for which they were intended and validated.

If a computerized system being used for the clinical study is part of a system normally used for other purposes, efforts should be made to ensure that the study software is logically and physically isolated as necessary to preclude unintended interaction with non-study software. If any of the software programs are changed the system should be evaluated to determine the effect of the changes on logical security.

Controls should be in place to prevent, detect, and mitigate effects of computer viruses on study data and software.

## SYSTEM DEPENDABILITY

The sponsor should ensure and document that computerized systems conform to the sponsor's established requirements for completeness, accuracy, reliability, and consistent intended performance.

A. Systems documentation should be readily available at the site where clinical trials are conducted. Such documentation should provide an overall description of computerized systems and the relationship of hardware, software, and physical environment.

B. FDA may inspect documentation, possessed by a regulated company, that demonstrates validation of software. The study sponsor is responsible, if requested, for making such documentation available at the time of inspection at the site where software is used. Clinical investigators are not generally responsible for validation unless they originated or modified software.

1. For software purchased off-the-shelf, most of the validation should have been done by the company that wrote the software. The sponsor or contract research organization should have documentation (either original validation documents or on-site vendor audit documents) of this design level validation by the vendor, and should have itself performed functional testing (e.g., by use of test data sets) and researched known software limitations, problems, and defect corrections.

In the special case of database and spreadsheet software that is (1) purchased off-the-shelf, (2) designed for and widely used for general purposes, (3) unmodified, and (4) not being used for direct entry of data, the sponsor or contract research organization may not have documentation of design level validation. However, the sponsor or contract research organization should have itself performed functional testing (e.g., by use of test data sets) and researched known software limitations, problems, and defect corrections.

2. Documentation important to demonstrate software validation includes:

Written design specification that describes what the software is intended to do and how it is intended to do it;

A written test plan based on the design specification, including both structural and functional analysis; and,

Test results and an evaluation of how these results demonstrate that the predetermined design specification has been met.

C. Change Control

Written procedures should be in place to ensure that changes to the computerized system such as software upgrades, equipment or component replacement, or new instrumentation will maintain the integrity of the data or the integrity of protocols.

The impact of any change to the system should be evaluated and a decision made regarding the need to revalidate. Revalidation should be performed for changes that exceed operational limits or design specifications.

All changes to the system should be documented.

## IX. SYSTEM CONTROLS

A. Software Version Control

Measures should be in place to ensure that versions of software used to generate, collect, maintain, and transmit data are the versions that are stated in the systems documentation.

B. Contingency Plans

Written procedures should describe contingency plans for continuing the study by alternate means in the event of failure of the computerized system.

C. Backup and Recovery of Electronic Records

Backup and recovery procedures should be clearly outlined in the SOPs and be sufficient to protect against data loss. Records should be backed up regularly in a way that would prevent a catastrophic loss and ensure the quality and integrity of the data.

Backup records should be stored at a secure location specified in the SOPs. Storage is typically offsite or in a building separate from the original records.

Backup and recovery logs should be maintained to facilitate an assessment of the nature and scope of data loss resulting from a system failure.

## X. TRAINING OF PERSONNEL

A. Qualifications

Each person who enters or processes data should have the education, training, and experience or any combination thereof necessary to perform the assigned functions.

Individuals responsible for monitoring the trial should have education, training, and experience in the use of the computerized system necessary to adequately monitor the trial.

B. Training

Training should be provided to individuals in the specific operations that they are to perform.

Training should be conducted by qualified individuals on a continuing basis, as needed, to ensure familiarity with the computerized system and with any changes to the system during the course of the study.

C. Documentation

Employee education, training, and experience should be documented.

## XI. RECORDS INSPECTION

A. FDA may inspect all records that are intended to support submissions to the Agency, regardless of how they were created or maintained. Therefore, systems should be able to generate accurate and complete copies of records in both human readable and electronic form suitable for inspection, review, and copying by the Agency. Persons should contact the Agency if there is any doubt about what file formats and media the Agency can read and copy.

B. The sponsor should be able to provide hardware and software as necessary for FDA personnel to inspect the electronic documents and audit trail at the site where an FDA inspection is taking place.

## XII. CERTIFICATION OF ELECTRONIC SIGNATURES

As required by 21 CFR 11.100(c), persons using electronic signatures to meet an FDA signature requirement shall, prior to or at the time of such use, certify to the agency that the electronic signatures in their system, used on or after August 20, 1997, are intended to be the legally binding equivalent of traditional handwritten signatures.

As set forth in 21 CFR 11.100(c), the certification shall be submitted in paper form signed with a traditional handwritten signature to the Office of Regional Operations (HFC-100), 5600 Fishers Lane, Rockville Maryland 20857. The certification is to be submitted prior to or at the time electronic signatures are used. However, a single certification may cover all electronic signatures used by persons in a given organization. This certification is a legal document created by persons to acknowledge that their electronic signatures have the same legal significance as their traditional handwritten signatures. An acceptable certification may take the following form:

"Pursuant to Section 11.100 of Title 21 of the Code of Federal Regulations, this is to certify that [name of organization] intends that all electronic signatures executed by our employees, agents, or representatives, located anywhere in the world, are the legally binding equivalent of traditional handwritten signatures."

## XIII. REFERENCES

FDA, *Software Development Activities*, 1987.

FDA, *Guideline for the Monitoring of Clinical Investigations*, 1988.

FDA, *Guidance for Industry: Good Target Animal Practices: Clinical Investigators and Monitors*, 1997.

FDA, *Compliance Program Guidance Manual*, "Compliance Program 7348.810 - Sponsors, Contract Research Organizations and Monitors," October 30, 1998.

FDA, *Compliance Program Guidance Manual*, "Compliance Program 7348.811 - Bioresearch Monitoring - Clinical Investigators," September 2, 1998.

FDA, *Information Sheets for Institutional Review Boards and Clinical Investigators*, 1998.

FDA, *Glossary of Computerized System and Software Development Terminology*, 1995.

FDA, *21 CFR Part 11, Electronic Records; Electronic Signatures; Final Rule*. Federal Register Vol. 62, No. 54, 13429, March 20, 1997.

FDA, *[draft] Guidance for Industry: General Principles of Software Validation*, draft 1997.

International Conference on Harmonisation, *Good Clinical Practice: Consolidated Guideline*, Federal Register Vol 62, No. 90, 25711, May 9, 1997.


Sec. 425.100 Computerized Drug Processing; CGMP Applicability To Hardware and Software* (CPG 7132a.11)


BACKGROUND:


The use of computers in the production and control of drug products is quickly increasing. Questions have been raised as to the applicability of various sections of the Current Good Manufacturing Practice Regulations to the physical devices (hardware) which constitute the computer systems and to the instructions (software) which make them function.

POLICY:

Where a computer system is performing a function covered by the CGMP regulations then, in general, hardware will be regarded as equipment and applications software1 will be regarded as records. The kind of record (e.g., standard operating procedure, master production record) that the software constitutes and the kind of equipment (e.g., process controller, laboratory instrument) that the hardware constitutes will be governed by how the hardware and software are used in the manufacture, processing, packing, or holding of the drug product. Their exact use will then be used to determine and apply the appropriate sections of the regulations that address equipment and records.

1Applications software consists of programs written to specified user requirements for the purpose of performing a designated task such as process control, laboratory analyses, and acquisition/processing/storage of information required by the CGMP regulations.

*Material between asterisks is new or revised*

Issued: 10/19/84
Revised: 9/4/87

21 CFR PART 58

Title 21
CHAPTER I
SUBCHAPTER A
PART 58

PART 58 - GOOD LABORATORY PRACTICE FOR NONCLINICAL LABORATORY STUDIES
SUBPART A - GENERAL PROVISIONS

Sec.
58.1 Scope.
58.3 Definitions.
58.10 Applicability to studies performed under grants and
    contracts.
58.15 Inspection of a testing facility.
            SUBPART B - ORGANIZATION AND PERSONNEL
58.29 Personnel.
58.31 Testing facility management.
58.33 Study director.
58.35 Quality assurance unit.
            SUBPART C - FACILITIES
58.41 General.
58.43 Animal care facilities.
58.45 Animal supply facilities.
58.47 Facilities for handling test and control articles.
58.49 Laboratory operation areas.
58.51 Specimen and data storage facilities.
            SUBPART D - EQUIPMENT
58.61 Equipment design.
58.63 Maintenance and calibration of equipment.
            SUBPART E - TESTING FACILITIES OPERATION
58.81 Standard operating procedures.
58.83 Reagents and solutions.
58.90 Animal care.

SUBPART F - TEST AND CONTROL ARTICLES

Authority: Secs. 402, 406, 408, 409, 501, 502, 503, 505, 506, 507, 510, 512-516, 518-520, 701, 706, 801 of the Federal Food, Drug, and Cosmetic Act (21 U.S.C. 342, 346, 346a, 348, 351, 352, 353, 355, 356, 357, 360, 360b-360f, 360h-360j, 371, 376, 381); secs. 215, 351, 354-360F of the Public Health Service Act (42 U.S.C. 216, 262, 263b-263n).

Source: 43 FR 60013, Dec. 22, 1978, unless otherwise noted.


Subpart A - General Provisions


Sec. 58.1 Scope.

(a) This part prescribes good laboratory practices for conducting nonclinical laboratory studies that support or are intended to support applications for research or marketing permits for products regulated by the Food and Drug Administration, including food and color additives, animal food additives, human and animal drugs, medical devices for human use, biological products, and electronic products. Compliance with this part is intended to assure the quality and integrity of the safety data filed pursuant to sections 406, 408, 409, 502, 503, 505, 506, 507, 510, 512-516, 518-520, 706, and 801 of the Federal Food, Drug, and Cosmetic Act and sections 351 and 354-360F of the Public Health Service Act.

(b) References in this part to regulatory sections of the Code of Federal Regulations are to Chapter I of Title 21, unless otherwise noted.

(43 FR 60013, Dec. 22, 1978, as amended at 52 FR 33779, Sept. 4, 1987)


Sec. 58.3 Definitions.

As used in this part, the following terms shall have the meanings specified:

(a) Act means the Federal Food, Drug, and Cosmetic Act, as amended (secs. 201-902, 52 Stat. 1040 et seq., as amended (21

U.S.C. 321-392)).

(b) Test article means any food additive, color additive, drug, biological product, electronic product, medical device for human use, or any other article subject to regulation under the act or under sections 351 and 354-360F of the Public Health Service Act.

(c) Control article means any food additive, color additive, drug, biological product, electronic product, medical device for human use, or any article other than a test article, feed, or water that is administered to the test system in the course of a nonclinical laboratory study for the purpose of establishing a basis for comparison with the test article.

(d) Nonclinical laboratory study means in vivo or in vitro experiments in which test articles are studied prospectively in test systems under laboratory conditions to determine their safety. The term does not include studies utilizing human subjects or clinical studies or field trials in animals. The term does not include basic exploratory studies carried out to determine whether a test article has any potential utility or to determine physical or chemical characteristics of a test article.

(e) Application for research or marketing permit includes:

(1) A color additive petition, described in part 71.

(2) A food additive petition, described in parts 171 and 571.

(3) Data and information regarding a substance submitted as part of the procedures for establishing that a substance is generally recognized as safe for use, which use results or may reasonably be expected to result, directly or indirectly, in its becoming a component or otherwise affecting the characteristics of any food, described in Sec.70.35 and 570.35.

(4) Data and information regarding a food additive submitted as part of the procedures regarding food additives permitted to be used on an interim basis pending additional study, described in Sec. 180.1.

(5) An investigational new drug application, described in part 312 of this chapter.

(6) A new drug application, described in part 314.

(7) Data and information regarding an over-the-counter drug for human use, submitted as part of the procedures for classifying such drugs as generally recognized as safe and effective and not misbranded, described in part 330.

(8) Data and information about a substance submitted as part of the procedures for establishing a tolerance for unavoidable contaminants in food and food-packaging materials, described in parts 109 and 509.

(9) Data and information regarding an antibiotic drug submitted as part of the procedures for issuing, amending, or repealing regulations for such drugs, described in Sec. 314.300 of this chapter.

(10) A Notice of Claimed Investigational Exemption for a New Animal Drug, described in part 511.

(11) A new animal drug application, described in part 514.

(12) (Reserved)

(13) An application for a biological product license, described in part 601.

(14) An application for an investigational device exemption, described in part 812.

(15) An Application for Premarket Approval of a Medical Device, described in section 515 of the act.

(16) A Product Development Protocol for a Medical Device, described in section 515 of the act.

(17) Data and information regarding a medical device submitted as part of the procedures for classifying such devices, described in

part 860.

(18) Data and information regarding a medical device submitted as part of the procedures for establishing, amending, or repealing a performance standard for such devices, described in part 861.

(19) Data and information regarding an electronic product submitted as part of the procedures for obtaining an exemption from notification of a radiation safety defect or failure of compliance with a radiation safety performance standard, described in subpart D of part 1003.

(20) Data and information regarding an electronic product submitted as part of the procedures for establishing, amending, or repealing a standard for such product, described in section 358 of the Public Health Service Act.

(21) Data and information regarding an electronic product submitted as part of the procedures for obtaining a variance from any electronic product performance standard as described in Sec. 1010.4.

(22) Data and information regarding an electronic product submitted as part of the procedures for granting, amending, or extending an exemption from any electronic product performance standard, as described in Sec. 1010.5.

(f) Sponsor means:

(1) A person who initiates and supports, by provision of financial or other resources, a nonclinical laboratory study;

(2) A person who submits a nonclinical study to the Food and Drug Administration in support of an application for a research or marketing permit; or

(3) A testing facility, if it both initiates and actually conducts the study.

(g) Testing facility means a person who actually conducts a nonclinical laboratory study, i.e., actually uses the test article in a test system. Testing facility includes any establishment required to register under section 510 of the act that conducts nonclinical laboratory studies and any consulting laboratory described in section 704 of the act that conducts such studies. Testing facility encompasses only those operational units that are being or have been used to conduct nonclinical laboratory studies.

(h) Person includes an individual, partnership, corporation, association, scientific or academic establishment, government agency, or organizational unit thereof, and any other legal entity.

(i) Test system means any animal, plant, microorganism, or subparts thereof to which the test or control article is administered or added for study. Test system also includes appropriate groups or components of the system not treated with the test or control articles.

(j) Specimen means any material derived from a test system for examination or analysis.

(k) Raw data means any laboratory worksheets, records, memoranda, notes, or exact copies thereof, that are the result of original observations and activities of a nonclinical laboratory study and are necessary for the reconstruction and evaluation of the report of that study. In the event that exact transcripts of raw data have been prepared (e.g., tapes which have been transcribed verbatim, dated, and verified accurate by signature), the exact copy or exact transcript may be substituted for the original source as raw data. Raw data may include photographs, microfilm or microfiche copies, computer printouts, magnetic media, including dictated observations, and recorded data from automated instruments.

(l) Quality assurance unit means any person or organizational element, except the study director, designated by testing facility management to perform the duties relating to quality assurance of nonclinical laboratory studies.

(m) Study director means the individual responsible for the overall conduct of a nonclinical laboratory study.

(n) Batch means a specific quantity or lot of a test or control article that has been characterized according to Sec. 58.105(a).

(o) Study initiation date means the date the protocol is signed by the study director.

(p) Study completion date means the date the final report is signed by the study director.

(43 FR 60013, Dec. 22, 1978, as amended at 52 FR 33779, Sept. 4, 1987; 54 FR 9039, Mar. 3, 1989)

Sec. 58.10 Applicability to studies performed under grants and contracts.

When a sponsor conducting a nonclinical laboratory study intended to be submitted to or reviewed by the Food and Drug Administration utilizes the services of a consulting laboratory, contractor, or grantee to perform an analysis or other service, it shall notify the consulting laboratory, contractor, or grantee that the service is part of a nonclinical laboratory study that must be conducted in compliance with the provisions of this part.

Sec. 58.15 Inspection of a testing facility.

(a) A testing facility shall permit an authorized employee of the Food and Drug Administration, at reasonable times and in a reasonable manner, to inspect the facility and to inspect (and in the case of records also to copy) all records and specimens required to be maintained regarding studies within the scope of this part. The records inspection and copying requirements shall not apply to quality assurance unit records of findings and problems, or to actions recommended and taken.

(b) The Food and Drug Administration will not consider a nonclinical laboratory study in support of an application for a research or marketing permit if the testing facility refuses to permit inspection . The determination that a nonclinical laboratory study will not be considered in support of an application for a research or marketing permit does not, however, relieve the applicant for such a permit of any obligation under any applicable statute or regulation to submit the results of the study to the Food and Drug Administration.

Subpart B - Organization and Personnel

Sec. 58.29 Personnel.

(a) Each individual engaged in the conduct of or responsible for the supervision of a nonclinical laboratory study shall have education, training, and experience, or combination thereof, to enable that individual to perform the assigned functions.

(b) Each testing facility shall maintain a current summary of training and experience and job description for each individual engaged in or supervising the conduct of a nonclinical laboratory study.

(c) There shall be a sufficient number of personnel for the timely and proper conduct of the study according to the protocol.

(d) Personnel shall take necessary personal sanitation and health precautions designed to avoid contamination of test and control articles and test systems.

(e) Personnel engaged in a nonclinical laboratory study shall wear clothing appropriate for the duties they perform. Such clothing shall be changed as often as necessary to prevent microbiological, radiological, or chemical contamination of test systems and test and control articles.

(f) Any individual found at any time to have an illness that may adversely affect the quality and integrity of the nonclinical laboratory study shall be excluded from direct contact with test systems, test and control articles and any other operation or function that may adversely affect the study until the condition is corrected. All personnel shall be instructed to report to their immediate supervisors any health or medical conditions that may reasonably be considered to have an adverse effect on a nonclinical laboratory study.


Sec. 58.31  Testing facility management.


For each nonclinical laboratory study, testing facility management shall:

(a) Designate a study director as described in Sec. 58.33, before the study is initiated.

(b) Replace the study director promptly if it becomes necessary to do so during the conduct of a study.

(c) Assure that there is a quality assurance unit as described in Sec. 58.35.

(d) Assure that test and control articles or mixtures have been appropriately tested for identity, strength, purity, stability, and uniformity, as applicable.

(e) Assure that personnel, resources, facilities, equipment, materials, and methodologies are available as scheduled.

(f) Assure that personnel clearly understand the functions they are to perform.

(g) Assure that any deviations from these regulations reported by the quality assurance unit are communicated to the study director and corrective actions are taken and documented.

(43 FR 60013, Dec. 22, 1978, as amended at 52 FR 33780, Sept. 4, 1987)


Sec. 58.33  Study director.


For each nonclinical laboratory study, a scientist or other professional of appropriate education, training, and experience, or combination thereof, shall be identified as the study director. The study director has overall responsibility for the technical conduct of the study, as well as for the interpretation, analysis, documentation and reporting of results, and represents the single point of study control. The study director shall assure that:

(a) The protocol, including any change, is approved as provided by Sec. 58 .120 and is followed.

(b) All experimental data, including observations of unanticipated responses of the test system are accurately recorded and verified.

(c) Unforeseen circumstances that may affect the quality and integrity of the nonclinical laboratory study are noted when they occur, and corrective action is taken and documented.

(d) Test systems are as specified in the protocol.

(e) All applicable good laboratory practice regulations are followed.

(f) All raw data, documentation, protocols, specimens, and final reports are transferred to the archives during or at the close of the study.

(43 FR 60013, Dec. 22, 1978; 44 FR 17657, Mar. 23, 1979)

Sec. 58.35 Quality assurance unit.

(a) A testing facility shall have a quality assurance unit which shall be responsible for monitoring each study to assure management that the facilities, equipment, personnel, methods, practices , records, and controls are in conformance with the regulations in this part. For any given study, the quality assurance unit shall be entirely separate from and independent of the personnel engaged in the direction and conduct of that study.

(b) The quality assurance unit shall:

(1) Maintain a copy of a master schedule sheet of all nonclinical laboratory studies conducted at the testing facility indexed by test article and containing the test system, nature of study, date study was initiated, current status of each study, identity of the sponsor, and name of the study director.

(2) Maintain copies of all protocols pertaining to all nonclinical laboratory studies for which the unit is responsible.

(3) Inspect each nonclinical laboratory study at intervals adequate to assure the integrity of the study and maintain written and properly signed records of each periodic inspection showing the date of the inspection, the study inspected, the phase or segment of the study inspected, the person performing the inspection, findings and problems, action recommended and taken to resolve existing problems, and any scheduled date for reinspection. Any problems found during the course of an inspection which are likely to affect study integrity shall be brought to the attention of the study director and management immediately.

(4) Periodically submit to management and the study director written status reports on each study, noting any problems and the corrective actions taken.

(5) Determine that no deviations from approved protocols or standard operating procedures were made without proper authorization and documentation.

(6) Review the final study report to assure that such report accurately describes the methods and standard operating procedures, and that the reported results accurately reflect the raw data of the nonclinical laboratory study.

(7) Prepare and sign a statement to be included with the final study report which shall specify the dates inspections were made and findings reported to management and to the study director.

(c) The responsibilities and procedures applicable to the quality assurance unit, the records maintained by the quality assurance unit, and the method of indexing such records shall be in writing and shall be maintained. These items including inspection dates, the study inspected, the phase or segment of the study inspected, and the name of the individual performing the inspection shall be made available for inspection to authorized employees of the Food and Drug Administration.

(d) A designated representative of the Food and Drug Administration shall have access to the written procedures established for the inspection and may request testing facility management to certify that inspections are being implemented, performed, documented, and followed-up in accordance with this paragraph.
(Information collection requirements approved by the Office of Management and Budget under control number 0910-0203)
(43 FR 60013, Dec. 22, 1978, as amended at 52 FR 33780, Sept. 4, 1987)


Subpart C - Facilities

Sec. 58.41 General.


Each testing facility shall be of suitable size and construction to facilitate the proper conduct of nonclinical laboratory studies. It shall be designed so that there is a degree of separation that will prevent any function or activity from having an adverse effect on the study.
(52 FR 33780, Sept. 4, 1987)


Sec. 58.43 Animal care facilities.


(a) A testing facility shall have a sufficient number of animal rooms or areas, as needed, to assure proper: (1) Separation of species or test systems, (2) isolation of individual projects, (3) quarantine of animals , and (4) routine or specialized housing of animals .

(b) A testing facility shall have a number of animal rooms or areas separate from those described in paragraph (a) of this section to ensure isolation of studies being done with test systems or test and control articles known to be biohazardous, including volatile substances, aerosols, radioactive materials, and infectious agents.

(c) Separate areas shall be provided, as appropriate, for the diagnosis, treatment, and control of laboratory animal diseases. These areas shall provide effective isolation for the housing of animals either known or suspected of being diseased, or of being carriers of disease, from other animals .

(d) When animals are housed, facilities shall exist for the collection and disposal of all animal waste and refuse or for safe sanitary storage of waste before removal from the testing facility. Disposal facilities shall be so provided and operated as to minimize vermin infestation, odors, disease hazards, and environmental contamination.
(43 FR 60013, Dec. 22, 1978, as amended at 52 FR 33780, Sept. 4, 1987)


Sec. 58.45 Animal supply facilities.


There shall be storage areas, as needed, for feed, bedding, supplies, and equipment. Storage areas for feed and bedding shall be separated from areas housing the test systems and shall be

protected against infestation or contamination. Perishable supplies shall be preserved by appropriate means.
(43 FR 60013, Dec. 22, 1978, as amended at 52 FR 33780, Sept. 4, 1987)


Sec. 58.47 Facilities for handling test and control articles.


(a) As necessary to prevent contamination or mixups, there shall be separate areas for:
(1) Receipt and storage of the test and control articles.
(2) Mixing of the test and control articles with a carrier, e.g., feed.
(3) Storage of the test and control article mixtures.
(b) Storage areas for the test and/or control article and test and control mixtures shall be separate from areas housing the test systems and shall be adequate to preserve the identity, strength, purity, and stability of the articles and mixtures.


Sec. 58.49  Laboratory operation areas.


Separate laboratory space shall be provided, as needed, for the performance of the routine and specialized procedures required by nonclinical laboratory studies.
(52 FR 33780, Sept. 4, 1987)


Sec. 58.51  Specimen and data storage facilities.


Space shall be provided for archives, limited to access by authorized personnel only, for the storage and retrieval of all raw data and specimens from completed studies.


Subpart D - Equipment

Sec. 58.61  Equipment design.


Equipment used in the generation, measurement, or assessment of data and equipment used for facility environmental control shall be of appropriate design and adequate capacity to function according to the protocol and shall be suitably located for operation, inspection, cleaning, and maintenance.
(52 FR 33780, Sept. 4, 1987)


Sec. 58.63 Maintenance and calibration of equipment .


(a) Equipment shall be adequately inspected, cleaned, and maintained. Equipment used for the generation, measurement, or assessment of data shall be adequately tested, calibrated and/or standardized.
(b) The written standard operating procedures required under Sec. 58.81(b)(11) shall set forth in sufficient detail the methods, materials, and schedules to be used in the routine inspection,

cleaning, maintenance, testing, calibration, and/or standardization of equipment , and shall specify, when appropriate, remedial action to be taken in the event of failure or malfunction of equipment . The written standard operating procedures shall designate the person responsible for the performance of each operation.

(c) Written records shall be maintained of all inspection, maintenance, testing, calibrating and/or standardizing operations. These records, containing the date of the operation, shall describe whether the maintenance operations were routine and followed the written standard operating procedures. Written records shall be kept of nonroutine repairs performed on equipment as a result of failure and malfunction. Such records shall document the nature of the defect, how and when the defect was discovered, and any remedial action taken in response to the defect.

(Information collection requirements approved by the Office of Management and Budget under control number 0910-0203)

(43 FR 60013, Dec. 22, 1978, as amended at 52 FR 33780, Sept. 4, 1987)

Subpart E - Testing Facilities Operation

Sec. 58.81  Standard operating procedures.

(a) A testing facility shall have standard operating procedures in writing setting forth nonclinical laboratory study methods that management is satisfied are adequate to insure the quality and integrity of the data generated in the course of a study. All deviations in a study from standard operating procedures shall be authorized by the study director and shall be documented in the raw data. Significant changes in established standard operating procedures shall be properly authorized in writing by management.

(b) Standard operating procedures shall be established for, but not limited to, the following:

(1) Animal room preparation.

(2) Animal care.

(3) Receipt, identification, storage, handling, mixing, and method of sampling of the test and control articles.

(4) Test system observations.

(5) Laboratory tests.

(6) Handling of animals found moribund or dead during study.

(7) Necropsy of animals or postmortem examination of animals.

(8) Collection and identification of specimens.

(9) Histopathology.

(10) Data handling, storage, and retrieval.

(11) Maintenance and calibration of equipment.

(12) Transfer, proper placement, and identification of animals.

(c) Each laboratory area shall have immediately available laboratory manuals and standard operating procedures relative to the laboratory procedures being performed. Published literature may be used as a supplement to standard operating procedures.

(d) A historical file of standard operating procedures, and all revisions thereof, including the dates of such revisions, shall be maintained.

(43 FR 60013, Dec. 22, 1978, as amended at 52 FR 33780, Sept. 4, 1987)

Sec. 58.83  Reagents and solutions.

All reagents and solutions in the laboratory areas shall be
labeled to indicate identity, titer or concentration, storage
requirements, and expiration date. Deteriorated or outdated
reagents and solutions shall not be used.


Sec. 58.90 Animal care.


(a) There shall be standard operating procedures for the housing,
feeding, handling, and care of animals.

(b) All newly received animals from outside sources shall be
isolated and their health status shall be evaluated in accordance
with acceptable veterinary medical practice .

(c) At the initiation of a nonclinical laboratory study, animals
shall be free of any disease or condition that might interfere with
the purpose or conduct of the study. If, during the course of the
study, the animals contract such a disease or condition, the
diseased animals shall be isolated, if necessary. These animals
may be treated for disease or signs of disease provided that such
treatment does not interfere with the study. The diagnosis,
authorizations of treatment, description of treatment, and each
date of treatment shall be documented and shall be retained.

(d) Warm-blooded animals, excluding suckling rodents, used in
laboratory procedures that require manipulations and observations
over an extended period of time or in studies that require the
animals to be removed from and returned to their home cages for any
reason (e.g., cage cleaning, treatment, etc.), shall receive
appropriate identification. All information needed to specifically
identify each animal within an animal-housing unit shall appear on
the outside of that unit.

(e) Animals of different species shall be housed in separate
rooms when necessary. Animals of the same species, but used in
different studies, should not ordinarily be housed in the same room
when inadvertent exposure to control or test articles or animal
mixup could affect the outcome of either study. If such mixed
housing is necessary, adequate differentiation by space and
identification shall be made.

(f) Animal cages, racks and accessory equipment shall be cleaned
and sanitized at appropriate intervals.

(g) Feed and water used for the animals shall be analyzed
periodically to ensure that contaminants known to be capable of
interfering with the study and reasonably expected to be present in
such feed or water are not present at levels above those specified
in the protocol. Documentation of such analyses shall be
maintained as raw data.

(h) Bedding used in animal cages or pens shall not interfere with
the purpose or conduct of the study and shall be changed as often
as necessary to keep the animals dry and clean.

(i) If any pest control materials are used, the use shall be
documented. Cleaning and pest control materials that interfere
with the study shall not be used.
(Information collection requirements approved by the Office of
Management and Budget under control number 0910-0203)
(43 FR 60013, Dec. 22, 1978, as amended at 52 FR 33780, Sept. 4,
1987; 54 FR 15924, Apr. 20, 1989; 56 FR 32088, July 15, 1991)


Subpart F - Test and Control Articles

Sec. 58.105  Test and control article characterization.

(a) The identity, strength, purity, and composition or other characteristics which will appropriately define the test or control article shall be determined for each batch and shall be documented. Methods of synthesis, fabrication, or derivation of the test and control articles shall be documented by the sponsor or the testing facility. In those cases where marketed products are used as control articles, such products will be characterized by their labeling.

(b) The stability of each test or control article shall be determined by the testing facility or by the sponsor either: (1) Before study initiation, or (2) concomitantly according to written standard operating procedures, which provide for periodic analysis of each batch.

(c) Each storage container for a test or control article shall be labeled by name, chemical abstract number or code number, batch number, expiration date, if any, and, where appropriate, storage conditions necessary to maintain the identity, strength, purity, and composition of the test or control article. Storage containers shall be assigned to a particular test article for the duration of the study.

(d) For studies of more than 4 weeks' duration, reserve samples from each batch of test and control articles shall be retained for the period of time provided by Sec. 58.195.
(Information collection requirements approved by the Office of Management and Budget under control number 0910-0203)
(43 FR 60013, Dec. 22, 1978, as amended at 52 FR 33781, Sept. 4, 1987)


Sec. 58.107  Test and control article handling.

Procedures shall be established for a system for the handling of the test and control articles to ensure that:

(a) There is proper storage.

(b) Distribution is made in a manner designed to preclude the possibility of contamination, deterioration, or damage.

(c) Proper identification is maintained throughout the distribution process.

(d) The receipt and distribution of each batch is documented. Such documentation shall include the date and quantity of each batch distributed or returned.


Sec. 58.113  Mixtures of articles with carriers.

(a) For each test or control article that is mixed with a carrier, tests by appropriate analytical methods shall be conducted:

(1) To determine the uniformity of the mixture and to determine, periodically, the concentration of the test or control article in the mixture .

(2) To determine the stability of the test and control articles in the mixture as required by the conditions of the study either:

(i) Before study initiation, or

(ii) Concomitantly according to written standard operating procedures which provide for periodic analysis of the test and control articles in the mixture .

(b) (Reserved)

(c) Where any of the components of the test or control article carrier mixture has an expiration date, that date shall be clearly shown on the container. If more than one component has an expiration date, the earliest date shall be shown.

(43 FR 60013, Dec. 22, 1978, as amended at 45 FR 24865, Apr. 11, 1980; 52 FR 33781, Sept. 4, 1987)

Subpart G - Protocol for and Conduct of a Nonclinical Laboratory Study.

Sec. 58.120  Protocol.

(a) Each study shall have an approved written protocol that clearly indicates the objectives and all methods for the conduct of the study.  The protocol shall contain, as applicable, the following information:

(1) A descriptive title and statement of the purpose of the study.

(2) Identification of the test and control articles by name, chemical abstract number, or code number.

(3) The name of the sponsor and the name and address of the testing facility at which the study is being conducted.

(4) The number, body weight range, sex, source of supply, species, strain, substrain, and age of the test system.

(5) The procedure for identification of the test system.

(6) A description of the experimental design, including the methods for the control of bias.

(7) A description and/or identification of the diet used in the study as well as solvents, emulsifiers, and/or other materials used to solubilize or suspend the test or control articles before mixing with the carrier.  The description shall include specifications for acceptable levels of contaminants that are reasonably expected to be present in the dietary materials and are known to be capable of interfering with the purpose or conduct of the study if present at levels greater than established by the specifications.

(8) Each dosage level, expressed in milligrams per kilogram of body weight or other appropriate units, of the test or control article to be administered and the method and frequency of administration.

(9) The type and frequency of tests, analyses, and measurements to be made.

(10) The records to be maintained.

(11) The date of approval of the protocol by the sponsor and the dated signature of the study director.

(12) A statement of the proposed statistical methods to be used.

(b) All changes in or revisions of an approved protocol and the reasons therefor shall be documented, signed by the study director, dated, and maintained with the protocol .

(Information collection requirements approved by the Office of Management and Budget under control number 0910-0203)

(43 FR 60013, Dec. 22, 1978, as amended at 52 FR 33781, Sept. 4, 1987)

Sec. 58.130 Conduct of a nonclinical laboratory study.

(a) The nonclinical laboratory study shall be conducted in

accordance with the protocol.

(b) The test systems shall be monitored in conformity with the protocol.

(c) Specimens shall be identified by test system, study, nature, and date of collection. This information shall be located on the specimen container or shall accompany the specimen in a manner that precludes error in the recording and storage of data.

(d) Records of gross findings for a specimen from postmortem observations should be available to a pathologist when examining that specimen histopathologically.

(e) All data generated during the conduct of a nonclinical laboratory study, except those that are generated by automated data collection systems, shall be recorded directly, promptly, and legibly in ink. All data entries shall be dated on the date of entry and signed or initialed by the person entering the data. Any change in entries shall be made so as not to obscure the original entry, shall indicate the reason for such change, and shall be dated and signed or identified at the time of the change. In automated data collection systems, the individual responsible for direct data input shall be identified at the time of data input. Any change in automated data entries shall be made so as not to obscure the original entry, shall indicate the reason for change, shall be dated, and the responsible individual shall be identified. (Information collection requirements approved by the Office of Management and Budget under control number 0910-0203) (43 FR 60013, Dec. 22, 1978, as amended at 52 FR 33781, Sept. 4, 1987)


Subpart J - Records and Reports

Sec. 58.185 Reporting of nonclinical laboratory study results.


(a) A final report shall be prepared for each nonclinical laboratory study and shall include, but not necessarily be limited to, the following:

(1) Name and address of the facility performing the study and the dates on which the study was initiated and completed.

(2) Objectives and procedures stated in the approved protocol, including any changes in the original protocol.

(3) Statistical methods employed for analyzing the data.

(4) The test and control articles identified by name, chemical abstracts number or code number, strength, purity, and composition or other appropriate characteristics.

(5) Stability of the test and control articles under the conditions of administration.

(6) A description of the methods used.

(7) A description of the test system used. Where applicable, the final report shall include the number of animals used, sex, body weight range, source of supply, species, strain and substrain, age, and procedure used for identification.

(8) A description of the dosage, dosage regimen, route of administration, and duration.

(9) A description of all cirmcumstances that may have affected the quality or integrity of the data.

(10) The name of the study director, the names of other scientists or professionals, and the names of all supervisory personnel, involved in the study.

(11) A description of the transformations, calculations, or operations performed on the data, a summary and analysis of the

data, and a statement of the conclusions drawn from the analysis.

(12) The signed and dated reports of each of the individual scientists or other professionals involved in the study.

(13) The locations where all specimens, raw data, and the final report are to be stored.

(14) The statement prepared and signed by the quality assurance unit as described in Sec. 58 .35(b)(7).

(b) The final report shall be signed and dated by the study director.

(c) Corrections or additions to a final report shall be in the form of an amendment by the study director. The amendment shall clearly identify that part of the final report that is being added to or corrected and the reasons for the correction or addition, and shall be signed and dated by the person responsible.

(43 FR 60013, Dec. 22, 1978, as amended at 52 FR 33781, Sept. 4, 1987)


Sec. 58.190 Storage and retrieval of records and data.


(a) All raw data, documentation, protocols, final reports, and specimens (except those specimens obtained from mutagenicity tests and wet specimens of blood, urine, feces, and biological fluids) generated as a result of a nonclinical laboratory study shall be retained.

(b) There shall be archives for orderly storage and expedient retrieval of all raw data, documentation, protocols, specimens, and interim and final reports. Conditions of storage shall minimize deterioration of the documents or specimens in accordance with the requirements for the time period of their retention and the nature of the documents or specimens. A testing facility may contract with commercial archives to provide a repository for all material to be retained. Raw data and specimens may be retained elsewhere provided that the archives have specific reference to those other locations.

(c) An individual shall be identified as responsible for the archives.

(d) Only authorized personnel shall enter the archives.

(e) Material retained or referred to in the archives shall be indexed to permit expedient retrieval.

(Information collection requirements approved by the Office of Management and Budget under control number 0910-0203)

(43 FR 60013, Dec. 22, 1978, as amended at 52 FR 33781, Sept. 4, 1987)


Sec. 58.195 Retention of records.


(a) Record retention requirements set forth in this section do not supersede the record retention requirements of any other regulations in this chapter.

(b) Except as provided in paragraph (c) of this section, documentation records, raw data and specimens pertaining to a nonclinical laboratory study and required to be made by this part shall be retained in the archive(s) for whichever of the following periods is shortest:

(1) A period of at least 2 years following the date on which an application for a research or marketing permit, in support of which the results of the nonclinical laboratory study were submitted, is

approved by the Food and Drug Administration. This requirement does not apply to studies supporting investigational new drug applications (IND's) or applications for investigational device exemptions (IDE's), records of which shall be governed by the provisions of paragraph (b)(2) of this section.

(2) A period of at least 5 years following the date on which the results of the nonclinical laboratory study are submitted to the Food and Drug Administration in support of an application for a research or marketing permit.

(3) In other situations (e.g., where the nonclinical laboratory study does not result in the submission of the study in support of an application for a research or marketing permit), a period of at least 2 years following the date on which the study is completed, terminated, or discontinued.

(c) Wet specimens (except those specimens obtained from mutagenicity tests and wet specimens of blood, urine, feces, and biological fluids), samples of test or control articles, and specially prepared material, which are relatively fragile and differ markedly in stability and quality during storage, shall be retained only as long as the quality of the preparation affords evaluation. In no case shall retention be required for longer periods than those set forth in paragraphs (a) and (b) of this section.

(d) The master schedule sheet, copies of protocols, and records of quality assurance inspections, as required by Sec. 58.35(c) shall be maintained by the quality assurance unit as an easily accessible system of records for the period of time specified in paragraphs (a) and (b) of this section.

(e) Summaries of training and experience and job descriptions required to be maintained by Sec. 58 . 29 (b) may be retained along with all other testing facility employment records for the length of time specified in paragraphs (a) and (b) of this section.

(f) Records and reports of the maintenance and calibration and inspection of equipment, as required by Sec. 58.63(b) and (c), shall be retained for the length of time specified in paragraph (b) of this section.

(g) Records required by this part may be retained either as original records or as true copies such as photocopies, microfilm, microfiche, or other accurate reproductions of the original records.

(h) If a facility conducting nonclinical testing goes out of business, all raw data, documentation, and other material specified in this section shall be transferred to the archives of the sponsor of the study. The Food and Drug Administration shall be notified in writing of such a transfer.

(43 FR 60013, Dec. 22, 1978, as amended at 52 FR 33781, Sept. 4, 1987; 54 FR 9039, Mar. 3, 1989)


Subpart K - Disqualification of Testing Facilities

Sec. 58.200 Purpose.


(a) The purposes of disqualification are: (1) To permit the exclusion from consideration of completed studies that were conducted by a testing facility which has failed to comply with the requirements of the good laboratory practice regulations until it can be adequately demonstrated that such noncompliance did not occur during, or did not affect the validity or acceptability of data generated by, a particular study; and (2) to exclude from consideration all studies completed after the date of disqualification until the facility can satisfy the Commissioner that it will conduct studies in compliance with such regulations.

(b) The determination that a nonclinical laboratory study may not be considered in support of an application for a research or marketing permit does not, however, relieve the applicant for such a permit of any obligation under any other applicable regulation to submit the results of the study to the Food and Drug Administration.

Sec. 58.202 Grounds for disqualification.

The Commissioner may disqualify a testing facility upon finding all of the following:

(a) The testing facility failed to comply with one or more of the regulations set forth in this part (or any other regulations regarding such facilities in this chapter);

(b) The noncompliance adversely affected the validity of the nonclinical laboratory studies; and

(c) Other lesser regulatory actions (e.g., warnings or rejection of individual studies) have not been or will probably not be adequate to achieve compliance with the good laboratory practice regulations.

Sec. 58.204 Notice of and opportunity for hearing on proposed disqualification.

(a) Whenever the Commissioner has information indicating that grounds exist under Sec. 58.202 which in his opinion justify disqualification of a testing facility, he may issue to the testing facility a written notice proposing that the facility be disqualified.

(b) A hearing on the disqualification shall be conducted in accordance with the requirements for a regulatory hearing set forth in part 16 of this chapter.

Sec. 58.206 Final order on disqualification.

(a) If the Commissioner, after the regulatory hearing, or after the time for requesting a hearing expires without a request being made, upon an evaulation of the administrative record of the disqualification proceeding, makes the findings required in Sec. 58.202, he shall issue a final order disqualifying the facility. Such order shall include a statement of the basis for that determination. Upon issuing a final order, the Commissioner shall notify (with a copy of the order) the testing facility of the action.

(b) If the Commissioner, after a regulatory hearing or after the time for requesting a hearing expires without a request being made, upon an evaluation of the administrative record of the disqualification proceeding, does not make the findings required in Sec. 58.202, he shall issue a final order terminating the disqualification proceeding. Such order shall include a statement of the basis for that determination. Upon issuing a final order the Commissioner shall notify the testing facility and provide a copy of the order.

Sec. 58.210 Actions upon disqualification.

(a) Once a testing facility has been disqualified, each application for a research or marketing permit, whether approved or not, containing or relying upon any nonclinical laboratory study conducted by the disqualified testing facility may be examined to determine whether such study was or would be essential to a decision. If it is determined that a study was or would be essential, the Food and Drug Administration shall also determine whether the study is acceptable, notwithstanding the disqualification of the facility. Any study done by a testing facility before or after disqualification may be presumed to be unacceptable, and the person relying on the study may be required to establish that the study was not affected by the circumstances that led to the disqualification, e.g., by submitting validating information. If the study is then determined to be unacceptable, such data such be eliminated from consideration in support of the application; and such elimination may serve as new information justifying the termination or withdrawal of approval of the application.

(b) No nonclinical laboratory study begun by a testing facility after the date of the facility's disqualification shall be considered in support of any application for a research or marketing permit, unless the facility has been reinstated under Sec. 58 .219. The determination that a study may not be considered in support of an application for a research or marketing permit does not, however, relieve the applicant for such a permit of any obligation under any other applicable regulation to submit the results of the study to the Food and Drug Administration.

Sec. 58.213 Public disclosure of information regarding disqualification.

(a) Upon issuance of a final order disqualifying a testing facility under Sec. 58 .206(a), the Commissioner may notify all or any interested persons. Such notice may be given at the discretion of the Commissioner whenever he believes that such disclosure would further the public interest or would promote compliance with the good laboratory practice regulations set forth in this part. Such notice, if given, shall include a copy of the final order issued under Sec. 58 .206(a) and shall state that the disqualification constitutes a determination by the Food and Drug Administration that nonclinical laboratory studies performed by the facility will not be considered by the Food and Drug Administration in support of any application for a research or marketing permit. If such notice is sent to another Federal Government agency, the Food and Drug Administration will recommend that the agency also consider whether or not it should accept nonclinical laboratory studies performed by the testing facility. If such notice is not sent to any other person, it shall state that it is given because of the relationship between the testing facility and the person being notified and that the Food and Drug Administration is not advising or recommending that any action be taken by the person notified.

(b) A determination that a testing facility has been disqualified and the administrative record regarding such determination are disclosable to the public under part 20 of this chapter.

Sec. 58.215 Alternative or additional actions to disqualification.

(a) Disqualification of a testing facility under this subpart is independent of, and neither in lieu of nor a precondition to, other proceedings or actions authorized by the act. The Food and Drug Administration may, at any time, institute against a testing facility and/or against the sponsor of a nonclinical laboratory study that has been submitted to the Food and Drug Administration any appropriate judicial proceedings (civil or criminal) and any other appropriate regulatory action, in addition to or in lieu of, and prior to, simultaneously with, or subsequent to, disqualification. The Food and Drug Administration may also refer the matter to another Federal, State, or local government law enforcement or regulatory agency for such action as that agency deems appropriate.

(b) The Food and Drug Administration may refuse to consider any particular nonclinical laboratory study in support of an application for a research or marketing permit, if it finds that the study was not conducted in accordance with the good laboratory practice regulations set forth in this part, without disqualifying the testing facility that conducted the study or undertaking other regulatory action.

Sec. 58.217 Suspension or termination of a testing facility by a sponsor.

Termination of a testing facility by a sponsor is independent of, and neither in lieu of nor a precondition to, proceedings or actions authorized by this subpart. If a sponsor terminates or suspends a testing facility from further participation in a nonclinical laboratory study that is being conducted as part of any application for a research or marketing permit that has been submitted to any Center of the Food and Drug Administration (whether approved or not), it shall notify that Center in writing within 15 working days of the action; the notice shall include a statement of the reasons for such action. Suspension or termination of a testing facility by a sponsor does not relieve it of any obligation under any other applicable regulation to submit the results of the study to the Food and Drug Administration. (43 FR FR 60013, Dec. 22, 1978, as amended at 50 FR 8995, Mar. 6, 1985)

Sec. 58.219 Reinstatement of a disqualified testing facility.

A testing facility that has been disqualified may be reinstated as an acceptable source of nonclinical laboratory studies to be submitted to the Food and Drug Administration if the Commissioner determines, upon an evaluation of the submission of the testing facility, that the facility can adequately assure that it will conduct future nonclinical laboratory studies in compliance with the good laboratory practice regulations set forth in this part and, if any studies are currently being conducted, that the quality and integrity of such studies have not been seriously compromised. A disqualified testing facility that wishes to be so reinstated shall present in writing to the Commissioner reasons why it believes it should be reinstated and a detailed description of the corrective actions it has taken or intends to take to assure that the acts or omissions which led to its disqualification will not recur. The Commissioner may condition reinstatement upon the testing facility being found in compliance with the good laboratory practice regulations upon an inspection. If a testing facility is reinstated, the Commissioner shall so notify the testing facility and all organizations and persons who were notified, under Sec. 58 .213 of the disqualification of the testing facility. A determination that a testing facility has been reinstated is disclosable to the public under part 20 of this chapter.

21 CFR 210 and 211

21 Code of Federal Regulations
Parts 210 and 211
Part 210 - CURRENT GOOD MANUFACTURING PRACTICE IN MANUFACTURING, PROCESSING, PACKING, OR HOLDING OF DRUGS; GENERAL Part 211 - CURRENT GOOD MANUFACTURING PRACTICE FOR FINISHED PHARMACEUTICALS

-----------------------------------------------------------------------------

Part 210 - CURRENT GOOD MANUFACTURING PRACTICE IN MANUFACTURING, PROCESSING, PACKING, OR HOLDING OF DRUGS; GENERAL

Sec.

210.1 Status of current good manufacturing practice regulations.

210.2 Applicability of current good manufacturing practice regulations.

210.3 Definitions.

AUTHORITY: Secs. 201, 501, 502, 505, 506, 507, 512, 701, 704 of the Federal Food, Drug, and Cosmetic Act (21 U.S.C. 321, 351, 352, 355, 356, 357, 360b, 371, 374).

SOURCE: 43 FR 45076, Sept. 29, 1978, unless otherwise noted.

§ 210.1 Status of current good manufacturing practice regulations.

(a) The regulations set forth in this part and in Parts 211 through 226 of this chapter contain the minimum current good manufacturing practice for methods to be used in, and the facilities or controls to be used for, the manufacture, processing, packing, or holding of a drug to assure that such drug meets the requirements of the act as to safety, and has the identity and strength and meets the quality and purity characteristics that it purports or is represented to possess.

(b) The failure to comply with any regulation set forth in this part and in Parts 211 through 226 of this chapter in the manufacture, processing, packing, or holding of a drug shall render such drug to be adulterated under section 501(a)(2)(B) of the act and such drug, as well as the person who is responsible for the failure to comply, shall be subject to regulatory action.

§ 210.2 Applicability of current good manufacturing practice regulations.

(a) The regulations in this part and in Parts 211 through 226 of this chapter as they may pertain to a drug and in Parts 600 through 680 of this chapter as they may pertain to a biological product for human use, shall be considered to supplement, not supersede, each other, unless the regulations explicitly provide otherwise. In the event that it is impossible to comply with all applicable regulations in these parts, the regulations specifically applicable to the drug in question shall supersede the more general.

(b) If a person engages in only some operations subject to the regulations in this part and in Parts 211 through 226 and Parts 600 through 680 of this chapter, and not in others, that person need only comply with those regulations applicable to the operations in which he or she is engaged.

§ 210.3 Definitions.

(a) The definitions and interpretations contained in section 201 of the act shall be applicable to such terms when used in this part and in Parts 211 through 226 of this chapter.

(b) The following definitions of terms apply to this part and to Parts 211 through 226 of this chapter.

(1) Act means the Federal Food, Drug, and Cosmetic Act, as amended (21 U.S.C. 301 et seq.).

(2) Batch means a specific quantity of a drug or other material that is intended to have uniform character and quality, within specified limits, and is produced according to a single manufacturing order during the same cycle of manufacture.

(3) Component means any ingredient intended for use in the manufacture of a drug product, including those that may not appear in such drug product.

(4) Drug product means a finished dosage form, for example, tablet, capsule, solution, etc., that contains an active drug ingredient generally, but not necessarily, in association with inactive ingredients. The term also includes a finished dosage form that does not contain an active ingredient but is intended to be used as a placebo.

(5) Fiber means any particulate contaminant with a length at least three times greater than its width.

(6) Non-fiber-releasing filter means any filter, which after any appropriate pretreatment such as washing or flushing, will not release fibers into the component or drug product that is being filtered. All filters composed of asbestos are deemed to be fiber-releasing filters.

(7) Active ingredient means any component that is intended to furnish pharmacological activity or other direct effect in the diagnosis, cure, mitigation, treatment, or prevention of disease, or to affect the structure or any function of the body of man or other animals. The term includes those components that may undergo chemical change in the manufacture of the drug product and be present in the drug product in a modified form intended to furnish the specified activity or effect.

(8) Inactive ingredient means any component other than an ``active ingredient."

(9) In-process material means any material fabricated, compounded, blended, or derived by chemical reaction that is produced for, and used in, the preparation of the drug product.

(10) Lot means a batch, or a specific identified portion of a batch, having uniform character and quality within specified limits; or, in the case of a drug product produced by continuous process, it is a specific identified amount produced in a unit of time or quantity in a manner that assures its having uniform character and quality within specified limits.

(11) Lot number, control number, or batch number means any distinctive combination of letters, numbers, or symbols, or any combination of them, from which the complete history of the manufacture, processing, packing, holding, and distribution of a batch or lot of drug product or other material can be determined.

(12) Manufacture, processing, packing, or holding of a drug product includes packaging and labeling operations, testing, and quality control of drug products.

(13) The term medicated feed means any Type B or Type C medicated feed as defined in 558.3 of this chapter. The feed contains one or more drugs as defined in section 201(g) of the act. The manufacture of medicated feeds is subject to the requirements of Part 225 of this chapter.

(14) The term medicated premix means a Type A medicated article as defined in 558.3 of this chapter. The article contains one or more drugs as defined in section 201(g) of the act. The manufacture of medicated premixes is subject to the requirements of Part 226 of this chapter.

(15) Quality control unit means any person or organizational element designated by the firm to be responsible for the duties relating to quality control.

(16) Strength means:

(I) The concentration of the drug substance (for example, weight/weight, weight/volume, or unit dose/volume basis), and/or

(ii) The potency, that is, the therapeutic activity of the drug product as indicated by appropriate laboratory tests or by adequately developed and controlled clinical data (expressed, for example, in terms of units by reference to a standard).

(17) Theoretical yield means the quantity that would be produced at any appropriate phase of manufacture, processing, or packing of a particular drug product, based upon the quantity of components to be used, in the absence of any loss or error in actual production.

(18) Actual yield means the quantity that is actually produced at any appropriate phase of manufacture, processing, or packing of a particular drug product.

(19) Percentage of theoretical yield means the ratio of the actual yield (at any appropriate phase of manufacture, processing, or packing of a particular drug product) to the theoretical yield (at the same phase), stated as a percentage.

(20) Acceptance criteria means the product specifications and acceptance/rejection criteria, such as acceptable quality level and unacceptable quality level, with an associated sampling plan, that are necessary for making a decision to accept or reject a lot or batch (or any other convenient subgroups of manufactured units).

(21) Representative sample means a sample that consists of a number of units that are drawn based on rational criteria such as random sampling and intended to assure that the sample accurately portrays the material being sampled.

(22) Gang-printed labeling means labeling derived from a sheet of material on which more than one item of labeling is printed.

[43 FR 45076, Sept. 29, 1978, as amended at 51 FR 7389, Mar. 3, 1986; 58 FR 41353, Aug. 3, 1993]

EFFECTIVE DATE NOTE: At 58 FR 41353, Aug. 8, 1993, 210.3 was amended by adding paragraph (b)(22) effective Aug. 3, 1994.

--------------------------------------------------------------------------------

Part 211 -CURRENT GOOD MANUFACTURING PRACTICE FOR FINISHED PHARMACEUTICALS

(21 CFR Part 211 As of April, 1996)

Authority: Secs. 201, 501, 502, 505, 506, 507, 512, 701, 704 of the Federal Food, Drug, and Cosmetic Act (21 U.S.C. 321, 351, 352, 355, 356, 357, 360b, 371, 374).

Source: 43 FR 45077, Sept. 29, 1978, unless otherwise noted.

PART 211 - CURRENT GOOD MANUFACTURING PRACTICE FOR FINISHED PHARMACEUTICALS

Subpart A - General Provisions
Sec.

211.1 Scope

211.3 Definitions

211.204 Returned drug products.

211.208 Drug product salvaging.

Subpart A-General Provisions
§ 211.1 Scope

(a) The regulations in this part contain the minimum current good manufacturing practice for preparation of drug products for administration to humans or animals.

(b) The current good manufacturing practice regulations in this chapter, as they pertain to drug products, and in parts 600 through 680 of this chapter, as they pertain to biological products for human use, shall be considered to supplement, not supersede, the regulations in this part unless the regulations explicitly provide otherwise. In the event it is impossible to comply with applicable regulations both in this part and in other parts of this chapter or in parts 600 through 680 of this chapter, the regulation specifically applicable to the drug product in question shall supersede the regulation in this part.

(c) Pending consideration of a proposed exemption, published in the Federal Register of September 29, 1978, the requirements in this part shall not be enforced for OTC drug products if the products and all their ingredients are ordinarily marketed and consumed as human foods, and which products may also fall within the legal definition of drugs by virtue of their intended use. Therefore, until further notice, regulations under part 110 of this chapter, and where applicable, parts 113 to 129 of this chapter, shall be applied in determining whether these OTC drug products that are also foods are manufactured, processed, packed, or held under current good manufacturing practice.

§ 211.3 Definitions.

The definitions set forth in § 210.3 of this chapter apply in this part.

Subpart B-Organization and Personnel
§ 211.22 Responsibilities of quality control unit.

(a) There shall be a quality control unit that shall have the responsibility and authority to approve or reject all components, drug product containers, closures, in-process materials, packaging material, labeling, and drug products, and the authority to review production records to assure that no errors have occurred or, if errors have occurred, that they have been fully investigated. The quality control unit shall be responsible for approving or rejecting drug products manufactured, processed, packed, or held under contract by another company.

(b) Adequate laboratory facilities for the testing and approval (or rejection) of components, drug product containers, closures, packaging materials, in-process materials, and drug products shall be available to the quality control unit.

(c) The quality control unit shall have the responsibility for approving or rejecting all procedures or specifications impacting on the identity, strength, quality, and purity of the drug product.

(d) The responsibilities and procedures applicable to the quality control unit shall be in writing; such written procedures shall be followed.

§ 211.25 Personnel qualifications.

(a) Each person engaged in the manufacture, processing, packing, or holding of a drug product shall have education, training, and experience, or any combination thereof, to enable that person to perform the assigned functions. Training shall be in the particular operations that the employee performs and in current good manufacturing practice (including the current good manufacturing practice regulations in this chapter and written procedures required by these regulations) as they relate to the employee's functions. Training in current good manufacturing practice shall be conducted by qualified individuals on a continuing basis and with sufficient frequency to assure that employees remain familiar with CGMP requirements applicable to them.

(b) Each person responsible for supervising the manufacture, processing, packing, or holding of a drug product shall have the education, training, and experience, or any combination thereof, to perform assigned functions in such a manner as to provide assurance that the drug product has the safety, identity, strength, quality, and purity that it purports or is represented to possess.

(c) There shall be an adequate number of qualified personnel to perform and supervise the manufacture, processing, packing, or holding of each drug product.

§ 211.28 Personnel responsibilities.

(a) Personnel engaged in the manufacture, processing, packing, or holding of a drug product shall wear clean clothing appropriate for the duties they perform. Protective apparel, such as head, face, hand, and arm coverings, shall be worn as necessary to protect drug products from contamination.

(b) Personnel shall practice good sanitation and health habits.

(c) Only personnel authorized by supervisory personnel shall enter those areas of the buildings and facilities designated as limited-access areas.

(d) Any person shown at any time (either by medical examination or supervisory observation) to have an apparent illness or open lesions that may adversely affect the safety or quality of drug products shall be excluded from direct contact with components, drug product containers, closures, in-process materials, and drug products until the condition is corrected or determined by competent medical personnel not to jeopardize the safety or quality of drug products. All personnel shall be instructed to report to supervisory personnel any health conditions that may have an adverse effect on drug products.

§ 211.34 Consultants.

Consultants advising on the manufacture, processing, packing, or holding of drug products shall have sufficient education, training, and experience, or any combination thereof, to advise on the subject for which they are retained. Records shall be maintained stating the name, address, and qualifications of any consultants and the type of service they provide.

Subpart C-Buildings and Facilities
§ 211.42 Design and construction features.

(a) Any building or buildings used in the manufacture, processing, packing, or holding of a drug product shall be of suitable size, construction and location to facilitate cleaning, maintenance, and proper operations.

(b) Any such building shall have adequate space for the orderly placement of equipment and materials to prevent mixups between different components, drug product containers, closures, labeling, in-process materials, or drug products, and to prevent contamination. The flow of components, drug product containers, closures, labeling, in-process materials, and drug products through the building or buildings shall be designed to prevent contamination.

(c) Operations shall be performed within specifically defined areas of adequate size. There shall be separate or defined areas for the firm's operations to prevent contamination or mixups as follows:

(1) Receipt, identification, storage, and withholding from use of components, drug product containers, closures, and labeling, pending the appropriate sampling, testing, or examination by the quality control unit before release for manufacturing or packaging;

(2) Holding rejected components, drug product containers, closures, and labeling before disposition;

(3) Storage of released components, drug product containers, closures, and labeling;

(4) Storage of in-process materials;

(5) Manufacturing and processing operations;

(6) Packaging and labeling operations;

(7) Quarantine storage before release of drug products;

(8) Storage of drug products after release;

(9) Control and laboratory operations;

(10) Aseptic processing, which includes as appropriate:

(I) Floors, walls, and ceilings of smooth, hard surfaces that are easily cleanable;

(ii) Temperature and humidity controls;

(iii) An air supply filtered through high-efficiency particulate air filters under positive pressure, regardless of whether flow is laminar or nonlaminar;

(iv) A system for monitoring environmental conditions;

(v) A system for cleaning and disinfecting the room and equipment to produce aseptic conditions;

(vi) A system for maintaining any equipment used to control the aseptic conditions.

(d) Operations relating to the manufacture, processing, and packing of penicillin shall be performed in facilities separate from those used for other drug products for human use.

[43 FR 45077, Sept. 29, 1978, as amended at 60 FR 4091, Jan. 20, 1995]

§ 211.44 Lighting.

Adequate lighting shall be provided in all areas.

§ 211.46 Ventilation, air filtration, air heating and cooling.

(a) Adequate ventilation shall be provided.

(b) Equipment for adequate control over air pressure, micro-organisms, dust, humidity, and temperature shall be provided when appropriate for the manufacture, processing, packing, or holding of a drug product.

(c) Air filtration systems, including prefilters and particulate matter air filters, shall be used when appropriate on air supplies to production areas. If air is recirculated to production areas, measures shall be taken to control recirculation of dust from production. In areas where air contamination occurs during production, there shall be adequate exhaust systems or other systems adequate to control contaminants.

(d) Air-handling systems for the manufacture, processing, and packing of penicillin shall be completely separate from those for other drug products for human use.

§ 211.48 Plumbing.

(a) Potable water shall be supplied under continuous positive pressure in a plumbing system free of defects that could contribute contamination to any drug product. Potable water shall meet the standards prescribed in the Environmental Protection Agency's Primary Drinking Water Regulations set forth in 40 CFR part 141. Water not meeting such standards shall not be permitted in the potable water system.

(b) Drains shall be of adequate size and, where connected directly to a sewer, shall be provided with an air break or other mechanical device to prevent back-siphonage.

[43 FR 45077, Sept. 29, 1978, as amended at 48 FR 11426, Mar. 18, 1983]

§ 211.50 Sewage and refuse.

Sewage, trash, and other refuse in and from the building and immediate premises shall be disposed of in a safe and sanitary manner.

§ 211.52 Washing and toilet facilities.

Adequate washing facilities shall be provided, including hot and cold water, soap or detergent, air driers or single-service towels, and clean toilet facilities easily accessible to working areas.

§ 211.56 Sanitation.

(a) Any building used in the manufacture, processing, packing, or holding of a drug product shall be maintained in a clean and sanitary condition, Any such building shall be free of infestation by rodents, birds, insects, and other vermin (other than laboratory animals). Trash and organic waste matter shall be held and disposed of in a timely and sanitary manner.

(b) There shall be written procedures assigning responsibility for sanitation and describing in sufficient detail the cleaning schedules, methods, equipment, and materials to be used in cleaning the buildings and facilities; such written procedures shall be followed.

(c) There shall be written procedures for use of suitable rodenticides, insecticides, fungicides, fumigating agents, and cleaning and sanitizing agents. Such written procedures shall be designed to prevent the contamination of equipment, components, drug product containers, closures, packaging, labeling materials, or drug products and shall be followed. Rodenticides, insecticides, and fungicides shall not be used unless registered and used in accordance with the Federal Insecticide, Fungicide, and Rodenticide Act (7 U.S.C. 135).

(d) Sanitation procedures shall apply to work performed by contractors or temporary employees as well as work performed by full-time employees during the ordinary course of operations.

§ 211.58 Maintenance.

Any building used in the manufacture, processing, packing, or holding of a drug product shall be maintained in a good state of repair.

Subpart D-Equipment
§ 211.63 Equipment design, size, and location.

Equipment used in the manufacture, processing, packing, or holding of a drug product shall be of appropriate design, adequate size, and suitably located to facilitate operations for its intended use and for its cleaning and maintenance.

§ 211.65 Equipment construction.

(a) Equipment shall be constructed so that surfaces that contact components, in-process materials, or drug products shall not be reactive, additive, or absorptive so as to alter the safety, identity, strength, quality, or purity of the drug product beyond the official or other established requirements.

(b) Any substances required for operation, such as lubricants or coolants, shall not come into contact with components, drug product containers, closures, in-process materials, or drug products so as to alter the safety, identity, strength, quality, or purity of the drug product beyond the official or other established requirements.

§ 211.67 Equipment cleaning and maintenance.

(a) Equipment and utensils shall be cleaned, maintained, and sanitized at appropriate intervals to prevent malfunctions or contamination that would alter the safety, identity, strength, quality, or purity of the drug product beyond the official or other established requirements.

(b) Written procedures shall be established and followed for cleaning and maintenance of equipment, including utensils, used in the manufacture, processing, packing, or holding of a drug product. These procedures shall include, but are not necessarily limited to, the following:

(1) Assignment of responsibility for cleaning and maintaining equipment;

(2) Maintenance and cleaning schedules, including, where appropriate, sanitizing schedules;

(3) A description in sufficient detail of the methods, equipment, and materials used in cleaning and maintenance operations, and the methods of disassembling and reassembling equipment as necessary to assure proper cleaning and maintenance;

(4) Removal or obliteration of previous batch identification;

(5) Protection of clean equipment from contamination prior to use;

(6) Inspection of equipment for cleanliness immediately before use.

(c) Records shall be kept of maintenance, cleaning, sanitizing, and inspection as specified in §§ 211.180 and 211.182.

§ 211.68 Automatic, mechanical, and electronic equipment.

(a) Automatic, mechanical, or electronic equipment or other types of equipment, including computers, or related systems that will perform a function satisfactorily, may be used in the manufacture, processing, packing, and holding of a drug product. If such equipment is so used, it shall be routinely calibrated, inspected, or checked according to a written program designed to assure proper performance. Written records of those calibration checks and inspections shall be maintained.

(b) Appropriate controls shall be exercised over computer or related systems to assure that changes in master production and control records or other records are instituted only by authorized personnel. Input to and output from the computer or related system of formulas or other records or data shall be checked for accuracy. The degree and frequency of input/output verification shall be based on the complexity and reliability of the computer or related system. A backup file of data entered into the computer or related system shall be maintained except where certain data, such as calculations performed in connection with laboratory analysis, are eliminated by computerization or other automated processes. In such instances a written record of the program shall be maintained along with appropriate validation data. Hard copy or alternative systems, such as duplicates, tapes, or microfilm, designed to assure that backup data are exact and complete and that it is secure from alteration, inadvertent erasures, or loss shall be maintained.

[43 FR 45077, Sept. 29, 1978, as amended at 60 FR 4091, Jan. 20, 1995]

§ 211.72 Filters.

Filters for liquid filtration used in the manufacture, processing, or packing of injectable drug products intended for human use shall not release fibers into such products. Fiber-releasing filters may not be used in the manufacture, processing, or packing of these injectable drug products unless it is not possible to manufacture such drug products without the use of such filters. If use of a fiber-releasing filter is necessary, an additional non-fiber-releasing filter of 0.22 micron maximum mean porosity (0.45 micron if the manufacturing conditions so dictate) shall subsequently be used to reduce the content of particles in the injectable drug product. Use of an asbestos-containing filter, with or without subsequent use of a specific non-fiber-releasing filter, is permissible only upon submission of proof to the appropriate bureau of the Food and Drug Administration that use of a non-fiber-releasing filter will, or is likely to, compromise the safety or effectiveness of the injectable drug product.

Subpart E-Control of Components and Drug Product Containers and Closures
§ 211.80 General requirements.

(a) There shall be written procedures describing in sufficient detail the receipt, identification, storage, handling, sampling, testing, and approval or rejection of components and drug product containers and closures; such written procedures shall be followed.

(b) Components and drug product containers and closures shall at all times be handled and stored in a manner to prevent contamination.

(c) Bagged or boxed components of drug product containers, or closures shall be stored off the floor and suitably spaced to permit cleaning and inspection.

(d) Each container or grouping of containers for components or drug product containers, or closures shall be identified with a distinctive code for each lot in each shipment received. This code shall be used in recording the disposition of each lot. Each lot shall be appropriately identified as to its status (i.e., quarantined, approved, or rejected).

§ 211.82 Receipt and storage of untested components, drug product containers, and closures.

(a) Upon receipt and before acceptance, each container or grouping of containers of components, drug product containers, and closures shall be examined visually for appropriate labeling as to contents, container damage or broken seals, and contamination.

(b) Components, drug product containers, and closures shall be stored under quarantine until they have been tested or examined, as appropriate, and released. Storage within the area shall conform to the requirements of §211.80.

§ 211.84 Testing and approval or rejection of components, drug product containers, and closures.

(a) Each lot of components, drug product containers, and closures shall be withheld from use until the lot has been sampled, tested, or examined, as appropriate, and released for use by the quality control unit.

(b) Representative samples of each shipment of each lot shall be collected for testing or examination. The number of containers to be sampled, and the amount of material to be taken from each container, shall be based upon appropriate criteria such as statistical criteria for component variability, confidence levels, and degree of precision desired, the past quality history of the supplier, and the quantity needed for analysis and reserve where required by § 211.170.

(c) Samples shall be collected in accordance with the following procedures:

(1) The containers of components selected shall be cleaned where necessary, by appropriate means.

(2) The containers shall be opened, sampled, and resealed in a manner designed to prevent contamination of their contents and contamination of other components, drug product containers, or closures.

(3) Sterile equipment and aseptic sampling techniques shall be used when necessary.

(4) If it is necessary to sample a component from the top, middle, and bottom of its container, such sample subdivisions shall not be composited for testing.

(5) Sample containers shall be identified so that the following information can be determined: name of the material sampled, the lot number, the container from which the sample was taken, the date on which the sample was taken, and the name of the person who collected the sample.

(6) Containers from which samples have been taken shall be marked to show that samples have been removed from them.

(d) Samples shall be examined and tested as follows:

(1) At least one test shall be conducted to verify the identity of each component of a drug product. Specific identity tests, if they exist, shall be used.

(2) Each component shall be tested for conformity with all appropriate written specifications for purity, strength, and quality. In lieu of such testing by the manufacturer, a report of analysis may be accepted from the supplier of a component, provided that at least one specific identity test is conducted on such component by the manufacturer, and provided that the manufacturer establishes the reliability of the supplier's analyses through appropriate validation of the supplier's test results at appropriate intervals.

(3) Containers and closures shall be tested for conformance with all appropriate written procedures. In lieu of such testing by the manufacturer, a certificate of testing may be accepted from the supplier, provided that at least a visual identification is conducted on such containers/closures by the manufacturer and provided that the manufacturer establishes the reliability of the supplier's test results through appropriate validation of the supplier's test results at appropriate intervals.

(4) When appropriate, components shall be microscopically examined.

(5) Each lot of a component, drug product container, or closure that is liable to contamination with filth, insect infestation, or other extraneous adulterant shall be examined against established specifications for such contamination.

(6) Each lot of a component, drug product container, or closure that is liable to microbiological contamination that is objectionable in view of its intended use shall be subjected to microbiological tests before use.

(e) Any lot of components, drug product containers, or closures that meets the appropriate written specifications of identity, strength, quality, and purity and related tests under paragraph (d) of this section may be approved and released for use. Any lot of such material that does not meet such specifications shall be rejected.

§ 211.86 Use of approved components, drug product containers, and closures.

Components, drug product containers, and closures approved for use shall be rotated so that the oldest approved stock is used first. Deviation from this requirement is permitted if such deviation is temporary and appropriate.

§ 211.87 Retesting of approved components, drug product containers, and closures.

Components, drug product containers, and closures shall be retested or reexamined, as appropriate, for identity, strength, quality, and purity and approved or rejected by the quality control unit in accordance with § 211.84 as necessary, e.g., after storage for long periods or after exposure to air, heat or other conditions that might adversely affect the component, drug product container, or closure.

§ 211.89 Rejected components, drug product containers, and closures.

Rejected components, drug product containers, and closures shall be identified and controlled under a quarantine system designed to prevent their use in manufacturing or processing operations for which they are unsuitable.

§ 211.94 Drug product containers and closures.

(a) Drug product containers and closures shall not be reactive, additive, or absorptive so as to alter the safety, identity, strength, quality, or purity of the drug beyond the official or established requirements.

(b) Container closure systems shall provide adequate protection against foreseeable external factors in storage and use that can cause deterioration or contamination of the drug product. (c) Drug product containers and closures shall be clean and, where indicated by the nature of the drug, sterilized and processed to remove pyrogenic properties to assure that they are suitable for their intended use.

(d) Standards or specifications, methods of testing, and, where indicated, methods of cleaning, sterilizing, and processing to remove pyrogenic properties shall be written and followed for drug product containers and closures.

Subpart F-Production and Process Controls
§ 211.100 Written procedures; deviations.

(a) There shall be written procedures for production and process control designed to assure that the drug products have the identity, strength, quality, and purity they purport or are represented to possess. Such procedures shall include all requirements in this subpart. These written procedures, including any changes, shall be drafted, reviewed, and approved by the appropriate organizational units and reviewed and approved by the quality control unit.

(b) Written production and process control procedures shall be followed in the execution of the various production and process control functions and shall be documented at the time of performance. Any deviation from the written procedures shall be recorded and justified.

§ 211.101 Charge-in of components.

Written production and control procedures shall include the following, which are designed to assure that the drug products produced have the identity, strength, quality, and purity they purport or are represented to possess:

(a) The batch shall be formulated with the intent to provide not less than 100 percent of the labeled or established amount of active ingredient.

(b) Components for drug product manufacturing shall be weighed, measured, or subdivided as appropriate. If a component is removed from the original container to another, the new container shall be identified with the following information:

(1) Component name or item code;

(2) Receiving or control number;

(3) Weight or measure in new container;

(4) Batch for which component was dispensed, including its product name, strength, and lot number.

(c) Weighing, measuring, or subdividing operations for components shall be adequately supervised. Each container of component dispensed to manufacturing shall be examined by a second person to assure that:

(1) The component was released by the quality control unit;

(2) The weight or measure is correct as stated in the batch production records;

(3) The containers are properly identified.

(d) Each component shall be added to the batch by one person and verified by a second person.

§ 211.103 Calculation of yield.

Actual yields and percentages of theoretical yield shall be determined at the conclusion of each appropriate phase of manufacturing, processing, packaging, or holding of the drug product. Such calculations shall be performed by one person and independently verified by a second person.

§ 211.105 Equipment identification.

(a) All compounding and storage containers, processing lines, and major equipment used during the production of a batch of a drug product shall be properly identified at all times to indicate their contents and, when necessary, the phase of processing of the batch.

(b) Major equipment shall be identified by a distinctive identification number or code that shall be recorded in the batch production record to show the specific equipment used in the manufacture of each batch of a drug product. In cases where only one of a particular type of equipment exists in a manufacturing facility, the name of the equipment may be used in lieu of a distinctive identification number or code.

§ 211.110 Sampling and testing of in-process materials and drug products.

(a) To assure batch uniformity and integrity of drug products, written procedures shall be established and followed that describe the in-process controls, and tests, or examinations to be conducted on appropriate samples of in-process materials of each batch. Such control procedures shall be established to monitor the output and to validate the performance of those manufacturing processes that may be responsible for causing variability in the characteristics of in-process material and the drug product. Such control procedures shall include, but are not limited to, the following, where appropriate:

(1) Tablet or capsule weight variation;

(2) Disintegration time;

(3) Adequacy of mixing to assure uniformity and homogeneity;

(4) Dissolution time and rate;

(5) Clarity, completeness, or pH of solutions.

(b) Valid in-process specifications for such characteristics shall be consistent with drug product final specifications and shall be derived from previous acceptable process average and process variability estimates where possible and determined by the application of suitable statistical procedures where appropriate. Examination and testing of samples shall assure that the drug product and in-process material conform to specifications.

(c) In-process materials shall be tested for identity, strength, quality, and purity as appropriate, and approved or rejected by the quality control unit, during the production process, e.g., at commencement or completion of significant phases or after storage for long periods.

(d) Rejected in-process materials shall be identified and controlled under a quarantine system designed to prevent their use in manufacturing or processing operations for which they are unsuitable.

§ 211.111 Time limitations on production.

When appropriate, time limits for the completion of each phase of production shall be established to assure the quality of the drug product. Deviation from established time limits may be acceptable if such deviation does not compromise the quality of the drug product. Such deviation shall be justified and documented.

§ 211.113 Control of microbiological contamination.

(a) Appropriate written procedures, designed to prevent objectionable microorganisms in drug products not required to be sterile, shall be established and followed.

(b) Appropriate written procedures, designed to prevent microbiological contamination of drug products purporting to be sterile, shall be established and followed. Such procedures shall include validation of any sterilization process.

§ 211.115 Reprocessing.

(a) Written procedures shall be established and followed prescribing a system for reprocessing batches that do not conform to standards or specifications and the steps to be taken to insure that the reprocessed batches will conform with all established standards, specifications, and characteristics.

(b) Reprocessing shall not be performed without the review and approval of the quality control unit.

Subpart G-Packaging and Labeling Control
§ 211.122 Materials examination and usage criteria.

(a) There shall be written procedures describing in sufficient detail the receipt, identification, storage, handling, sampling, examination, and/or testing of labeling and packaging materials; such written procedures shall be followed. Labeling and packaging materials shall be representatively sampled, and examined or tested upon receipt and before use in packaging or labeling of a drug product.

(b) Any labeling or packaging materials meeting appropriate written specifications may be approved and released for use. Any labeling or packaging materials that do not meet such specifications shall be rejected to prevent their use in operations for which they are unsuitable.

(c) Records shall be maintained for each shipment received of each different labeling and packaging material indicating receipt, examination or testing, and whether accepted or rejected.

(d) Labels and other labeling materials for each different drug product, strength, dosage form, or quantity of contents shall be stored separately with suitable identification. Access to the storage area shall be limited to authorized personnel.

(e) Obsolete and outdated labels, labeling, and other packaging materials shall be destroyed.

(f) Use of gang printing of labeling for different drug products or different strengths or net contents of the same drug product, is prohibited unless the labeling from gang-printed sheets is adequately differentiated by size, shape, or color.

(g) If cut labeling is used, packaging and labeling operations shall include one of the following special control procedures:

(1) Dedication of labeling and packaging lines to each different strength of each different drug product.

(2) Use of appropriate electronic or electromechanical equipment to conduct a 100-percent examination for correct labeling during or after completion of finishing operations; or

(3) Use of visual inspection to conduct a 100-percent examination for correct labeling during or after completion of finishing operations for hand-applied labeling. Such examination shall be performed by one person and independently verified by a second person.

(h) Printing devices on, or associated with, manufacturing lines used to imprint labeling upon the drug product unit label or case shall be monitored to assure that all imprinting conforms to the print specified in the batch production record.

[43 FR 45077, Sept. 29, 1978, as amended at 58 FR 41353, Aug. 3, 1993]

§ 211.125 Labeling issuance.

(a) Strict control shall be exercised over labeling issued for use in drug product labeling operations.

(b) Labeling materials issued for a batch shall be carefully examined for identity and conformity to the labeling specified in the master or batch production records.

(c) Procedures shall be utilized to reconcile the quantities of labeling issued, used, and returned, and shall require evaluation of discrepancies found between the quantity of drug product finished and the quantity of labeling issued when such discrepancies are outside narrow preset limits based on historical operating data. Such discrepancies shall be investigated in accordance with § 211.192. Labeling reconciliation is waived for cut or roll labeling if a 100-percent examination for correct labeling is performed in accordance with § 211.122(g)(2).

(d) All excess labeling bearing lot or control numbers shall be destroyed.

(e) Returned labeling shall be maintained and stored in a manner to prevent mixups and provide proper identification.

(f) Procedures shall be written describing in sufficient detail the control procedures employed for the issuance of labeling; such written procedures shall be followed.

[43 FR 45077, Sept. 29, 1978, as amended at 58 FR 41345, Aug. 3, 1993]

§ 211.130 Packaging and labeling operations.

There shall be written procedures designed to assure that correct labels, labeling, and packaging materials are used for drug products; such written procedures shall be followed. These procedures shall incorporate the following features:

(a) Prevention of mixups and cross-contamination by physical or spatial separation from operations on other drug products.

(b) Identification and handling of filled drug product containers that are set aside and held in unlabeled condition for future labeling operations to preclude mislabeling of individual containers, lots, or portions of lots. Identification need not be applied to each individual container but shall be sufficient to determine name, strength, quantity of contents, and lot or control number of each container.

(c) Identification of the drug product with a lot or control number that permits determination of the history of the manufacture and control of the batch.

(d) Examination of packaging and labeling materials for suitability and correctness before packaging operations, and documentation of such examination in the batch production record.

(e) Inspection of the packaging and labeling facilities immediately before use to assure that all drug products have been removed from previous operations. Inspection shall also be made to assure that packaging and labeling materials not suitable for subsequent operations have been removed. Results of inspection shall be documented in the batch production records.

[43 FR 45077, Sept. 29, 1978, as amended at 58 FR 41354, Aug. 3, 1993]

§ 211.132 Tamper-resistant packaging requirements for over-the-counter (OTC) human drug products.

(a) General. The Food and Drug Administration has the authority under the Federal Food, Drug, and Cosmetic Act (the act) to establish a uniform national requirement for tamper-resistant packaging of OTC drug products that will improve the security of OTC drug packaging and help assure the safety and effectiveness of OTC drug products. An OTC drug product (except a dermatological, dentifrice, insulin, or throat lozenge product) for retail sale that is not packaged in a tamper-resistant package or that is not properly labeled under this section is adulterated under section 501 of the act or misbranded under section 502 of the act, or both.

(b) Requirement for tamper-resistant package. Each manufacturer and packer who packages an OTC drug product (except a dermatological, dentifrice, insulin, or throat lozenge product) for retail sale shall package the product in a tamper-resistant package, if this product is accessible to the public while held for sale. A tamper-resistant package is one having one or more indicators or barriers to entry which, if breached or missing, can reasonably be expected to provide visible evidence to consumers that tampering has occurred. To reduce the likelihood of successful tampering and to increase the likelihood that consumers will discover if a product has been tampered with, the package is required to be distinctive by design (e.g., an aerosol product container) or by the use of one or more indicators or barriers to entry that employ an identifying characteristic (e.g., a pattern, name, registered trademark, logo, or picture). For purposes of this section, the term "distinctive by design" means the packaging cannot be duplicated with commonly available materials or through commonly available processes. For purposes of this section, the term "aerosol product" means a product which depends upon the power of a liquified or compressed gas to expel the contents from the container. A tamper-resistant package may involve an immediate-container and closure system or secondary- container or carton system or any combination of systems intended to provide a visual indication of package integrity. The tamper- resistant feature shall be designed to and shall remain intact when handled in a reasonable manner during manufacture, distribution, and retail display.

(1) For two-piece, hard gelatin capsule products subject to this requirement, a minimum of two tamper-resistant packaging features is required, unless the capsules are sealed by a tamper- resistant technology.

(2) For all other products subject to this requirement, including two-piece, hard gelatin capsules that are sealed by a tamper- resistant technology, a minimum of one tamper-resistant feature is required.

(c) Labeling. Each retail package of an OTC drug product covered by this section, except ammonia inhalant in crushable glass ampules, aerosol products as defined in paragraph (b) of this section, or containers of compressed medical oxygen, is required to bear a statement that is prominently placed so that consumers are alerted to the specific tamper-resistant feature of the package. The labeling statement is also required to be so placed that it will be unaffected if the tamper-resistant feature of the package is breached or missing. If the tamper-resistant feature chosen to meet the requirement in paragraph (b) of this section is one that uses an identifying characteristic, that characteristic is required to be referred to in the labeling statement. For example, the labeling statement on a bottle with a shrink band could say "For your protection, this bottle has an imprinted seal around the neck."

(d) Request for exemptions from packaging and labeling requirements. A manufacturer or packer may request an exemption from the packaging and labeling requirements of this section. A request for an exemption is required to be submitted in the form of a citizen petition under § 10.30 of this chapter and should be clearly identified on the envelope as a "Request for Exemption from Tamper-Resistant Rule." The petition is required to contain the following:

(1) The name of the drug product or, if the petition seeks an exemption for a drug class, the name of the drug class, and a list of products within that class.

(2) The reasons that the drug product's compliance with the tamper-resistant packaging or labeling requirements of this section is unnecessary or cannot be achieved.

(3) A description of alternative steps that are available, or that the petitioner has already taken, to reduce the likelihood that the product or drug class will be the subject of malicious adulteration.

(4) Other information justifying an exemption.

(e) OTC drug products subject to approved new drug applications. Holders of approved new drug applications for OTC drug products are required under § 314.70 of this chapter to provide the agency with notification of changes in packaging and labeling to comply with the requirements of this section. Changes in packaging and labeling required by this regulation may be made before FDA approval, as provided under § 314.70(c) of this chapter. Manufacturing changes by which capsules are to be sealed require prior FDA approval under § 314.70(b) of this chapter.

(f) Poison Prevention Packaging Act of 1970. This section does not affect any requirements for "special packaging" as defined under § 310.3(l) of this chapter and required under the Poison Prevention Packaging Act of 1970.

(Approved by the Office of Management and Budget under OMB control number 0910-0149)

[54 FR 5228, Feb. 2, 1989]

§ 211.134 Drug product inspection.

(a) Packaged and labeled products shall be examined during finishing operations to provide assurance that containers and packages in the lot have the correct label.

(b) A representative sample of units shall be collected at the completion of finishing operations and shall be visually examined for correct labeling.

(c) Results of these examinations shall be recorded in the batch production or control records.

§ 211.137 Expiration dating.

(a) To assure that a drug product meets applicable standards of identity, strength, quality, and purity at the time of use, it shall bear an expiration date determined by appropriate stability testing described in § 211.166.

(b) Expiration dates shall be related to any storage conditions stated on the labeling, as determined by stability studies described in §211.166.

(c) If the drug product is to be reconstituted at the time of dispensing, its labeling shall bear expiration information for both the reconstituted and unreconstituted drug products.

(d) Expiration dates shall appear on labeling in accordance with the requirements of § 201.17 of this chapter.

(e) Homeopathic drug products shall be exempt from the requirements of this section.

(f) Allergenic extracts that are labeled "No U.S. Standard of Potency" are exempt from the requirements of this section.

(g) New drug products for investigational use are exempt from the requirements of this section, provided that they meet appropriate standards or specifications as demonstrated by stability studies during their use in clinical investigations. Where new drug products for investigational use are to be reconstituted at the time of dispensing, their labeling shall bear expiration information for the reconstituted drug product.

(h) Pending consideration of a proposed exemption, published in the Federal Register of September 29, 1978, the requirements in this section shall not be enforced for human OTC drug products if their labeling does not bear dosage limitations and they are stable for at least 3 years as supported by appropriate stability data.

[43 FR 45077, Sept. 29, 1978, as amended at 46 FR 56412, Nov. 17, 1981; 60 FR 4091, Jan. 20, 1995]

Subpart H-Holding and Distribution
§ 211.142 Warehousing procedures.

Written procedures describing the warehousing of drug products shall be established and followed. They shall include:

(a) Quarantine of drug products before release by the quality control unit.

(b) Storage of drug products under appropriate conditions of temperature, humidity, and light so that the identity, strength, quality, and purity of the drug products are not affected.

§ 211.150 Distribution procedures.

Written procedures shall be established, and followed, describing the distribution of drug products. They shall include:

(a) A procedure whereby the oldest approved stock of a drug product is distributed first. Deviation from this requirement is permitted if such deviation is temporary and appropriate.

(b) A system by which the distribution of each lot of drug product can be readily determined to facilitate its recall if necessary.

Subpart I-Laboratory Controls
§ 211.160 General requirements.

(a) The establishment of any specifications, standards, sampling plans, test procedures, or other laboratory control mechanisms required by this subpart, including any change in such specifications, standards, sampling plans, test procedures, or other laboratory control mechanisms, shall be drafted by the appropriate organizational unit and reviewed and approved by the quality control unit. The requirements in this subpart shall be followed and shall be documented at the time of performance. Any deviation from the written specifications, standards, sampling plans, test procedures, or other laboratory control mechanisms shall be recorded and justified.

(b) Laboratory controls shall include the establishment of scientifically sound and appropriate specifications, standards, sampling plans, and test procedures designed to assure that components, drug product containers, closures, in-process materials, labeling, and drug products conform to appropriate standards of identity, strength, quality, and purity. Laboratory controls shall include:

(1) Determination of conformance to appropriate written specifications for the acceptance of each lot within each shipment of components, drug product containers, closures, and labeling used in the manufacture, processing, packing, or holding of drug products. The specifications shall include a description of the sampling and testing procedures used. Samples shall be representative and adequately identified. Such procedures shall also require appropriate retesting of any component, drug product container, or closure that is subject to deterioration.

(2) Determination of conformance to written specifications and a description of sampling and testing procedures for in-process materials. Such samples shall be representative and properly identified.

(3) Determination of conformance to written descriptions of sampling procedures and appropriate specifications for drug products. Such samples shall be representative and properly identified.

(4) The calibration of instruments, apparatus, gauges, and recording devices at suitable intervals in accordance with an established written program containing specific directions, schedules, limits for accuracy and precision, and provisions for remedial action in the event accuracy and/or precision limits are not met. Instruments, apparatus, gauges, and recording devices not meeting established specifications shall not be used.

§ 211.165 Testing and release for distribution.

(a) For each batch of drug product, there shall be appropriate laboratory determination of satisfactory conformance to final specifications for the drug product, including the identity and strength of each active ingredient, prior to release. Where sterility and/or pyrogen testing are conducted on specific batches of shortlived radiopharmaceuticals, such batches may be released prior to completion of sterility and/or pyrogen testing, provided such testing is completed as soon as possible.

(b) There shall be appropriate laboratory testing, as necessary, of each batch of drug product required to be free of objectionable microorganisms.

(c) Any sampling and testing plans shall be described in written procedures that shall include the method of sampling and the number of units per batch to be tested; such written procedure shall be followed.

(d) Acceptance criteria for the sampling and testing conducted by the quality control unit shall be adequate to assure that batches of drug products meet each appropriate specification and appropriate statistical quality control criteria as a condition for their approval and release. The statistical quality control criteria shall include appropriate acceptance levels and/or appropriate rejection levels.

(e) The accuracy, sensitivity, specificity, and reproducibility of test methods employed by the firm shall be established and documented. Such validation and documentation may be accomplished in accordance with § 211.194(a)(2).

(f) Drug products failing to meet established standards or specifications and any other relevant quality control criteria shall be rejected. Reprocessing may be performed. Prior to acceptance and use, reprocessed material must meet appropriate standards, specifications, and any other relevant criteria.

§ 211.166 Stability testing.

(a) There shall be a written testing program designed to assess the stability characteristics of drug products. The results of such stability testing shall be used in determining appropriate storage conditions and expiration dates. The written program shall be followed and shall include:

(1) Sample size and test intervals based on statistical criteria for each attribute examined to assure valid estimates of stability;

(2) Storage conditions for samples retained for testing;

(3) Reliable, meaningful, and specific test methods;

(4) Testing of the drug product in the same container-closure system as that in which the drug product is marketed;

(5) Testing of drug products for reconstitution at the time of dispensing (as directed in the labeling) as well as after they are reconstituted.

(b) An adequate number of batches of each drug product shall be tested to determine an appropriate expiration date and a record of such data shall be maintained. Accelerated studies, combined with basic stability information on the components, drug products, and container-closure system, may be used to support tentative expiration dates provided full shelf life studies are not available and are being conducted. Where data from accelerated studies are used to project a tentative expiration date that is beyond a date supported by actual shelf life studies, there must be stability studies conducted, including drug product testing at appropriate intervals, until the tentative expiration date is verified or the appropriate expiration date determined.

(c) For homeopathic drug products, the requirements of this section are as follows:

(1) There shall be a written assessment of stability based at least on testing or examination of the drug product for compatibility of the ingredients, and based on marketing experience with the drug product to indicate that there is no degradation of the product for the normal or expected period of use.

(2) Evaluation of stability shall be based on the same container-closure system in which the drug product is being marketed.

(d) Allergenic extracts that are labeled "No U.S. Standard of Potency" are exempt from the requirements of this section.

[43 FR 45077, Sept. 29, 1978, as amended at 46 FR 56412, Nov. 17, 1981]

§ 211.167 Special testing requirements.

(a) For each batch of drug product purporting to be sterile and/or pyrogen-free, there shall be appropriate laboratory testing to determine conformance to such requirements. The test procedures shall be in writing and shall be followed.

(b) For each batch of ophthalmic ointment, there shall be appropriate testing to determine conformance to specifications regarding the presence of foreign particles and harsh or abrasive substances. The test procedures shall be in writing and shall be followed.

(c) For each batch of controlled-release dosage form, there shall be appropriate laboratory testing to determine conformance to the specifications for the rate of release of each active ingredient. The test procedures shall be in writing and shall be followed.

§ 211.170 Reserve samples.

(a) An appropriately identified reserve sample that is representative of each lot in each shipment of each active ingredient shall be retained. The reserve sample consists of at least twice the quantity necessary for all tests required to determine whether the active ingredient meets its established specifications, except for sterility and pyrogen testing. The retention time is as follows:

(1) For an active ingredient in a drug product other than those described in paragraphs (a) (2) and (3) of this section, the reserve sample shall be retained for 1 year after the expiration date of the last lot of the drug product containing the active ingredient.

(2) For an active ingredient in a radioactive drug product, except for nonradioactive reagent kits, the reserve sample shall be retained for:

(I) Three months after the expiration date of the last lot of the drug product containing the active ingredient if the expiration dating period of the drug product is 30 days or less; or

(ii) Six months after the expiration date of the last lot of the drug product containing the active ingredient if the expiration dating period of the drug product is more than 30 days.

(3) For an active ingredient in an OTC drug product that is exempt from bearing an expiration date under § 211.137, the reserve sample shall be retained for 3 years after distribution of the last lot of the drug product containing the active ingredient.

(b) An appropriately identified reserve sample that is representative of each lot or batch of drug product shall be retained and stored under conditions consistent with product labeling. The reserve sample shall be stored in the same immediate container-closure system in which the drug product is marketed or in one that has essentially the same characteristics. The reserve sample consists of at least twice the quantity necessary to perform all the required tests, except those for sterility and pyrogens. Except for those drug products described in paragraph (b)(2) of this section, reserve samples from representative sample lots or batches selected by acceptable statistical procedures shall be examined visually at least once a year for evidence of deterioration unless visual examination would affect the integrity of the reserve sample. Any evidence of reserve sample deterioration shall be investigated in accordance with § 211.192. The results of examination shall be recorded and maintained with other stability data on the drug product. Reserve samples of compressed medical gases need not be retained. The retention time is as follows:

(1) For a drug product other than those described in paragraphs (b) (2) and (3) of this section, the reserve sample shall be retained for 1 year after the expiration date of the drug product.

(2) For a radioactive drug product, except for nonradioactive reagent kits, the reserve sample shall be retained for:

(I) Three months after the expiration date of the drug product if the expiration dating period of the drug product is 30 days or less; or

(ii) Six months after the expiration date of the drug product if the expiration dating period of the drug product is more than 30 days.

(3) For an OTC drug product that is exempt for bearing an expiration date under § 211.137, the reserve sample must be retained for 3 years after the lot or batch of drug product is distributed.

[48 FR 13025, Mar. 29, 1983, as amended at 60 FR 4091, Jan. 20, 1995]

§ 211.173 Laboratory animals.

Animals used in testing components, in-process materials, or drug products for compliance with established specifications shall be maintained and controlled in a manner that assures their suitability for their intended use. They shall be identified, and adequate records shall be maintained showing the history of their use.

§ 211.176 Penicillin contamination.

If a reasonable possibility exists that a non-penicillin drug product has been exposed to cross-contamination with penicillin, the non-penicillin drug product shall be tested for the presence of penicillin. Such drug product shall not be marketed if detectable levels are found when tested according to procedures specified in 'Procedures for Detecting and Measuring Penicillin Contamination in Drugs,' which is incorporated by reference. Copies are available from the Division of Research and Testing (HFD-470), Center for Drug Evaluation and Research, Food and Drug Administration, 200 C St. SW., Washington, DC 20204, or available for inspection at the Office of the Federal Register, 800 North Capitol Street, NW., suite 700, Washington, DC 20408.

[43 FR 45077, Sept. 29, 1978, as amended at 47 FR 9396, Mar. 5, 1982; 50 FR 8996, Mar. 6, 1985; 55 FR 11577, Mar. 29, 1990]

Subpart J-Records and Reports
§ 211.180 General requirements.

(a) Any production, control, or distribution record that is required to be maintained in compliance with this part and is specifically associated with a batch of a drug product shall be retained for at least 1 year after the expiration date of the batch or, in the case of certain OTC drug products lacking expiration dating because they meet the criteria for exemption under § 211.137, 3 years after distribution of the batch.

(b) Records shall be maintained for all components, drug product containers, closures, and labeling for at least 1 year after the expiration date or, in the case of certain OTC drug products lacking expiration dating because they meet the criteria for exemption under § 211.137, 3 years after distribution of the last lot of drug product incorporating the component or using the container, closure, or labeling.

(c) All records required under this part, or copies of such records, shall be readily available for authorized inspection during the retention period at the establishment where the activities described in such records occurred. These records or copies thereof shall be subject to photocopying or other means of reproduction as part of such inspection. Records that can be immediately retrieved from another location by computer or other electronic means shall be considered as meeting the requirements of this paragraph.

(d) Records required under this part may be retained either as original records or as true copies such as photocopies, microfilm, microfiche, or other accurate reproductions of the original records. Where reduction techniques, such as microfilming, are used, suitable reader and photocopying equipment shall be readily available.

(e) Written records required by this part shall be maintained so that data therein can be used for evaluating, at least annually, the quality standards of each drug product to determine the need for changes in drug product specifications or manufacturing or control procedures. Written procedures shall be established and followed for such evaluations and shall include provisions for:

(1) A review of a representative number of batches, whether approved or rejected, and, where applicable, records associated with the batch.

(2) A review of complaints, recalls, returned or salvaged drug products, and investigations conducted under § 211.192 for each drug product.

(f) Procedures shall be established to assure that the responsible officials of the firm, if they are not personally involved in or immediately aware of such actions, are notified in writing of any investigations conducted under §§ 211.198, 211.204, or 211.208 of these regulations, any recalls, reports of inspectional observations issued by the Food and Drug Administration, or any regulatory actions relating to good manufacturing practices brought by the Food and Drug Administration.

[43 FR 45077, Sept. 29, 1978, as amended at 60 FR 4901, Jan. 20, 1995]

§ 211.182 Equipment cleaning and use log.

A written record of major equipment cleaning, maintenance (except routine maintenance such as lubrication and adjustments), and use shall be included in individual equipment logs that show the date, time, product, and lot number of each batch processed. If equipment is dedicated to manufacture of one product, then individual equipment logs are not required, provided that lots or batches of such product follow in numerical order and are manufactured in numerical sequence. In cases where dedicated equipment is employed, the records of cleaning, maintenance, and use shall be part of the batch record. The persons performing and double-checking the cleaning and maintenance shall date and sign or initial the log indicating that the work was performed. Entries in the log shall be in chronological order.

§ 211.184 Component, drug product container, closure, and labeling records.

These records shall include the following:

(a) The identity and quantity of each shipment of each lot of components, drug product containers, closures, and labeling; the name of the supplier; the supplier's lot number(s) if known; the receiving code as specified in § 211.80; and the date of receipt. The name and location of the prime manufacturer, if different from the supplier, shall be listed if known.

(b) The results of any test or examination performed (including those performed as required by § 211.82(a), § 211.84(d), or §211.122(a)) and the conclusions derived therefrom.

(c) An individual inventory record of each component, drug product container, and closure and, for each component, a reconciliation of the use of each lot of such component. The inventory record shall contain sufficient information to allow determination of any batch or lot of drug product associated with the use of each component, drug product container, and closure.

(d) Documentation of the examination and review of labels and labeling for conformity with established specifications in accord with §§ 211.122(c) and 211.130(c).

(e) The disposition of rejected components, drug product containers, closure, and labeling.

§ 211.186 Master production and control records.

(a) To assure uniformity from batch to batch, master production and control records for each drug product, including each batch size thereof, shall be prepared, dated, and signed (full signature, handwritten) by one person and independently checked, dated, and signed by a second person. The preparation of master production and control records shall be described in a written procedure and such written procedure shall be followed.

(b) Master production and control records shall include:

(1) The name and strength of the product and a description of the dosage form;

(2) The name and weight or measure of each active ingredient per dosage unit or per unit of weight or measure of the drug product, and a statement of the total weight or measure of any dosage unit;

(3) A complete list of components designated by names or codes sufficiently specific to indicate any special quality characteristic;

(4) An accurate statement of the weight or measure of each component, using the same weight system (metric, avoirdupois, or apothecary) for each component. Reasonable variations may be permitted, however, in the amount of components necessary for the preparation in the dosage form, provided they are justified in the master production and control records;

(5) A statement concerning any calculated excess of component;

(6) A statement of theoretical weight or measure at appropriate phases of processing;

(7) A statement of theoretical yield, including the maximum and minimum percentages of theoretical yield beyond which investigation according to § 211.192 is required;

(8) A description of the drug product containers, closures, and packaging materials, including a specimen or copy of each label and all other labeling signed and dated by the person or persons responsible for approval of such labeling;

(9) Complete manufacturing and control instructions, sampling and testing procedures, specifications, special notations, and precautions to be followed.

§ 211.188 Batch production and control records.

Batch production and control records shall be prepared for each batch of drug product produced and shall include complete information relating to the production and control of each batch. These records shall include:

(a) An accurate reproduction of the appropriate master production or control record, checked for accuracy, dated, and signed;

(b) Documentation that each significant step in the manufacture, processing, packing, or holding of the batch was accomplished, including:

(1) Dates;

(2) Identity of individual major equipment and lines used;

(3) Specific identification of each batch of component or in-process material used;

(4) Weights and measures of components used in the course of processing;

(5) In-process and laboratory control results;

(6) Inspection of the packaging and labeling area before and after use;

(7) A statement of the actual yield and a statement of the percentage of theoretical yield at appropriate phases of processing;

(8) Complete labeling control records, including specimens or copies of all labeling used;

(9) Description of drug product containers and closures;

(10) Any sampling performed;

(11) Identification of the persons performing and directly supervising or checking each significant step in the operation;

(12) Any investigation made according to § 211.192.

(13) Results of examinations made in accordance with § 211.134.

§ 211.192 Production record review.

All drug product production and control records, including those for packaging and labeling, shall be reviewed and approved by the quality control unit to determine compliance with all established, approved written procedures before a batch is released or distributed. Any unexplained discrepancy (including a percentage of theoretical yield exceeding the maximum or minimum percentages established in master production and control records) or the failure of a batch or any of its components to meet any of its specifications shall be thoroughly investigated, whether or not the batch has already been distributed. The investigation shall extend to other batches of the same drug product and other drug products that may have been associated with the specific failure or discrepancy. A written record of the investigation shall be made and shall include the conclusions and followup.

§ 211.194 Laboratory records.

(a) Laboratory records shall include complete data derived from all tests necessary to assure compliance with established specifications and standards, including examinations and assays, as follows:

(1) A description of the sample received for testing with identification of source (that is, location from where sample was obtained), quantity, lot number or other distinctive code, date sample was taken, and date sample was received for testing.

(2) A statement of each method used in the testing of the sample. The statement shall indicate the location of data that establish that the methods used in the testing of the sample meet proper standards of accuracy and reliability as applied to the product tested. (If the method employed is in the current revision of the United States Pharmacopeia, National Formulary, Association of Official Analytical Chemists, Book of Methods,{2} or in other recognized standard references, or is detailed in an approved new drug application and the referenced method is not modified, a statement indicating the method and reference will suffice). The suitability of all testing methods used shall be verified under actual conditions of use.

{2} Copies may be obtained from: Association of Official Analytical Chemists, 2200 Wilson Blvd., Suite 400, Arlington, VA 22201-3301.

(3) A statement of the weight or measure of sample used for each test, where appropriate.

(4) A complete record of all data secured in the course of each test, including all graphs, charts, and spectra from laboratory instrumentation, properly identified to show the specific component, drug product container, closure, in-process material, or drug product, and lot tested.

(5) A record of all calculations performed in connection with the test, including units of measure, conversion factors, and equivalency factors.

(6) A statement of the results of tests and how the results compare with established standards of identity, strength, quality, and purity for the component, drug product container, closure, in-process material, or drug product tested.

(7) The initials or signature of the person who performs each test and the date(s) the tests were performed.

(8) The initials or signature of a second person showing that the original records have been reviewed for accuracy, completeness, and compliance with established standards.

(b) Complete records shall be maintained of any modification of an established method employed in testing. Such records shall include the reason for the modification and data to verify that the modification produced results that are at least as accurate and reliable for the material being tested as the established method.

(c) Complete records shall be maintained of any testing and standardization of laboratory reference standards, reagents, and standard solutions.

(d) Complete records shall be maintained of the periodic calibration of laboratory instruments, apparatus, gauges, and recording devices required by § 211.160(b)(4).

(e) Complete records shall be maintained of all stability testing performed in accordance with § 211.166.

[43 FR 45077, Sept. 29, 1978, as amended at 55 FR 11577, Mar. 29, 1990]

§ 211.196 Distribution records.

Distribution records shall contain the name and strength of the product and description of the dosage form, name and address of the consignee, date and quantity shipped, and lot or control number of the drug product. For compressed medical gas products, distribution records are not required to contain lot or control numbers.

(Approved by the Office of Management and Budget under control number 0910-0139)

[49 FR 9865, Mar. 16, 1984]
§ 211.198 Complaint files.

(a) Written procedures describing the handling of all written and oral complaints regarding a drug product shall be established and followed. Such procedures shall include provisions for review by the quality control unit, of any complaint involving the possible failure of a drug product to meet any of its specifications and, for such drug products, a determination as to the need for an investigation in accordance with § 211.192. Such procedures shall include provisions for review to determine whether the complaint represents a serious and unexpected adverse drug experience which is required to be reported to the Food and Drug Administration in accordance with § 310.305 of this chapter.

(b) A written record of each complaint shall be maintained in a file designated for drug product complaints. The file regarding such drug product complaints shall be maintained at the establishment where the drug product involved was manufactured, processed, or packed, or such file may be maintained at another facility if the written records in such files are readily available for inspection at that other facility. Written records involving a drug product shall be maintained until at least 1 year after the expiration date of the drug product, or 1 year after the date that the complaint was received, whichever is longer. In the case of certain OTC drug products lacking expiration dating because they meet the criteria for exemption under § 211.137, such written records shall be maintained for 3 years after distribution of the drug product.

(1) The written record shall include the following information, where known: the name and strength of the drug product, lot number, name of complainant, nature of complaint, and reply to complainant.

(2) Where an investigation under § 211.192 is conducted, the written record shall include the findings of the investigation and followup. The record or copy of the record of the investigation shall be maintained at the establishment where the investigation occurred in accordance with § 211.180(c).

(3) Where an investigation under § 211.192 is not conducted, the written record shall include the reason that an investigation was found not to be necessary and the name of the responsible person making such a determination.

[43 FR 45077, Sept. 29, 1978, as amended at 51 FR 24479, July 3, 1986]

Subpart K-Returned and Salvaged Drug Products
§ 211.204 Returned drug products.

Returned drug products shall be identified as such and held. If the conditions under which returned drug products have been held, stored, or shipped before or during their return, or if the condition of the drug product, its container, carton, or labeling, as a result of storage or shipping, casts doubt on the safety, identity, strength, quality or purity of the drug product, the returned drug product shall be destroyed unless examination, testing, or other investigations prove the drug product meets appropriate standards of safety, identity, strength, quality, or purity. A drug product may be reprocessed provided the subsequent drug product meets appropriate standards, specifications, and characteristics. Records of returned drug products shall be maintained and shall include the name and label potency of the drug product dosage form, lot number (or control number or batch number), reason for the return, quantity returned, date of disposition, and ultimate disposition of the returned drug product. If the reason for a drug product being returned implicates associated batches, an appropriate investigation shall be conducted in accordance with the requirements of § 211.192. Procedures for the holding, testing, and reprocessing of returned drug products shall be in writing and shall be followed.

§ 211.208 Drug product salvaging.

Drug products that have been subjected to improper storage conditions including extremes in temperature, humidity, smoke, fumes, pressure, age, or radiation due to natural disasters, fires, accidents, or equipment failures shall not be salvaged and returned to the marketplace. Whenever there is a question whether drug products have been subjected to such conditions, salvaging operations may be conducted only if there is (a) evidence from laboratory tests and assays (including animal feeding studies where applicable) that the drug products meet all applicable standards of identity, strength, quality, and purity and (b) evidence from inspection of the premises that the drug products and their associated packaging were not subjected to improper storage conditions as a result of the disaster or accident. Organoleptic examinations shall be acceptable only as supplemental evidence that the drug products meet appropriate standards of identity, strength, quality, and purity. Records including name, lot number, and disposition shall be maintained for drug products subject to this section.